I Am! I Can!

Keys to Quality Child Care

A Guide for Directors

I Am! I Can!

Keys to Quality Child Care

A Guide for Directors

New and Revised

Grace L. Mitchell
Nancy C. Bailey
Lois F. Dewsnap

TelShare Publishing Company, Inc.
Chelsea, Mass.

Printed in the United States of America
Library of Congress Catalog Card Number: 91-67111
ISBN: 0-910287-09-0

Cover design by Graves Fowler Associates, Silver Spring, MD 20906

Dedicated to

Donald Bates Mitchell

1906-1988

As a husband, father, mentor, and friend,
he provided steady and constant support
for our work.

As a teacher, he motivated
generations of students
to reach for and achieve high standards
and to enjoy pride in their accomplishments.

ACKNOWLEDGEMENTS

The authors wish to express their gratitude to the many teachers who contributed their original ideas, creative efforts, and practical suggestions to this work. To list them all would be an impossible task—rather let it be said that their generosity is symbolic of the spirit of sharing which is typical of our profession.

We wish to thank the many people—from Maine to Alaska, from Florida to Hawaii—who arranged for us to visit centers and meet with leaders in the field of child care. We traveled for eighteen months, making an independent national survey of child care, and have compressed what we learned into the substance of this book.

As we prepared to do this revision, we asked people who had been using the earlier edition to make suggestions for changes and improvements. We are especially grateful to Edith Counter Duran, Kathy Knowler, Susan Pollack, and Charlyne Taylor for giving so generously of their time in their responses.

In this revised edition Harriet Chmela has devoted her efforts to Volume 2, *A Preschool Curriculum*, but her sensitivity and humor are clearly reflected in this volume as well.

We would be remiss indeed if we did not give special thanks to Larry and Leah Rood, whose practical advice was surpassed only by their warm encouragement. Our gratitude also to Donald Ludgin, who began as our typesetter for this volume and ended up as our advisor, sharing generously his many years of experience as an editor.

CONTENTS

ABOUT THIS BOOK

We decided to avoid problems with personal pronouns by arbitrarily alternating between male and female pronouns from one chapter to the next. When the pronouns do not refer to a named child or teacher, we have used male pronouns for children and female pronouns for teachers in odd-numbered chapters and the reverse in even-numbered ones.

You will find a number of references in this book to Green Acres, and a word of explanation is in order. Grace Mitchell started a small school in Waltham, Massachusetts, in 1933 that grew to be the widely-known Green Acres Day School and Day Camp. Before the school closed in 1987, its hours had been extended to full days to accommodate working parents. The spirit and philosophy of the school are now carried on by the Green Acres Foundation, which puts on three Saturday workshops a year to help early childhood teachers in their professional growth.

Part One of this book was written by Nancy Bailey, who has set up and managed more than fifty child care centers. It is meant to help people just getting started to avoid the costly lessons Nancy learned through experience. It can also be very helpful to someone who is expanding to a second or third center.

Part Two is written to help directors in the daily operation of a child care center, with the emphasis on quality. There is much in this part that directors will want to share with the rest of the staff.

This book is Volume One of the new and revised *I Am! I Can!* Volume Two, *A Preschool Curriculum*, is a book of activities for teachers to use. You will find a number of references to it in this volume.

All of the forms in Chapter 9, pages 35 through 50, may be duplicated, as well as the last two pages in Chapter 40, pages 179 and 180. You are also free to copy "Ten Commandments for Teachers," page 132, and the posters that appear on pages 88, 92, 121, 122, 186, and 192. We have expressly not claimed copyright on the material on these pages.

PART ONE

STARTING A CENTER

INTRODUCTION

Whether you are an owner or a director (or both), and whether you are planning to open a child care center, thinking of expanding your current operations, or considering adding additional centers, you will have to devote your constant attention to most of the issues described in this book. Changing regulations, building codes, and economic conditions can seriously affect your business if you are not consistently well-informed.

The very first thing you must do is a market analysis. It isn't enough that friends have said, "You're so good with children—you ought to start a child care center." This is a highly competitive field and, in most areas, a highly regulated one. Until you are reasonably sure that there is a market for this service, and that there *will be* a market three, or four, or five years from now; until you know whether other centers in the area have waiting lists or cannot enroll enough children to cover their expenses; until you know what the business picture is in your area—you are not ready to make any costly moves. Chapter 1 will guide you through the steps of analyzing the market in your area.

If prospects look good, you next develop a business plan. Opening a center, even if you own a site and a building, is an expensive proposition. A business plan is a good reality check for you, and it is essential if you are going to a bank or other source for a loan. It not only helps *you* understand what is involved, but also helps you provide the information the bank needs to evaluate your proposal. Chapter 2 will help you prepare a business plan.

Once you know you are going ahead, and once you know you can get the money you need, then you need to know the tasks that lie between your dream and reality. You will need to schedule these tasks in the order in which they must be completed, and the order is crucial. If you do not do things in the right order, it will cost you money later. Chapter 3 explains the process in detail, and a schedule of pre-opening tasks appears in Chapter 9.

Marketing and promotion (covered in Chapter 4) are the means you use to let parents in your area know that you are offering sound child care services. These tasks will have to go on at the same time as such operational tasks as selecting and ordering equipment (explained in Chapter 5). Juggling these activities will take great care on your part.

No matter how attractive your site or how well-equipped your facility, your center will not prosper without the right staff, and finding the right teachers and other staff is by no means easy. Chapter 6 (*Job Descriptions*) and Chapter 7 (*Staff Selection*) will help you through this vital step.

Finally, you must persuade parents in your area that this is where they want their children to be. Once they are ready to make that decision, the way you handle the enrollment interview can assure a smooth relationship and avoid future problems. Chapter 8 explains enrollment procedures in detail.

Chapter 9 contains a number of the forms you will need in starting a center. You are free to copy these forms for your own use.

Chapter 1   MARKET ANALYSIS

Gathering data about local markets is your critical first step. A sample analysis form is provided on pages 35 and 36.

Licensing agencies   One of the sources to call is the state or local licensing agency, from which you should also obtain the regulations governing group child care centers. Ask also for regulations for family-based or home-based child care for comparison. You may discover that these regulations are far less stringent, and more compatible with your goals.

Ask for information about the number of centers offering the services you propose to offer, such as preschool, infant and toddler, and school-age care. Ask as well for any data on the number of slots available in these categories in existing centers.

Local census data   Request from city or town offices the most recent local census data for the numbers of children under the age of six, the numbers of families with incomes considered average in the area, and concentrations of these families within a one-mile, three-mile, and five-mile radius of your proposed site. If you are counting on full-time enrollments to meet your financial objectives, you will also need to know how many families are headed by two working parents.

Local schools forecast   Consult the local school systems to learn whether they forecast an increasing, stable, or decreasing number of young children in the coming three to five years. This information should indicate the trends anticipated, whereas the census data provide information about a particular point in the past. Learn also about any plans the public schools have to offer more programs for children younger than kindergarten or for children in need of after-school care. You might have difficulty competing with these publicly funded programs.

Local centers   Survey the local child care centers in your proposed market area. Start by telephoning centers listed in the Yellow Pages. Some people call and pretend to be parents shopping for care, asking their questions under this guise. You might prefer to be open with the director of the center you talk to. She may try to discourage you from becoming competition, or *may* encourage you to join in providing a much-needed service in the area. You will have to judge by the way she responds whether the answers to your survey are useful to your decision-making process. You can obtain some of this data from local resource-and-referral agencies, but more subtle information will be gained by making telephone inquiries yourself.

Organizations of child care providers   Look for local organizations of child care providers, as well as chapters of national organizations such as the National Association for the

Education of Young Children (NAEYC) and the National Child Care Association (NCCA). Ask about their perception of the need for more child care in the local market. Membership in these organizations is essential for owners and program administrators of child care and early childhood programs.

Local employers It is wise to consult with business organizations such as the Chamber of Commerce, as well as with major employers in the area. Be sure to ask whether executives of these businesses expect to expand or shrink the size of their workforces in the next three to five years. The health of your business depends directly upon the health of the economy in your market area.

Available staff The other side of the picture is the availability of staff. A study of the help wanted section of the local paper will give you some useful clues. If half the centers in the area are advertising for help, that's an indication that good teachers are scarce. You might also call college and other job placement offices and resource-and-referral agencies, as well as some of the larger centers.

In sum Before going on, then, collect as much information as you can about the availability of the particular services you propose to offer, the prices charged, and the number of openings or the number on waiting lists in those centers offering programs and services similar to those you are planning. When you have collected this information, you next must determine from the market analysis whether there is a sufficient number of potential consumers who might use your center not only in the coming months, but also in the long term, five or ten years from now. In some communities, centers which offer flexible hours for working families, welcome children under the age of three, or provide some other added service will succeed where traditional nursery schools have closed.

Stop now and write a business plan. Whether you plan to use private funds or seek outside public or private financing, you must create a working plan which will take you step by step to your desired goal. The purpose of a business plan is to show the person or institution from whom you seek funding that you have a clear understanding of all that is involved in opening a child care center. The process of gathering the information needed will help you to gain that understanding, and you will be prepared to make an effective presentation and answer questions with assurance.

You can find a number of books in your local town or college libraries that explain the process of developing a financial plan. Some provide outlines of plans you may wish to adapt. Others simply define the items your plan should include. In completing your own written plan, you will want to personalize the presentation to show how it applies your philosophy and your program to the local market. We provide an outline on page 37. As you develop your business plan, check often with your financial advisor and ask for suggestions.

Organization   In the context of this book, *organization* means the form in which your business will operate—a partnership, a corporation, or a part of a government agency, for example.

Let us assume that you have determined that there is a need for the services you propose to offer and a group of consumers willing and able to pay what you will charge for these services. (See the suggested operating budget on pages 40 and 41 for help in arriving at this figure.) If you have not already decided which form of organization to choose, consult next with both an attorney and a tax advisor, making sure that both are familiar with the options available to you in terms of the laws under which you must operate. Carefully weigh all the long-term consequences of choosing one form of organization, gathering as much information as possible about potential changes in the law which might affect you in the future.

It happened:

Helen and Rosa formed a private, non-profit organization in order to open a center on a desirable site. They chose this form because local zoning laws would not allow a business to operate in that neighborhood, but state laws allowed a non-profit educational institution to operate without regard to zoning restrictions. Now that state has passed a law allowing child care centers, as well, to operate without zoning restrictions, regardless of their form of organization, but Helen and Rosa cannot reverse their decision. As a result, the potential for expanding their business has been hurt. They have had to pass up the opportunity to form a partnership with an individual looking to invest a substantial sum of money in starting a proprietary center in a nearby community.

In some areas you may not have a choice of operating a for-profit center at your chosen site, or you may find that tax advantages or the possibility of funding from various government or employer-sponsored agencies will influence your decision. Information about these funding sources should be available through government departments of social services or child welfare, as well as from local provider networks.

Budgets Before you can approach outside sources for funding, you must estimate how much money you will need to open your center, to operate it for the first year, and to operate it for the first three years. The suggested budgets in Chapter 9 include most items and expenses essential to setting up and operating a child care center. Review your budget carefully, however, to be sure you have not omitted anything! Once your plan is underway and you are hard at work, you do not want to encounter any unpleasant surprises.

Professional services Begin by allowing sufficient money for the professional advice you will need from a lawyer and an accountant, as well as for all the fees necessary to form an organization. In some metropolitan areas of the United States, the federal Small Business Administration can put you in touch with retired business executives who will provide these professional services for you for very modest fees. They are part of a group called SCORE (Service Corps of Retired Executives). Look for the Small Business Administration in the list of federal government agencies in the telephone book.

Insurance Allow for the insurance you will need for property, for liability, for your employees (such as workers' compensation), and for transportation if you must offer this service. *You should work with an insurance agent* to be certain that you purchase the necessary coverage.

Site development Whether you are designing a new building or renovating existing space, you will need professional expertise from the building trades. Let us caution you to begin with free advice from the inspectors who will approve the finished product. Ask the building, fire, and plumbing inspectors to visit the proposed site and review your plans before you finalize your budget.

These experts will know what codes or regulations are apt to change and how you can plan to meet them *now*, while you can include these items in your financial planning. For example, will the fire marshall tell you that you will be required to install a sprinkler system a year from now? It has been our experience that these individuals will offer invaluable advice. If, on the other hand, you encounter an inspector who is going to be difficult to work with, you will have to figure out how you are going to win him over—and plan on some delays in completing the site development.

Licenses and permits   Determine at this time how much to budget for the fees each agency or department will charge for the permits required for child care centers. The fees may range from $10 for a permit to serve milk to $100 for a building inspection.

Learn about local regulations governing signs. You may have a good building and playground, but parents need to be able to identify your site as a child care center as they drive past it. It is essential to have a sign large enough for the words "child care" and your telephone number to be read easily from a moving car.

Prepaid deposits   Inquire about deposits which might be required by a landlord and by utility companies for new businesses. These deposits may tie up hundreds of dollars for as much as a year.

Equipment   Many vendors of products for child care centers offer booklets, and sometimes seminars, to assist with planning equipment needs and budgets. Be sure you look at your equipment needs in stages. For example, during the pre-opening phase, you will need office and reception area furniture, some kitchen items, and educational equipment and materials for marketing purposes, long before you will need all the equipment with which to run a center.

During your first year, you will need the equipment necessary for the numbers of children you expect to enroll in each age category. Then, in subsequent years, you can add needed equipment or enrichment materials when you are more certain of the numbers in each age group.

Let us offer a caution here. Weigh carefully the question of quality versus quantity. You must select furniture for safety first, then for durability and ease of maintenance. Some vendors will offer financing assistance if you order above a certain dollar limit. Even if their materials cost a little more, you may find them worth buying if their credit terms are attractive.

Facility design   Items to consider:
- a doorbell at the main entrance to allow you to control access to the center (make sure it can be heard by two or more staff during the early and late hours) and a buzzer that sounds when an exit door opens should a child wander out unnoticed.
- movable high and low partitions, rather than permanent interior walls, so you can use the classroom space most effectively and meet the changing needs of the children.
- sturdy windows low enough for the children to see out without climbing on the furniture.
- window coverings which will not tempt children to pull or swing on them and which are easy to keep clean—not draperies.
- low sinks just outside the children's toilet room, allowing easy supervision of hand-washing.
- floor coverings which can be kept clean and sanitary, especially where infants will crawl.

It happened:

Our first new buildings, designed for a hundred children, were carpeted over almost all the floor area. We thought that the carpet would give a warm, homelike appearance and that it would reduce the noise factor in the classrooms. Within the first year, we discovered that paint, mud, milk, juice, and bodily excretions had left stains too difficult to remove. Even after a thorough shampooing, the floors looked disgraceful. We spent thousands of dollars removing the carpet and replacing it with tiles or sheet goods. We learned that these are the best permanent floor coverings. We used small (four feet by six feet or six feet by nine feet) area rugs to add warmth and color. They could be replaced when they could no longer be cleaned.

Work carefully on your site plan. When you think you have plans that show all the important details of inside layout and outside play and parking areas, ask your licensor to review them *before* you begin construction.

Marketing

A significant expense in your budget should be for marketing. Word of mouth recommendations from happy parents using your services are indeed *the* best form of advertising, but that source will not necessarily bring you enough new business during the first few months you are open. You will need to tell your story to as many potential customers as possible. A simple brochure or poster may be just as effective as more expensive printed materials, but you should budget for several mailings, as well as displays in stores and on local employers' bulletin boards.

Include in your budget an advertisement in the Yellow Pages of the local telephone directories of a size comparable with those of the other centers with which you would compare yours. Also include the cost of business cards for the director—and for an assistant director if you have one. Other forms of paid advertising might be worth considering, especially before opening and during the first few months of operation.

Of significantly greater value than paid ads are the free stories you may get in local papers, but you would be wise not to depend on this source alone. You should, however, plan on spending some money on creating newsworthy events.

Payroll

A major item in your pre-opening expense budget should be for payroll, whether or not you include the owners or principals.

You should budget for someone to answer the telephone during an eight- or nine-hour day. An answering service or answering machine is not the ideal arrangement, but is better than no coverage at all. Busy parents will respond more positively to speaking to a real person.

You should budget for key staff members for orientation and staff training, as well as for open houses and other opportunities for parents to meet the teachers. They are more crucial to your marketing program than any other component of your center.

You should include in your budget for staff training enough to cover first aid and/or CPR training, required by many states. You may have to pay for this training in order for your staff to meet the requirements for a license to operate. However, since a record of this training is something staff members can take with them if they leave, you may choose to require that they reimburse you for a portion of this cost after they are employed.

Operating deficit   Even if you have chosen to open your center at the most advantageous time of year, usually September, you may not enroll enough children to operate at breakeven during the first few months. Allow for a percentage of shortfall in your projected revenues, and be prepared to meet payment schedules for fixed expenses and payroll from your capital funds, rather than from operating income.

Sample budgets   We have included three sample budgets in Chapter 9. They are offered as guidelines only, and should be modified for your particular operation. The first budget (on page 38) lists the most common expenses you will encounter before opening a center; the second (on page 39) summarizes the cash flow required during the three months immediately before the center opens. The third budget (pages 40 and 41) shows revenues and expenses for the first twelve-month period. We do not give hard numbers in these worksheets, because all centers are different. Only you can fill in the spaces with numbers.

    We have not included a set-up budget for real estate expenses. There are too many variables related to site development—legal and financial expenses, architectural fees, and construction costs, for example—for us to cover in this book.

    Some of the terms used in the budgets require explanation.

    Full-time equivalents (FTE's)—Sometimes referred to as "slots," full-time equivalents are calculated by combining part-time and full-time enrollments.

    Average percentage of enrollment—Only a center with an extensive waiting list can count on operating at capacity. Therefore, assume a realistic percentage of capacity (80 percent to 92 percent) when projecting total revenue.

    Average FTE's—Assuming that your center serves more than one age group, and charges different rates of tuition for the groups, you must assume percentages of total enrollment. Our sample shows infants, toddlers, and preschool, but you may add after school, vacation weeks, and summer programs to reflect the sources of your revenues.

    Average weekly tuition—The tuitions paid by each child are added and then averaged to arrive at the average tuition per slot, calculated using the rates that apply to each age group.

    Space is allowed in the far right column for you to estimate the percentages of revenue you should spend on each expense category. The two major expenses that will influence how much you must charge for services are the *costs of occupancy* (rent, taxes, utilities, insurance, and repairs) and *payroll expense.* The latter will depend upon the staff/child ratios required by your state's regulations and the mix of infants and toddlers, of preschool and after-school children, you expect to enroll. If you have no experience in designing a staffing schedule and budget, hire a consultant with a successful track record to help determine this line item.

Sources of funding
Assuming that you do not have enough money available from your personal assets or from a partnership, you will have to look for other sources. If you and your associates cannot, or choose not to, take out personal loans to fund your program, you may apply for public funding or for private foundation grants. Look in your local library for publications on the availability of private foundation money and on how to write a grant proposal. Seek help from the government child welfare, education, human resources, or social service offices in learning about the availability of public funds for child care programs. As of this writing, employers in the private sector do not appear to be a readily available source of start-up funds. Investigate this matter carefully, but line up additional sources before you commit much of your own money to creating an organization.

Whether you are applying to a financial institution, a government agency, or a private lender, you will need several copies of your completed business plan, the accompanying market analysis and budget projections, and your schedule of pre-opening tasks. You will also need personal and business references vouching for your ability to operate a business successfully and for your integrity and good standing in the community.

Prepare for several meetings and presentations to the decision-makers to whom you are applying for funds. Ask in advance how much time you should allow for completing each step of the process. Plan for unexpected delays, and budget for any expenses these delays may cost. Remember, "the best-laid plans ... ."

Timing   It is generally agreed that the best time to open or expand a child care program is in September, or the month when public schools begin the school year. Most parents plan for their children's care in school-year cycles and will look for new choices at this time. Some programs have opened in January, but it is a less desirable choice than September. It might be a good time for expanding your program, if you have determined that there is pent-up demand for your service.

Schedule   Once you have set your target date for opening or expanding, consider the length of time needed to complete the schedule of tasks we have suggested. If our timetable does not appear to match yours, adjust it accordingly, but again let us caution you to allow for unexpected delays. Your licensor may be the best person to ask about the length of time to allow for completion of major tasks.

Enlarge the Schedule of Pre-Opening Tasks on pages 42 and 43 to hang on a bulletin board; also, make copies for each member of the team to use to track progress and note delays and accomplishments during the preopening period. Indicate who will be responsible for seeing each task through to completion.

The tasks are presented in three major categories: Construction, Marketing and Promotion, and Operations. Completion periods are denoted in one-month or three-month (quarterly) periods. How many weeks you should allow for each set of tasks will depend on how complex the site development and construction will be, and on whether you (as owner) and a partner are going to do all of the work or plan to hire a director to complete some of the Operations tasks.

One reason for posting the total schedule is to allow each member of the team to see how tasks interrelate and how the progress of one depends on completion of another. For example, marketing requires business cards, brochures, fliers, and other material, as well as an office, a telephone, and similar basics.

Construction   Most of the work depends on the expertise and reliability of the contractor hired to build or renovate your facility. The schedule gives you the approximate time period by which each phase *must* be completed in order to coordinate with your other steps to complete the center. Some of the terms used in this part of the schedule require explanation:

•   *Building construction*—the dates when your contractor begins and completes work on your building if you are putting up a new center.
•   *Fit-out*—the dates when your contractor begins and completes work renovating your building if you are converting an older edifice.
•   *Utilities in*—the date by which the contractor should have heat, water, gas, and electricity ready for use.

• *Occupancy permit*—the date when you can move into the building to organize your office, hold interviews, and install furnishings.
• *Utilities on*—the date on which you assume financial responsibility for the utility bills.
• *License received*—the date before which children cannot be cared for at your center.

With luck, you and your contractor will work smoothly together. But you will learn all too soon that you must check on construction progress at least every other day!

Marketing Involve others in marketing effort, but you should plan and control the budget for marketing and should have some experience in buying advertising, working with designers on brochures, and pursuing every public relations opportunity. Among the tasks listed, the Yellow Pages are among the most effective forms of advertising, but the directories are published only once a year. As soon as you decide to set up your center, reserve a telephone number (for a modest monthly fee) and sign up for the next directory printing.

Operations This schedule begins and ends with a meeting with your licensor. If you heed this person's advice on how to meet government regulations, your final meeting prior to opening, the license review, should go smoothly, especially if you have kept in touch every few weeks.

You will find some suggestions with which to plan your first two weeks of operation in Volume 2, *A Preschool Curriculum*, Sequence One. But you should also have a written contingency plan to provide for the unexpected. *What if* on Day One your lead teacher calls in sick? *What if* the power fails? *What if* you have an emergency and can't be at the center yourself? You are the person who has to think of these things, and you should share your plan with other key members of the staff.

Simultaneous needs As you review the schedule, you will discover that many pre-opening activities must be carried out at the same time, especially marketing and enrolling children. Once the center is operating, there will be many times when your responsibilities require attention to program, marketing, handling money, and meeting with a parent or licensor almost simultaneously! If you are considering a partnership or sharing the job with a co-director, be very sure that you take sufficient time to establish a workable division of responsibilities. We strongly recommend that you write separate job descriptions for each person so there will be a clear understanding between partners, and so staff and parents will know to whom to bring specific concerns. We also urge you to meet at least once a week to discuss and evaluate the operation.

If the partnership has been formed with each person bringing capital to the business, there well may be disagreements over the use of funds. Look for a third person you both know and respect whom you can call in to arbitrate or act as a tie-breaker when you cannot agree on a critical decision.

Your marketing activities are most intense during the six months before your center opens and the first six months of operation; they are an ongoing part of your job. Although you may buy advertisements and mail out brochures that will stimulate inquiries about your center, you should go out and introduce yourself to the community. You must make yourself visible. Offer to speak about child care to various groups and local businesses. Most important of all, however, you must meet with prospective customers, so either you or your partner must be at the center to talk to walk-ins and to make appointments in response to telephone inquiries.

Free publicity is most effective—especially stories in the local media or in company newsletters distributed to employees in the area. To receive this publicity, you must create newsworthy events, such as the purchase of your site (with sketches of your planned facility), appointment of key staff members from the local community (with photos), and the date for an open house.

People to visit   The following is a list of offices, agencies, and businesses you should plan to visit. Leave your business card at each one.

- Editors and feature writers at the local newspaper
- Officials of the local government
- State, provincial, or county representatives
- Municipal services: the school board or school committee, the library, the fire department and police department
- Directors of boys or girls clubs and Y's, local Scouting leaders
- Administrators of public and private schools
- Administrators at institutions of higher education
- Deans and teachers of early childhood education
- Presidents of elementary school parent-teacher organizations
- Leaders of the Chamber of Commerce
- Heads of fraternal and civic organizations
- The hospital administrator and directors of nursing and social services
- Administrators of nursing homes, health services, and clinics
- Obstetricians, pediatricians, and pediatric dentists
- Directors of job placement agencies, public and private
- Managers of temporary help placement agencies
- Managers of human resources at local industries and banks
- Real estate agents and relocation specialists
- Managers of apartment or condominium complexes
- Managers of furniture leasing companies
- Local clergy and heads of religious schools
- The head of the League of Women Voters

- Directors of women's resource centers and child care referral agencies
- Managers of health clubs and weight-loss centers
- Managers of hotels, restaurants, and shopping malls
- Managers of taxi services, beauty salons, and service stations

Do not ask to place a poster in a business establishment on your first visit unless you see other business posters and fliers displayed. After you have introduced yourself and explained a little about your program, leave; plan to write a brief note as a follow-up to your visit. You may make a list of those businesses to which you will return to discuss mutually beneficial arrangements—you offer to advertise their services in exchange for similar assistance from them. For example, you could give out a flier or coupon offering diaper services and the diaper service could include your flier with its next billing statements.

At the end of each week—at least once a month—complete a marketing activity checklist (see the sample on page 44). Focus on the results each item produced, so you can repeat the most productive ones. Remember—without enrollment, you have no business!

Open house   Plan an open house to introduce yourself and your center to the people in your area. Prepare a mailing list of local officials, professionals, and heads of local businesses, including their titles, addresses, and phone numbers. Set a date, prepare the wording of the invitations, and work out a schedule of the events you plan for that day. Mail your invitations three weeks prior to the event, including a map showing the entrance to your center and the parking area. Place an Open House ad in the local papers during the week before the event.

Well in advance, make sure you have on hand whatever brochures or other promotional literature you want to hand out, as well as coupons or other promotional items. Check on your coffee urn and make sure you have adequate supplies of food and paper goods. Put a guest book in a prominent place—you can build your mailing list from the names and addresses entered in it.

Hire someone to come the day before the event to mow grass, trim shrubs, weed gardens, and pick up litter. Then, an hour before the open house, have someone make a last tour around the playground, parking, and entrance areas to pick up any debris that may have blown in.

Schedule extra hours for the custodian to ensure that the building is clean—that it smells clean!—bright, and beautiful.

Ask the cook to arrive an hour before the visitors to prepare coffee, tea, juice, and some kind of healthy snack. Arrange a serving area with adult-size chairs away from the entrance door, so your visitors won't form a bottleneck around the refreshments.

Assign members of the staff to greet guests, make sure they sign the guest book, serve refreshments, and explain the curriculum. If necessary, hire one or two extra teachers to free your lead teachers to cover the curriculum and help you host the event.

Set up a display area, with a table for brochures and newsletters, a map showing how transportation to the center can be arranged, and a display of pictures of your teaching staff, arranged by teams.

Arrange to have someone take black-and-white photographs, in case the local paper does not send a photographer. Make sure the person with a camera records the names of children, parents, and staff in any group pictures. Have photo release forms for parents to sign in case you want to use the pictures for publicity.

If the local paper sends a reporter, hand out your prepared background information on the center. If the local press does not attend, take a copy of your story to the editorial office, together with five-by-seven-inch black-and-white photos. A story you carry in is more likely to be used than one you mail in.

Within a week after the open house, call all the prospective clients who signed the guest book to arrange a visit and personal interview. Write notes to managers of local businesses, thanking them in advance for referrals to your center.

Ongoing marketing at the center

No matter how many years you have been operating a successful business, never cease to survey your satisfied customers as well as those who did not choose your services. On page 49 we offer a sample questionnaire you may adapt for this purpose, changing the questions to ask why a parent did *not* choose your center. Some of these responses may give you ideas for enhancing your services; others may reveal something about your operation or facility that you did not recognize. Acknowledge comments from all respondents with a phone call or brief note. Add these people to your mailing list. Some parents may change their arrangements if they become dissatisfied with their initial choice, and your center will be one they will want to revisit.

Consumers love winners. A customer is twice as likely to purchase from a winner as from someone else. Workers are three times as likely to work for a winner as from someone else. Your center can be perceived as a winner from the start, based on your efforts and the reputations of members of your staff drawn from the local community.

To differentiate your center from others like it, highlight staff credentials, qualifications, and continuing professional development. Make a display for each team area, with a picture of each member, labeled to show name and position. Include your student teachers, with the names of the schools they attend. Make a "We are so proud of ..." display on which you can show certificates from center workshops or area conferences, honors members of the staff have received, or newspaper articles about their activities. Change the displays often enough to keep them eye-catching and interesting.

Post the agenda of your monthly staff meeting if it includes a special topic or guest speaker. Invite parents to attend two or three times a year—let them listen in on staff training. If your guest is newsworthy, send the story to the local paper. Highlight it in your own newsletter as well. The newsletter is a good place to include stories about workshops or conferences you or members of your staff have attended.

For classrooms We urge you to purchase durable, educationally sound equipment, even if it means buying fewer items at a time. In considering furniture, look for the manufacturers' specifications and other written materials that indicate the ages for which the items are recommended. They are labelled to protect the manufacturer from liability whenever possible, which leaves you vulnerable if you have chosen unwisely. Some furniture may be colorful but lightweight and would be inappropriate for young children who would climb or pull on it. You should consider how easy the furniture will be to maintain—including how much the children will be asked to do to care for their environment.

You will notice in the Schedule of Pre-Opening Tasks on pages 42 and 43 that you do not actually order equipment until the ninth month. If you order too soon, you will have to store everything safely until your center is ready—and will have to expend time, money, and hard work moving it to the center from storage. However, you can study catalogues and choose vendors long before you order. Deciding on what you want and can afford, and making out orders, is a time-consuming task, and should be done when you have time to give it careful thought.

Before you begin selecting the specific items you want to order, read the licensing regulations to see whether they contain any requirements that would dictate what equipment you must purchase. We feel that there are items which should be priorities, although tables and chairs are not necessarily at the top of the list. (The tables you do purchase should have adjustable legs to allow you to use them for toddlers or preschool children.)

Top priorities A good-quality set of wooden unit blocks, with sufficient variety and numbers of each shape, should top the list for preschoolers. A sand table and a large container suitable for water play would also rate high on our list. You can borrow good children's books from your library, though they will have to be changed regularly to fit the curriculum themes (see the monthly themes in Vol. 2).

Safety Think a long time before building your own equipment. Think an equally long time before accepting donated items for use in your center. Quality furniture and equipment manufactured by reliable vendors has been designed by professionals for safety and age appropriateness. In using second-hand or poorly constructed materials, you are ignoring your first priority, which is the safety and well-being of children. You are also likely to find that it doesn't even make sense financially.

Some other safety concerns you should consider:

• Select dolls which are appropriate for each age group. Movable eyes and stranded hair generally are not appropriate for children younger than three. These items can easily be pulled out and put in the mouth, causing choking.

• Purchase blocks made of hard wood, which will last longer than those of soft wood.

• Use a *no-choke tube*, available in most vendors' catalogues, to test all small pieces of toys.

• Ask for written evidence that painted furniture and equipment is coated with lead-free paint. It is wise to have this evidence available to show parents. Many of them are aware of the long-term damage chewing on lead paint can cause to children.

• Pull hard on knobs, handles, the wheels of toy vehicles, movable limbs of wooden, rubber, or plastic dolls—in other words, any item of construction which can cause harm to children or just deteriorate faster than you can pay for it.

Balance You need to strive for balance in selecting equipment for the various interest centers (see *Interest Centers*, Chapter 31). You should also consider the wealth of activities which require more time than money but which may, in fact, be educationally more rewarding and even more fun than those depending on items purchased from catalogues. We have found that when teachers put their own time and talent into creating math and reading materials, for instance, they are more apt to teach the children how to make them last.

Infant furniture If you are planning to offer infant or toddler care, read the licensing regulations to determine the number of cribs, high chairs, and other items required for each group. Some regulations allow you to purchase one crib per FTE (full-time equivalent) as long as you have a procedure for sanitizing each crib between uses. For example, nine babies cared for, but only seven in attendance at one time, need only seven cribs.

Some regulations specify whether cots or mats are to be used at nap time, sometimes indicating different requirements for different age groups or for half-day and full-day programs. Again a caution. While high-quality infant furniture may cost as much as three times what you would spend in the local toy or department store, we have found that the cribs and high chairs sold for family use do not last very long. They are not designed for *institutional* use—several children using them each day, every day, for months on end.

You should purchase at least one crib equipped with reinforced wheels for use in evacuation. Consult the regulations to determine how many are required for each group of infants.

For the playground Look at licensing regulations to determine requirements for fencing the playground, as well as the location and number of gates. Ask for the exact specifications for latches and where on the gates they should be located. Should they be high enough so only adults can reach them or low enough so children can push on them to escape in an emergency? (We were told both by different inspectors in the same town!)

Playground priorities A large sandbox (covered when not in use) and sturdy climbing equip ment are priorities for the outside play area. Our playgrounds do not include swing sets unless there are many other choices while children wait for their turn. Also, the area around the swings which must be protected for the safety of children playing nearby takes up a lot of sometimes precious outdoor space. Another item which should be viewed with great caution is a slide. It really requires the exclusive attention of one adult to ensure that children do not fall off or hurt themselves in other ways before landing safely.

Surfaces Many regulations now include specific requirements, or at least suggestions, for surfaces under swings, slides, and climbing equipment. A depth of six inches of sand, mulch, peastone, or similar material is strongly recommended, based upon studies which have shown that the depth and resilience of the material can affect the seriousness of a child's fall. Peastone is widely used because sand can be packed down and mulch can be too easily blown away, reducing the required six-inch resilience. Falling onto peastone may cause surface abrasions, but reduces the risk of broken bones or serious head injuries.

Where appropriate, consult your local agricultural authority for a list of poisonous plants which should not be allowed in your fenced-in play area. Once you have removed them, you must be vigilant to keep them from returning.

For adults How your center looks when a visitor first enters affects how that person will feel about whether this will be a happy, comfortable place to work—or to enroll a child. You send a clear message about the standards you intend to maintain for children by the way you provide for adults in the environment.

The office area Select modestly-priced, standard-sized desks, chairs, display shelves, and filing cabinets for the business area of your center. If you buy or bring in used furniture for the reception area and director's office, take the time to clean, polish, paint, or refinish it. A few plants will do much to make the area attractive and homey—a plus in parents' minds. (Consider using silk plants if this area does not get the appropriate exposure or if keeping plants healthy is a problem. Better no plants at all than ones with wilting or dead leaves.) The neat, organized appearance and comfort of this area state that this is a center which values and respects the people who spend their days here.

The director and the office workers who will use them can be given some say in choosing the office chairs. Each of us has a different shape where we sit, and comfort is important to productivity. Adults' needs are too often ignored or put too low on the list of priorities when the equipment budget is prepared.

Classrooms Consider, too, the number of adults who will be in the classroom during program, snack time, and lunch time. Many adults like to brag that they can still sit on the children's chairs, but it may not be best for everyone's posture. It can be awkward to downright embarrassing for tall people to have to sit with their knees under their chins and participate in the activities, let alone look as though they are having fun!

It happened:

> *Not until the first day of school did Irene and Frank realize that they had forgotten to provide chairs for the teaching staff in their new center. All during staff training, they had joked about how everyone could still get down without creaking bones to sit at the children's tables. No one had realized that when the children gathered for their snack, they would occupy all the chairs. Everyone laughed, but it took some scrounging to find chairs for the teachers, and then for parents who had been urged to drop by any time.*

Staff resource area   You should provide a staff resource area where books, pamphlets, magazines, tapes, and other materials for training and planning can be organized and used regularly. It may be one set of shelves or display racks, or an alcove with a small table and a few chairs, or a room set aside for weekly or monthly team meetings. Organization of materials, not space, is the priority.

––––––––––––––––––––

As this book goes to press, federal regulations implementing the new Americans with Disabilities Act (ADA) include requirements that may affect some of our recommendations. You should get a copy of the ADA and review the requirements with your licensor.

Chapter 6   STAFF QUALIFICATIONS AND JOB DESCRIPTIONS

Director   If you are the director, use this section to help yourself understand what your position entails.

General   Maintaining contact with government regulatory agencies.
Conforming to health, safety, and licensing regulations.
Handling all problems related to the administration of the center.
Keeping records that pertain to the administration of the center.
Planning and implementing a program for professional growth for all members of the staff.
Keeping informed about new developments in the field of child care.
Planning and scheduling administrative responsibilities.
Supervising the management of classroom schedules.
Scheduling the use of shared classroom space and equipment.
Scheduling the responsibilities of the staff.
Designating one lead teacher as acting director in the director's absence, announcing this designation, and putting it in writing.

Marketing and enrollment   Being alert to enrollment needs at all times.
Maximizing the center's enrollment capacity at all times.
Conducting an ongoing public relations effort to keep the center in a favorable light in the community.
Interviewing parents of prospective enrollees.
Enrolling children according to the policies of the center.
Familiarizing parents with the center's policies.

Fiscal   Operating the center within budget requirements.
Ordering equipment and supplies.
Collecting tuitions and fees.
Handling petty cash and the food budget.
Preparing a year-end budget analysis.

Health   Planning and implementing a health program for the center, including the cleanliness of the building.
Keeping health history records and physicians' reports for all children and for all members of the staff.
Maintaining contact with agencies able to help children with special needs.
Maintaining a referral system for children with special needs.

Safety   Planning and implementing a safety program for the center.
Keeping informed of the center's legal responsibilities and liabilities, both as a care provider and as an employer.
Implementing a program of playground safety.
Planning and conducting drills for emergencies.

Children	Planning for developmentally appropriate program and routines for children.
	Evaluating program through first-hand observation.
	Planning for the evaluation of children in relation to their progress, abilities, and special needs.
	Arranging a sound nutritional program using the services of a nutrition consultant.
	Arranging for rest and relaxation for children.
Parents	Planning ways to explain the policies of the center to parents.
	Planning and administering a parent participation program.
	Communicating with parents in a wide variety of ways.
Staff	Preparing center-specific job descriptions.
	Recruiting and selecting staff members for employment.
	Arranging for substitute help as needed.
	Conducting regularly-scheduled staff meetings.
	Planning and implementing in-service training programs for staff.
	Assisting staff in preparing weekly, monthly, and yearly plans.
	Planning activities that promote wholesome interpersonal relationships among members of the staff.
	Assisting staff in planning individual programs for professional growth and career development.
	Assisting staff with keeping accurate classroom records and records on individual children.
	Keeping personnel records.
Community	Welcoming visitors to the center and arranging for visits to be pleasant and worthwhile.
	Planning and administering a student teaching program in cooperation with local educational institutions.
	Attending and participating in professional conferences and other local educational events
	Being available to community groups for public events that pertain to early childhood and to family life as a whole.
Space and equipment	Planning for and equipping outdoor and indoor areas.
	Arranging for repairs and maintenance.
	Replacing supplies and equipment as necessary.
	Keeping inventory records.
Lead teacher	Meeting the state's required qualifications for the position.
	Supervising teachers and assistants in the team.
	Implementing the curriculum and philosophy of the center.
	Using developmentally appropriate approaches to curriculum and to discipline.
	Assigning responsibility for groups of children to team members.
	Reviewing all children's progress reports three times a year.
	Acting as a role model for co-workers.

Maintaining the upkeep and cleanliness of areas assigned to the team and assigning workjobs to members of the team.

Maintaining a sufficient supply of materials and equipment and anticipating the need for additional supplies.

Following through on appropriate recommendations from teachers assigned to complete the monthly safety check.

Maintaining accurate records of children's attendance.

Conducting stimulating and nourishing team meetings.

Bringing the team's suggestions to meetings with the director.

Supporting the director in encouraging professional growth of all members of the staff, but particularly members of the team.

Teacher Meeting the state's required qualifications for the position.

Implementing the philosophy and curriculum of the center.

Handling discipline properly under the supervision of the lead teacher at all times.

Supervising and guiding the teaching assistants and encouraging their professional growth.

Teaching assistant Meeting the minimum age requirement, usually sixteen years of age.

Working under the direct supervision of a teacher or lead teacher at all times.

Participating in team planning and implementation of the philosophy and curriculum of the center.

Handling discipline only by reporting the problem to the lead teacher or teacher in the team.

Acting director Assuming the duties, responsibilities, and accountability of the director when the director is absent.

All staff Assuming responsibility for attention to health and safety conditions.

Assuming responsibility for daily housekeeping duties as assigned.

Orientation You need to review all policies and procedures with each new employee. The Employee Orientation Checklist on page 50 gives you a fairly comprehensive list of forms and procedures to review with each employee and, more important, to document that each has been completed within a reasonable period of time after hiring.

We use the term *orientation* to denote the first ninety days of each person's employment with the center. Avoid using the term *probation* for this period, because courts have ruled that employment beyond the probation period must be considered permanent—meaning that the employee is entitled to a lifetime job!

Progress reviews It is important to conduct and document employee progress reviews at least every thirty days during the orientation period. If you are pleased with the staff member's performance, it is important to say so—and to offer specific praise. If you note problems with a new employee, discuss them and offer specific suggestions for improvement at regular intervals—as often as once a week—during the orientation period. If, after sixty days, it is clear to one or both parties that the quality of work or the working conditions will not change, it is not necessary to wait the full ninety days to terminate employment.

In most businesses, a full-time employee is eligible for benefits after completing the ninety-day period successfully.

Employee handbook You may decide to print an employee handbook or you may choose to assemble the essential information and present it in a folder. Whether printed and bound or presented as loose sheets, the handbook should contain these four sections:

Introduction This section should state the center's philosophy, outline its history, and generally set the tone for the handbook.

Center policies The items listed here should be presented as more than guidelines, but not as grounds for dismissal:

Discipline: State clearly a developmentally appropriate approach and list prohibited actions, such as spanking or humiliation. (This policy should also appear in the material presented to parents.)

Attendance and punctuality: Outline specific procedures for calling in sick and for arranging for a substitute.

Professional growth: State clearly whether attendance at staff meetings and workshops is required or optional and whether you offer compensation for time or reimbursement for fees required if staff members attend conferences or take first aid training.

Dress: Be sure the policy is equally applicable to male and female members of the staff.

We ask that staff be constantly aware of how they appear to parents and visitors and to remember that they serve as role models to the children.

Center rules The items listed here should define prohibited actions which could result in disciplinary action or termination, such as:
- failing to report for work or to call in (no call—no show).
- engaging in or failing to report suspected child abuse.
- stealing the center's, children's, or co-worker's possessions.
- disclosing confidential information about families, co-workers, or the center.
- engaging in disruptive behavior or using offensive language.
- leaving the center or leaving an assigned work area without permission.
- falsifying records or timesheets.
- bringing, possessing, or using alcoholic beverages or drugs in the center, or any degree of intoxication on the premises.
- committing any unlawful act, on the premises or outside the workplace, which brings discredit on the center or affects its normal operations.

- giving unauthorized medical service.
- behaving in a manner inconsistent with stated discipline policies.

Wage and labor policies This section should begin with two basic statements, one about non-discriminatory hiring and compensation policies and one about each employee's responsibility to understand the policies and rules outlined in this handbook. For example, "Employees will be hired and compensated on the basis of the duties they perform, without regard to race, sex, religion, national origin, age, veteran status, or the presence of a mental, physical, or sensory handicap. Each employee must understand the work schedule, overtime, and record-keeping requirements (to ensure that there is no misunderstanding and to ensure full compliance with applicable laws) and the policies and rules outlined in this handbook."

You should then define and describe in detail such items as:

- the workday (the twenty-four hour period starting at 6:01 a.m.).
- the work week (seven consecutive days beginning with Monday).
- when and where work schedules will be available.
- how to document hours worked.
- when and where paychecks will be available.
- policies on overtime or compensatory time.
- policies on sick days, holidays, and vacations.
- policies on employing relatives to work on the same team.
- grievance procedures.
- reporting sexual harassment.
- when and how performance evaluations will take place.
- when and how wage reviews will take place.
- disciplinary procedures for those who violate written rules.
- termination of employment by employer or employee.

Review Before you print and hand out the employee handbook, have it reviewed by an attorney or someone knowledgeable about the current labor laws. It is essential that your policies be worded to protect both employer and employee from misunderstandings.

We offer detailed information in this chapter, because the *people* will make your center successful. Selecting the right person for each position is one of the most difficult decisions you will make, so take sufficient time to choose carefully among at least three applicants.

Interviewing   As you read this chapter, keep in mind that child care is a business and that businesses are regulated by government agencies. The cautions we offer here are meant to help you avoid hiring problems, not to intimidate or discourage you.

Before the interview   Ask all candidates to submit résumés or to complete employment applications in advance of the interview. Screen the papers to select candidates who meet your standards, as well as the licensing standards required for the position. Schedule interviews with the candidates far enough apart (at least thirty minutes to an hour) to enable you to spend enough time with each one.

When someone calls in response to your advertisement, avoid discussing wages except in general terms. You may say, "Our salaries and benefits are not comparable to public school compensation packages." In answer to such a question as "How much do you pay?' respond, "That would depend on the position I would assign to you" or "Since some of our positions are for part-time teachers, that would depend on your work schedule."

When the applicant arrives, allow enough time for her to become acquainted with your center by reading the following material:

- the brochure describing the organization, philosophy, and programs offered at your center;
- a job description and list of required qualifications; and
- a statement describing how the hiring decision will be made

At some centers, this information is assembled in a packet or book for applicants to review while waiting.

The interview   Consider the interview an opportunity to share information with the applicant, as well as an opportunity to gain information from her. It is also an initial opportunity for you to observe the candidate closely.

Help the applicant to feel comfortable by setting the tone for the interview. Instead of sitting behind your desk, sit in one of two arm chairs facing one another, with no barrier between, or at a small, low table. Have brochures and other materials readily available.

Talk for a few minutes, to get the interview going, then *listen!* To be fair, you must be sure to ask all applicants the same questions. After you have given the applicant a framework to speak to, listen for:

• The applicant's educational background and experiences with children. They should demonstrate agreement with your philosophy and program.

• The applicant's experiences working as a member of a team. These experiences should show understanding of shared responsibility for total program.

• The applicant's attitude toward former employers. An honest appraisal of another center with justifiable criticisms is acceptable, but highly subjective disparaging remarks about its program or director should make you skeptical.

• A healthy "I AM!" with openness to grow and learn from others.

• A realistic "I CAN!" combined with flexibility, the ability to complete a project, and a sense of pride in past accomplishments.

• Compatibility of personalities with people already on your staff. You must consider good chemistry as you gather people who will function comfortably and happily on a team.

• Contrary evidence. Be skeptical if an applicant assures you that he is flexible, then says he wants to work only with four-year-olds.

Things to ask about Ask about the applicant's experiences calling for the basic skills of the job, whether you are interviewing teachers or cooks. Phrase your questions to learn how the applicant has managed situations in the past. You can begin such questions with "Describe for me a time when ..." and go on with "... you had to meet a time commitment at work and faced an unexpected problem at home." Other examples: "... a child had you perplexed and at your wits end," "... you felt tension between yourself and someone else on the staff," or "... you came to work and found that the person on duty before you had left something important undone."

Two key areas to ask about: successes and failures. "Give me an example of an activity with a group of children that you felt was an outstanding success. What made it work?" Or, "Share with me a time when an activity was a flop. How did you handle that?" (Listen here for developmental appropriateness.)

Two other key areas: teamwork and leadership. "Tell me about times when you have worked as a member of a team" and "about a situation in which you were responsible for the actions of others."

Other questions • Where do you get your ideas for curriculum?

• If a child spends a lot of time wandering around with her thumb in her mouth, not participating in activities, what would you do?

• What would you do if a child who has come to the center happily for some time cries bitterly one morning when her parent leaves?

• Describe for me a structured environment.

• What would you do if a three-year-old painted her arms and hands with purple paint?

• Why did you leave your job (or why are you planning to leave)?

• Do you have a current first aid training certificate?

What you may not ask

An employment interview is considered a type of pre-employment test that must be conducted consistently and fairly. Some pre-employment inquiries are prohibited by law. Others are not specifically illegal but have been ruled discriminatory in employment rights decisions by the courts. These restrictions on the interview process are based on the recognition that individual differences make general personal characteristics unreliable—and unfair—predictors of job success. The key to measuring the validity of an interview question is job-relatedness.

You may not ask pre-employment questions about the following:

- *Race* or racial heritage
- *Sex* or sexual preference
- *Marital status*
- *Religion*
- *National origin* (or the national origin of the applicant's parents).
- *Pregnancy*—You cannot refuse to hire a woman solely because of pregnancy. You can reject a pregnant applicant if it can be shown that she does not meet valid, established physical requirements for the job.
- *Children or child care arrangements*—If you discriminate against women with children you must also refuse to hire men with children. Not all parents are unreliable in reporting to work, just as not all childless employees are dependable.
- *Transportation or living arrangements*—Where or with whom a person lives is not a relevant employment concern. You may discuss with applicants the lack of bus service, the cab fare from town, or any other special problems to consider when they decide whether to take the job. Your concern is that they get to work on time, not how.
- *Age*—You may ask about age only if the applicant is under 18 or over 70. A teen may need a work permit, may be allowed to work only limited hours, or may not be allowed to use certain equipment
- *Group or club membership*—Many clubs designate race, religion, or national origin. You may ask only whether an applicant belongs to a relevant professional organization, such as NAEYC, if that would be helpful to job performance.
- *Union membership*—You may not ask about past or present union membership or union activity.
- *Workers' compensation history*—You may not ask whether an applicant has ever filed a claim for workers' compensation.
- *Discrimination charges*—You may not ask whether an applicant has ever filed a discrimination suit or other legal complaint against a past employer.

You may ask some of these questions *after* you have hired the applicant if you have some business reason for needing the answer. For example, you need to know about marital status in order to know how to handle payroll tax deductions. You must accommodate an employee's religion or religious observance in scheduling work time unless it creates undue hardship on other employees or the operation of the business.

Don't let these restrictions bother you. By sticking to strictly job-related issues, you make wise use of your time, maintain a legal and fair posture, and gather the information you need to make a hiring decision. If the applicant begins to share unsolicited information that is not relevant, tactfully steer the conversation back to the pertinent issues. Never record such information, even when it is volunteered.

Things to cover Discuss *all* facets of the job—housekeeping duties, flexibility of schedules, and wages. Do not conclude an interview with someone you want to hire without discussing the compensation for the position and the approximate wages the applicant can expect to earn each week.

Non-verbal signals In addition to listening to what the applicant has to say, make certain to consider her physical appearance and posture. People often reveal how they feel about themselves by their body language—the way they stand or sit—and dress. Accepting a casual style of dress does not mean overlooking a sloppy appearance.

After the interview Make notes as soon as possible and attach them to the candidate's application. If you are interested in employing some of the applicants you have interviewed, suggest that they come back again, this time to observe the groups in which you have openings. Arrange these visits with the cooperation of the lead teachers involved, allowing them to become better acquainted with the candidates. You may ask them to assist in making the final decisions on which applicants to hire. Inviting the applicants to a second visit may imply that the position will be offered, and places the responsibility on you for explaining a decision *not* to hire.

Before hiring Check the references provided for *all* potential members of your staff and make sure that they have the necessary credentials to meet the licensing requirements for the positions. If you have to make an offer of employment before you can check the references, make clear to the candidate that, if you discover any irregularity in the background check which would tend to make the employee undesirable, you will have to consider it carefully. Should it develop that you would not have hired the person if you had known all the facts, employment will have to be terminated.

Children of staff Many directors do not allow members of their staff to enroll their own children in the program, fearing that a teacher, for example, might favor her child over others, causing resentment in other parents, or that the teacher's child might want to cling to the parent. Neither is a fair generalization. Many centers benefit from the extra care and enthusiasm given to the program by the teacher, cook, or custodian whose own child is enrolled.

It happened:
> *Sydonie, an outstanding teacher, chose to teach kindergarten in a private center for half the salary she could have earned in the public*

school because her baby could be enrolled in the infant program in the same center.

The cleanest facility we operated was maintained by Cliff, a public-school custodian who cleaned nights in exchange for a scholarship for his five-year-old daughter.

Avoid panic hiring You probably won't make your best choices in an emergency. Instead, hire substitutes while you screen and interview several candidates for any opening, no matter how urgent the need seems to be.

It is unwise to hire someone as a teaching assistant, expecting to keep her in that position, if she is qualified to be a lead teacher and feels she is capable of being one. If you have a realistic possibility that such a position may become available within a specified period of time, you can make that conditional offer.

Once a parent has decided to enroll a child, you will need to allow as much as an hour to explain the policies for tuition payment, daily program, health and safety, special events, and parent involvement. We have included a sample Statement of Tuition Policy on page 46 and an Enrollment Application on page 47. They include details common to most of the centers we have surveyed.

Parents need to understand the reasons for center policies before signing the application to avoid confusion later on. As you review each of the following points, read each policy statement aloud to the parents and look at them to be sure they agree (you should conduct this process as carefully as a banker reviews the terms and conditions of a loan with her client):

Tuition policies

Calendar—What weekly and daily schedule does the tuition payment cover?
- Annual enrollment fee (which may run between $25 and $50)—Is it refundable? Under what conditions?
- Tuition deposit—Will it be applied to the last week?
- Tuition payments—How often? If you charge a late payment fee, how do you define *late*?
- Returned check fee—How many will you accept before you demand cash?
- Absence, illness, vacation—Is tuition reduced or omitted?
- Withdrawal—How much notice do you require?

Enrollment application

Explain the information you require on the front of the form and have the parent sign it. Then explain each of the authorizations you need and ask for a signature for each after you have explained it. Do not accept one signature for all the authorizations. Remind the parent that those listed as emergency contacts or as authorized to pick up the child should be notified that someone from the center may telephone them in an emergency.

Parent handbook

We urge you to create a handbook rather than give out policies on loose sheets of paper. Some of the information may not at first have relevance to every parent, but at some later date you and the parent may wish to review some of the specific policies.

Begin your handbook with an introductory "Welcome!" a statement of the center's philosophy and a description of its program, and a statement of its non-discrimination policy. Add a request that the parent keep the handbook for easy reference during the year.

Review the wording

Some of these policies may be required by regulations. *Review the wording* with your licensor *before* you distribute the handbook.

Points to cover   • Describe procedures for drop-off (sign-in) and pick-up (sign-out) of children. Describe where parents may park and which entrance to use to enter the building.

State the center's policy about food brought from home—daily or on special occasions.

• Describe how children's birthdays will be acknowledged at the center and how holidays will be celebrated.

• Suggest appropriate clothing for everyday wear and list items of clothing to be kept at the center. Insist that each item be marked with the child's name.

• Describe opportunities for parent involvement, explaining which are required or optional, and which are formal or informal.

• State the center's schedule of parent conferences and parent meetings and explain how to request a conference with a teacher.

• Describe the center's discipline policy, stating how a child will be dealt with in response to specific behaviors.

• Describe the policies and procedures for closing because of problems at the facility or emergency weather conditions. Explain where children will be taken if they have to be evacuated from the center.

• Describe the procedure when a child arrives at the center with symptoms of an illness or develops symptoms during the day. Explain how parents are expected to respond.

• Describe the procedures the center will follow if a child is injured and requires either first aid or emergency medical treatment.

• Describe the center's procedures for reporting suspected child abuse, following your state's published guidelines, and include the telephone number for the child abuse hotline.

• State the parents' rights to know what information is in the child's folder, to amend that information, to obtain copies, and to control release of the information to people or agencies outside the center.

• List all the forms that must be completed and in your hands before the child can attend the center. Point out the information that must be updated annually, such as the names of the people to contact in emergencies and the record of a health examination.

The forms that appear on the following pages are among the ones you will need as you analyze the market for the services you plan to provide, apply for financial backing, prepare your center for its first clients, and then operate it.

Even though all the material in this book is covered by national and international copyright laws, we have specifically excluded the forms on these pages from copyright protection. Feel free to photocopy the forms and use them just as you find them here or photocopy them and adapt them to your center's particular needs.

The forms included here are:

MARKET ANALYSIS

Part One: Proposed Site

	within 1 mile	within 3 miles
Population	_____	_____
Children ages 0 to 4 in the last five years	_____	_____
Working mothers with at least one child age 0 to 4	_____	_____
Median income	_____	_____

Summary of competitor profiles (centers within three miles serving 35 or more children)

name	total capacity	total enrollment	percent of capacity	rates for infant	rates for toddler	rates for preschool
1 _____	_____	_____	_____	_____	_____	_____
2 _____	_____	_____	_____	_____	_____	_____
3 _____	_____	_____	_____	_____	_____	_____
4 _____	_____	_____	_____	_____	_____	_____
5 _____	_____	_____	_____	_____	_____	_____
6 _____	_____	_____	_____	_____	_____	_____
7 _____	_____	_____	_____	_____	_____	_____
8 _____	_____	_____	_____	_____	_____	_____
9 _____	_____	_____	_____	_____	_____	_____

Part Two: Profile for Each Competitor

Name: _____   Date: _____

Address: _____   Caller: _____

Telephone: _____

Name of contact: _____

Hours of operation: _____

Age range of children   _____

	Number of children:		Rates Full day	Half day
Infants	_____		_____	_____
Toddlers	_____		_____	_____
Preschool	_____		_____	_____
Kindergarten	_____		_____	_____
After school	_____		_____	_____

Total enrollment   _____   Licensed capacity   _____

	yes	no
Part of a chain?	☐	☐
Transportation to and from school?	☐	☐
Hot meals? Breakfast	☐	☐
Lunch	☐	☐
Snacks? Morning	☐	☐
Afternoon	☐	☐
Building constructed for child care?	☐	☐

Comments: _____

_____

_____

_____

_____

_____

OUTLINE FOR BUSINESS PLAN

AND FUNDING PRESENTATION

I. OVERVIEW

II. THE ORGANIZATION
- A. Brief background
- B. Objectives
- C. Management

III. THE MARKET
- A. Women entering the work force
- B. Two-income households
- C. Employer financial assistance
- D. The competition

IV. GENERAL OPERATIONS
- A. Five-year plan
  - 1. Total revenues
  - 2. Operating expenses
  - 3. Pretax income
- B. Organization chart
- C. Real estate
  - 1. Site selection
  - 2. Cost and cost control
  - 3. Funding

V. SERVICES AND PHILOSOPHY
- A. Age: six weeks to six years
- B. Curriculum
- C. Quality
- D. Affordability

VI. PERSONNEL
- A. Recruiting
- B. Training
- C. Retention and motivation
- D. Costs

VII. MARKETING AND ENROLLMENT
- A. Initial September opening
- B. Promotional program
- C. Enrollment process
- D. Tuition rates

VIII. FINANCIAL DATA
- A. Financial history
- B. Financial projections
- C. Current stockholders and number of shares

IX. INVESTMENT
- A. Capital sought
- B. Security and terms offered
- C. Use of funds
  - 1. Pre-opening expenses
  - 2. Operating loss during first six months
- D. Exit evaluation

X. MANAGEMENT AND ORGANIZATION
- A. Board of Directors
- B. Advisory Board
- C. Key management
- D. Organization chart
- E. Expansion plan

BUDGET FOR START-UP COSTS*

Center will serve _____ FTE's: ____ preschool, ____ toddler, ____ infant

Professional services	$ _____
Insurance	_____
Licenses and fees	_____
Educational furniture	_____
Educational equipment and supplies	_____
Playground equipment and fencing	_____
Office furniture	_____
Office equipment and supplies	_____
Telephone system	_____
Cleaning equipment	_____
Health, cleaning, and paper supplies	_____
Kitchen equipment	_____
Kitchen food and supplies	_____
Salaries and benefits	_____
Books, dues, and subscriptions	_____
Marketing and promotion	_____
Printing	_____
Postage	_____
Miscellaneous	_____
Total	$ _____

* Does not include real estate expense

BUDGET FOR PRE-OPENING OPERATING EXPENSES

AND CASH FLOW SUMMARY

	Month 1	Month 2	Month 3	Total
Director's Salary	$ _____	$ _____	$ _____	$ _____
Staff Salaries	_____	_____	_____	_____
Benefits	_____	_____	_____	_____
Promotion	_____	_____	_____	_____
Printing	_____	_____	_____	_____
Maintenance/Cleaning	_____	_____	_____	_____
Utilities/Telephone	_____	_____	_____	_____
Supplies	_____	_____	_____	_____
Miscellaneous	_____	_____	_____	_____
Rent	_____	_____	_____	_____
Taxes/License fees	_____	_____	_____	_____
Insurance	_____	_____	_____	_____
Vehicles	_____	_____	_____	_____
Total	$ _____	$ _____	$ _____	$ _____

BUDGET AND PLAN FOR FISCAL YEAR

beginning July 1 and ending June 30

	Jul	Aug	Sep	Oct	Nov	Dec	Jan	Feb	Mar	Apr	May	Jun
CAPACITY: FTE'S	___	___	___	___	___	___	___	___	___	___	___	___
AVERAGE % ENROLLMENT	___%	___%	___%	___%	___%	___%	___%	___%	___%	___%	___%	___%
AVERAGE FTE'S:												
Infants/Toddlers	___	___	___	___	___	___	___	___	___	___	___	___
Preschoolers	___	___	___	___	___	___	___	___	___	___	___	___
Total	___	___	___	___	___	___	___	___	___	___	___	___
AVERAGE WEEKLY TUITION:												
Infants/Toddlers	$___	___	___	___	___	___	___	___	___	___	___	___
Preschoolers	$___	___	___	___	___	___	___	___	___	___	___	___

	Jul	Aug	Sep	Oct	Nov	Dec	Jan	Feb	Mar	Apr	May	Jun	Total	Source by %
REVENUE Tuition														
Infants/Toddlers	$___	___	___	___	___	___	___	___	___	___	___	___	___	___%
Preschoolers	$___	___	___	___	___	___	___	___	___	___	___	___	___	___%
Registration Fees	$___	___	___	___	___	___	___	___	___	___	___	___	___	___%
Less discount for siblings	$___	___	___	___	___	___	___	___	___	___	___	___	___	___%
TOTAL REVENUE	$___	___	___	___	___	___	___	___	___	___	___	___	___	100%

EXPENSES		% of Revenue
Director's salary	$ ____	____ %
Teaching salaries	$ ____	____ %
Other salaries	$ ____	____ %
Benefits	$ ____	____ %
Professional services	$ ____	____ %
Equipment replacement	$ ____	____ %
Repairs	$ ____	____ %
Food	$ ____	____ %
Cleaning	$ ____	____ %
Telephone	$ ____	____ %
Utilities	$ ____	____ %
Education supplies	$ ____	____ %
Office supplies	$ ____	____ %
Paper/cleaning supplies	$ ____	____ %
Dues & subscriptions	$ ____	____ %
Miscellaneous	$ ____	____ %
Rent	$ ____	____ %
Real estate taxes	$ ____	____ %
License/Accreditation fees	$ ____	____ %
Property/Liability Insurance	$ ____	____ %
Depreciation	$ ____	____ %
Amortization	$ ____	____ %
Equipment rental	$ ____	____ %
TOTAL EXPENSES	$ ____	____ %
NET	$ ____	100%

SCHEDULE OF PRE-OPENING TASKS

	First Quarter			Second Quarter			Third Quarter			Fourth Quarter		
	1	2	3	4	5	6	7	8	9	10	11	12
CONSTRUCTION												
Meet with building inspector	x											
Conceptual design				x	x							
Cost estimate & contractor agreement					x							
Design freeze						x						
Construction schedule						x						
Building permit						x						
Begin construction/fit-out							x					
Completion date									x			
Playground/site work										x		
Utilities in									x			
Occupancy permit										x		
MARKETING AND PROMOTION												
Brochures & fliers									x			
Signs ordered									x			
Signs installed									x	x		
Direct mail: first & second mailings												
Advertising							*	*	*	*	*	*
Promotional events							Write a detailed schedule with dates for each					
Community meetings							step; coordinate with the director of operations.					
Media articles							*	*	*	*	*	*
Newsletter										x		
Yellow Pages: get publication date							x					
Visit information & referral agencies									x			
Visit local businesses									x			

OPERATIONS

	First Quarter			Second Quarter			Third Quarter			Fourth Quarter		
	1	2	3	4	5	6	7	8	9	10	11	12
Meet with licensor	x											
Telephone service installed							x				x	x
Answering service operational								x				
Printing									x			
Director hired									x			
Director's office furnished										x		
Utilities on										x		
Supplies & equipment ordered									x			
Supplies & equipment received										x		
Parent & staff handbooks prepared											x	
License application prepared											x	
Staff hired											x	
Pre-opening training for staff												x
Workplace events												x
Community meetings												
Newsletter											x	
Open houses											x	x
Playground ready											x	.
License review											x	
License received										x		
Enrollment										x	x	x
Written plan for 1st & 2nd week												x

Write a detailed schedule with dates for each step; coordinate with the director of operations.

MARKETING ACTIVITY CHECKLIST

Activity	Date	Result*
Phoned telephone inquirers	_____	_____
	_____	_____
Posted calendar of curriculum events	_____	_____
	_____	_____
Held daytime event for _____	_____	_____
	_____	_____
Held evening event for _____	_____	_____
	_____	_____
Mailed newsletter to parents	_____	_____
Advertised in _____	_____	_____
	_____	_____
Placed news story in _____	_____	_____
	_____	_____
Called on referral agency	_____	_____
	_____	_____
Called on real estate/rental agency	_____	_____
	_____	_____
Called on _____	_____	_____
	_____	_____
Attended meeting of _____	_____	_____
	_____	_____
Placed posters at _____	_____	_____
	_____	_____
Other	_____
	_____
	_____

*New enrollees or leads to them; news story or speaking engagement; and so on. Repeat the efforts with successful results and skip the ones not worth doing.

INQUIRY RECORD

Your objective in answering is to get the caller to visit our center.

1. In answering, identify the center and introduce yourself

2. Record the caller's name:

3. Ask what type of program the caller wants: _____

4. Ask for information about the child: _____

   Name: _____ Age: _____ Sex: _____

   Comments: _____

5. Invite the parent and child to visit:

   Day: _____ Date: _____ Time: _____

6. Ask how caller heard of the center:

   _____

7. Ask for caller's name, address, and phone number:

   Name: _____ Phone: _____

   Address: _____

8. Thank the caller for calling the center.

Follow-up answer by: _____ Date: _____

Comments: _____

_____

_____

_____

_____

_____

_____

_____

_____

_____

_____

TUITION POLICY

Calendar

The center will be open from Monday through Friday from 6:30 a.m. to 6:00 p.m. throughout the year. It will be closed on these legal holidays:

New Year's Day	Memorial Day	Independence Day
Labor Day	Thanksgiving Day	Christmas Day

Annual Enrollment Fee

A non-refundable enrollment fee is required when the child is first enrolled and on the anniversary of enrollment during successive years.

Deposit

A deposit of one week's tuition is required upon enrollment. The deposit will be applied to the tuition for the last week the child attends.

Tuition

Tuition is paid weekly. The fact that there will be holidays and absences due to illness has been figured into the overall tuition charges and does not change the tuition rate for a single week. These days may not be used for credit.

Tuition is due in advance, payable by Friday morning for the following week, by check or money order. Late payments must be accompanied by a $10.00 late charge. Dishonored checks must be replaced and must be accompanied by a $15.00 fee. After a second occurrence, only cash or money order will be accepted as payment. Accounts two weeks in arrears will result in immediate disenrollment.

Illness

No credit will be given for absences due to illness. These days may not be credited toward vacation.

Vacation

Parents will not be charged for an absence due to vacation if the center receives two weeks written notice in advance. Two weeks vacation, without responsibility for tuition, is permitted during the period from September through June. (A week is considered to be Monday through Friday.)

Program Changes

The center must receive two weeks written notice in advance of any change in program schedule. Changes affecting weekly tuition rates may not be made during a week which includes a legal holiday, because these days were taken into consideration when the tuition rates were established.

Withdrawal

Two weeks written notice is required for withdrawal—for any reason—and parents will be charged for that period. The deposit will be applied to the child's last week of attendance.

APPLICATION FOR ENROLLMENT

Name of child: _____ Date of birth: _____

Home address: _____

_____ Telephone: _____

Mother's name: _____ Telephone: _____

Home address: _____

Work: _____ Telephone: _____

Hours at work: _____

Father's name: _____ Telephone: _____

Home address: _____

Work: _____ Telephone: _____

Hours at work: _____

In case of emergency, give names of persons who can be called if we cannot reach parents (and be sure that these people know you have given us their names):

Name: _____ Telephone: _____

Address: _____ Relationship: _____

Name: _____ Telephone: _____

Address: _____ Relationship: _____

Names and ages of other children in the family:

Name: _____ Age: _____

Name: _____ Age: _____

Is there a physical or emotional problem which might interfere with your child's adjustment to this program? If so, please describe:

_____

I, _____ (parent/guardian), wish to enroll _____ in the child care program for the following schedule:

Days of the week: _____ Hours: _____

Enclosed is the enrollment fee (non-refundable if my child is accepted) and one week's tuition as a deposit. I understand that the tuition deposit will be applied to the last week my child attends. I have read and understand all policy information and agree to comply with these policies.

Signature: _____ Date: _____

AUTHORIZATIONS

The following authorizations are necessary for the center staff to act in your child's best interests at all times. Please complete and sign each one.

child's name: _____

PICK-UP AUTHORIZATION: I hereby authorize

name: _____ Relationship: _____

address: _____ Telephone: _____

name: _____ Relationship: _____

address: _____ Telephone: _____

to pick up my child from the center. If these instructions should change, I will let you know in advance and in writing. (Please note any special instructions and the names of persons not authorized to remove your child from the center.)

Signature of parent/guardian: _____ Date: _____

MEDICAL EMERGENCY PERMISSION:

I ☐ authorize ☐ do not authorize the center staff to administer first aid treatment to my child.

I ☐ authorize ☐ do not authorize the center staff to take my child.to _____ Hospital and authorize treatment by the doctor on call.

Signature of parent/guardian: _____ Date: _____

PHOTOGRAPHIC RELEASE:

I ☐ consent ☐ do not consent and authorize the child care center to use and reproduce photographs taken of my child and to circulate them for advertising and publicity purposes of every description.

Signature of parent/guardian: _____ Date: _____

_____

ENROLLMENT POLICY

Our child care center provides services to children and families without regard to race, sex, religion, cultural heritage, political beliefs, or marital status.

PARENT SURVEY

1. How did you first hear of this center?
   - ☐ Saw the sign.
   - ☐ Heard about it from a friend.
   - ☐ Saw it listed in the Yellow Pages.
   - ☐ Saw an ad in a newspaper. Which paper? _____
   - ☐ Referred by an agency or employer. Who? _____
   - ☐ Saw a poster or notice. Where? _____
   - ☐ Other: _____

2. Did you receive our brochure in the mail?　　　　☐ Yes　　　☐ No

3. Did you find the brochure
   - ☐ interesting and helpful
   - ☐ confusing
   - ☐ not informative enough
   - ☐ other: _____

4. Did you find it helpful to visit before your child entered?　☐ Yes　　　☐ No

5. Can you recall anything memorable — positive or negative — about the time you and your child visited the center?　　　　☐ Yes　　　☐ No

   What was it? _____

6. What was the most important thing you saw about us that you really liked or that made you decide to send your child here?

   _____

   _____

   _____

7. If we could offer any type of class, activity, or service to your child at the center, what would you like it to be?

   _____

   _____

   _____

8. Any other comments?　_____

   _____

   _____

We appreciate your telling friends and neighbors about us when you have the opportunity. Thank you

Your signature (if you wish)　_____

EMPLOYEE ORIENTATION CHECKLIST

Name: _____   Job title: _____

Supervisor: _____   Job title: _____

	employee's initials	date	supervisor's initials
Received copy and reviewed employee handbook	_____	_____	_____
Completed application on file	_____	_____	_____
Employee references on file	_____	_____	_____
Certification and credentials verified	_____	_____	_____
First aid certificate verified	_____	_____	_____
Medical history questionnaire and health screening done	_____	_____	_____
Payroll hire form completed	_____	_____	_____
Benefits package reviewed	_____	_____	_____
Job description reviewed and signed, copy received	_____	_____	_____
Review and performance evaluation procedures explained	_____	_____	_____
Time sheet procedures explained	_____	_____	_____
Attendance policy reviewed	_____	_____	_____
Dress code explained	_____	_____	_____
Emergency procedures, including evacuation plan, explained	_____	_____	_____
Accident/incident reporting procedure explained	_____	_____	_____
Parents' rights reviewed	_____	_____	_____
Infection control procedures explained	_____	_____	_____
Theft or child abuse reporting procedures explained	_____	_____	_____
No smoking policy explained	_____	_____	_____
Proper use of equipment (a-v, fire extinguisher) explained	_____	_____	_____
In-service training program explained	_____	_____	_____
Suggestions and complaint procedure explained	_____	_____	_____
Team and center organization explained	_____	_____	_____
Informed of confidentiality of children's records	_____	_____	_____
Facility tour	_____	_____	_____

Emergency contact: Name: _____   Relationship: _____

Phone number: _____

I have received and understand the policies, procedures, and information listed above.

Employee's signature _____   Date: _____

Supervisor's signature _____   Date: _____

PART TWO

OPERATING A CENTER

Three Keys to Quality:
People
Environment
Program

THE "I AM! I CAN!" PHILOSOPHY

PHYSICAL

EMOTIONAL

I AM!

I CAN!

SOCIAL

INTELLECTUAL

In Part II you will find many references to this diagram. It depicts a frame for the "I AM! I CAN!" philosophy. The four sides of the square represent the four areas of human growth and development.

A child grows in all four of the areas shown on the square, but growth will not be balanced or equal in all areas. At times, physical growth is rapid; at others, the child is bursting with ideas and creative energy. There come times when the need for the companionship of peers is uppermost, while emotional growth will reach highs and lows. A sudden spurt in one direction may be followed by a plateau—a quiet time when the growing individual seems to be absorbing and assimilating what has been experienced.

The four corners of the square can be compared to the sharp edges of a personality. On the social side of "becoming," we rub against others, learn to compromise and adjust, and little by little those sharp corners are honed away. The square moves in the direction of the circle.

The circle within the square, representing the "well-rounded" personality, is as mythical as the perfect human being. In a world abounding in variety and differences, there is a place for everyone. Each must seek the particular place in life which will allow the full use of individual skills, talents, and interests.

The "I AM!" comes through development of a healthy ego, through accepting oneself as a worthwhile human being—needed, wanted, liked, LOVED—and at all times, in all things, BEING ACCEPTED AS IS.

The arrows in the diagram indicate that when this is the case, the child can approach each new developmental task with confidence and meet with success. Each new success strengthens the "I CAN!" which in turn reinforces the "I AM!," and the beautiful circular motion thus established can go on *ad infinitum.*

The human personality in the developing process might be compared to the human figure in the growing process, bulging in one spot today, sticking out in another next week, or being completely lopsided for an extended period. The "I AM! I CAN!" philosophy does not seek to create perfect patterns of the square and circle, but uses the image symbolically to define a basic philosophy of education.

What happens to the very young, developing person who is constantly put down, denied inherent rights to physical and psychological protection, thwarted, discouraged, labeled by society as a misfit or a dropout? Continual assault on the "I AM!" will make it impossible for the child to become a competent, contributing member of society. The lack of decent self-image will destroy the "I AM!" and will cancel out any hope of developing the "I CAN!"

Teachers have a responsibility to constantly evaluate *total* development, to be aware of the progress of each child in each area of growth at *all* times. They observe children with this pattern in mind, seeing them as individuals, not just members of a group.

There will always be children who are at one end or the other of a continuum, either bright, attractive children who make teaching a joy, or the ones who, because of their behavior or personality, are hard to love. In between these two extremes are the "deprived" children, neither "good" nor "bad" enough to draw attention. They go through life unnoticed, never receiving the extra attention which might develop their full potential. The true teacher sees and appreciates each and every child. Though each one deserves and should receive a full share of time and attention, it is neither possible nor necessary that they all receive *equal shares*, since needs vary, both within groups and within individuals. The child who is suddenly bursting with creative energy after a month of easy social growth needs to be stimulated and challenged. The teacher who has kept lap and arms ready for the shy and insecure child intuitively senses when to pull back and let go, or when to give a gentle nudge of encouragement.

A teacher will know which child can climb the ladder on the slide, which one is poorly coordinated, which one is trying to find a friend, cautiously working toward becoming a social being. It is important also to recognize biting, kicking, and grabbing behavior as another form of social awakening. A teacher can "read" the frustration of a child through the language of behavior. As that child, guided by the teacher, accepts the fact that life is not always perfect, one of the sharp corners of the developmental square will be chipped away.

Each teacher thrills to see the glow of success on the face of a child, and strives to create opportunities for that success—EVERY DAY!

Each teacher works to stimulate healthy growth in all areas of development, enabling each child to say, "I AM! I CAN!"

Chapter 10   **STAFF TRAINING AND PREPARATION**

It is impossible to overemphasize the value of staff training. If you are opening a new center, and if you have been able to budget for staff payroll for the week before opening, you will find that expense to be a worthwhile investment. We trust that you will find the plan outlined here to be useful.

Whether you have hired experienced teachers or people starting their first jobs in child care, this week will serve several purposes:

It will give you the assurance that they will know the things that you, the owner-director, feel are essential in a well-run center.

It will introduce team teaching and establish the teams.

It will develop a feeling of unity, a feeling of pride in their center, and a sense of professionalism among all members of the staff.

If you cannot do this training in the framework we outline here, figure out another plan—but *do it.* Give the training in the evenings, give the training on a weekend retreat—but give it. Even if you have only three teachers, they need to begin to feel like a team, to become comfortable with one another, and to know what you expect of them.

As the director, you will probably want to present your own training program, but in a large center you may ask the assistant director, team leaders, or director of education to conduct some sessions.

Day One

Welcome   Welcome members of the staff and give a brief history of the center.

Philosophy   Explain the "I AM! I CAN!" philosophy, using the diagram on page 53.

Outline a day   Talk the staff through an entire day from the moment the door opens in the morning until it is locked at night. Use visual aids such as diagrams and floor plans. Personalize your talk by using names. "It is 6:45 a.m. Mary is the first to arrive. She will ... Then, at 7:00 Tony comes. His first job is ... The first child arrives at 7:00 ... At 7:30 Su Lee will come. By that time there may be as many as seven children. ..." Your listeners should be able to visualize the process. Lead a tour of the building, referring throughout to places mentioned in your description of the day's activities.

Team teaching	Explain the system of team teaching, in which most teams are made up of all the teachers working with the same age group. Introduce or identify all the members of each team in your center.
Snack time	Have members of each team sit together. Ask lead teachers to discuss the usual snack time procedures.
Health	Using Chapter 42, conduct a session on health. Have someone give a wrong-way and right-way demonstration of hand-washing.
Zoning	Explain zoning. Discuss lunch, toileting, and nap time, as described in Chapter 33, *Daily Schedules and Routines*, showing how zoning works.
Lunch	Have team members sit together at children's tables, with lead teachers playing the roles of their teachers. Ask members of the team to follow the procedures described, including clean-up.
Break	Take a breather.
Music	Teach a few name games and at least three songs and explain when and how they are used. Discuss music and its place in the curriculum.
Safety	Explain the center's safety policies. Allow time for detailed discussion, using material from Chapter 43, *Safety*.
Environment	Ask each team to go to its own area, where the lead teachers should talk about creating the right environment and maintaining it. Be sure they cover *voice control*, as described in Chapter 29, and mention housekeeping.
Review	Bring the entire group together again to review material covered that day through such devices as role playing. Ask open-ended questions that will stimulate thinking and communications.

Day Two

Ages and stages	Explain the term *developmentally appropriate* and how it applies to both curriculum and discipline. (Refer to page 2 of Sue Bredekamp's *Developmentally Appropriate Practice* [NAEYC].) Discuss small- and large-muscle development. Explain solitary, parallel, and group play.
Snack time	Demonstrate informal snack procedures.
Curriculum	Discuss how curriculum relates to the philosophy of your center. Describe a typical day for preschool group, toddler group, infant group, and school-age group (depending on the ones included in your center).
Lunch	Ask the newcomers to organize lunch and follow-up: hand-washing, table setting, clean-up, and a review of toileting and nap time.

Break	Take a breather.
Songs and finger plays	Teach several more songs and finger plays. (See the headings *Finger Plays* and *Songs* in the *Index* to Vol. 2.)
Supplies	Describe where general supplies are stored and what supplies are stored in each team area. Explain everyone's responsibility for the care and replacement of supplies.
Parent-teacher relationships	Describe relationships with parents, including your center's multi-cultural approach (respecting all cultures) and policies on confidentiality and separating social from professional relationships.
Review in teams	Have the teams meet to review and discuss the day's subjects.
Employee Handbook	Gather the entire group to go over the contents of the Employee Handbook, stressing appearance, promptness, and such problems as absenteeism, and allowing opportunities for questions and discussion.

Day Three

Discipline	Explain how the "I AM! I CAN!" philosophy relates to discipline. Discuss the definition and the Four Step Plan described in Chapter 28.
Snack time	
Observation and recording	Describe the process of observation and recording. Pass out the record cards for each teacher's group. Go over sample cards, explaining each kind of entry. Refer to Chapter 15, *Observation and Recording*.
Lunch	
Licensing and regulation	Review the regulations relevant to your center. Pass out copies of the regulations that directly concern members of the staff. Stress the importance of understanding the regulations and how they apply to the practices followed in the center.
Safety review	Ask questions based on the safety material you covered on Day One. Pass out copies of the safety checklists and discuss their contents.
Interest centers	Define interest centers. Discuss traditional versus integrated programs.
Prepare to set up	Break up into team meetings, at which lead teachers describe the division of responsibilities in setting up the center the next morning.
Keys to quality	At the final general meeting, talk about the three keys that will guide teachers —people, environment, and program—and close with a message of praise, encouragement, anticipation, and excitement!

Day Four

Preparation
Spend the morning preparing the rooms for the first parent-child visits. You and your lead teachers assist the new teachers and go over your own checklists.

Orientation
Afternoon: Meet with parents and children, as described in the next chapter, *Orientation Day*.

Day Five

Orientation
Morning: Repeat yesterday afternoon's process with other parents and children.

Final preparations
Afternoon: Complete your preparations for opening day. See Chapter 12, *Last Day Countdown*.

New staff during the year
It is fine when an entire staff can be employed and trained at one time —but it seldom happens that way! During the year, you may have to add more teachers or replace any who leave. How can you be sure that a newly hired teacher has been adequately trained in your practices and procedures? You may have the best intentions, you may even think you have covered all the bases, until the day when you see something that makes your blood run cold and the teacher protests, "But no one ever told me that!"

That was our motivation for creating a videotaped staff training program. In ten sessions, it covers the basics—the knowledge every person should have before being allowed to start working with children (see Chapter 44). With this tool, you can make up a training program and appoint a member of the staff to guide the newcomer through it. The appointed guide becomes the new teacher's coach.

Picture Sandy on her first day on the job. You greet her and introduce her to Virginia, explaining that Virginia will be her coach. "If you have questions about salaries or policies, come to me; other than that, talk to Virginia." Sandy will probably find it less intimidating to ask a co-worker, especially if she feels that her question may sound a bit stupid. Virginia will show Sandy where to hang her coat and put her personal property, tell her where the staff room is and how and when she will use it, point out the location of the bathroom, introduce her to the rest of the staff, and do whatever she can to make her feel comfortable. From that point on, she will guide Sandy through the entire training program, using a checklist to make sure she has covered every necessary bit of information.

The coach system has a dual benefit. The teacher you select for this important task feels he has moved a step up in status, which is good for his "I AM!" At the same time, when he teaches someone else, he strengthens and reinforces his own knowledge base.

Chapter 11   **ORIENTATION DAY**

It is important to have the child come to the center for orientation before his first day. The purpose is for him to become comfortable in his new surroundings while still secure in the company of his own parents. Attention to detail on this important occasion will pay dividends in the tranquility of the first day and the overall adjustment of the child.

The major purpose is for staff to get acquainted with individual children and vice versa before they come together as a group. The following suggestions should be applied for a new center just opening, but when children enter during the year it is important to see that they receive the same careful consideration.

Accommodating parent schedules

The procedure should be spread out over one or two days, with small groups coming at various times so the teachers can spend time with each child. Some directors will plan for a two-hour period in the morning and another in the afternoon. Others will schedule children to come for one hour, four at a time. Some parents can take time off at the beginning of the day and others will find it easier late in the afternoon. If the only time that a working parent can come is on a Saturday, a teacher should see that it is to her advantage to make this accommodation.

Name tags

The environment should be carefully arranged, with enough toys to make it interesting, but not enough to cause confusion. Each child should be given a name tag. Attractively decorated, it will become a special possession which he will wear with pride. Making or decorating the tag could be the first thing parent and child do together. In addition to the name tag he puts on, his name pinned or attached with Velcro to his back will help staff members address him by name, reinforcing his "I AM!" Putting the name on his back will give greater visibility as he bends over a table, stands at the easel, or sits on the floor.

Introduce routines

The child should be introduced to as many of the daily routines as possible. When he chooses his cubby, it is marked with his name and a symbol (a seal or sticker) or, even better, with a snapshot of him which the center had requested. If he has worn an outer garment, he should hang it on his very own hook (*Space of My Own*, Vol. 2, p. 6).

The child should be shown where the bathroom is and assured that "You can go any time you need to, but I will remind you in case you forget." It is best to show the child a rest mat or cot and explain about naps. Mealtime will be explained when snacks are served—when all the children sit down with their parents for juice.

Take pictures   If a staff member can take candid pictures of parent and child together at the open house, the pictures provide a helpful record to the director. During the first weeks teachers might use these pictures in name games, or might display them on an attractive poster, where the children can find their own pictures and begin to identify their new friends.

Store extra clothing   Extra clothing should be marked and stored where the child can see it. Decorated shoe boxes, uniform in size and marked with the same symbol as that on the child's cubby, can be stored on a high shelf.

Suggestions to parents   The director can make helpful suggestions to the parents:

- Make frequent casual references to the center, calling it by name.
- Stop by to visit the playground.
- Shop for new clothes to wear on the first day.

The word *casual* is the key. Overemphasis or exaggeration could back-fire. The intent is to ease the transition from the security of home and family to the new environment—not to push the child out of the nest.

It is 8:00 Friday morning. You have all day to make sure you have covered everything in this chapter. Then you can relax and enjoy the weekend before your center opens Monday morning.

People are ready　Everyone is ready, from the director who greets parents and children at the door, to the receptionist at the desk, to the teacher who smilingly calls each child by name.

What can the teacher do ahead of time to help the child have a good first day?

• Make sure you have a color-coded name tag for every child and match each child's color to her teacher's color.

• Study the record cards before school opens and know each child's name and something about her. "You have a baby sister. Do you help your mother take care of her?"

• Know whether this child comes to school with her mother, her father, or a driver. If she comes with a driver, know the driver's name. Know when this child comes and leaves.

• Talk about, rehearse, and memorize daily procedures so well that the first day will go like clockwork, and the atmosphere will be calm and serene.

Environment is ready　The whole center is sparkling clean. Interest centers are set up to be inviting without being overwhelming. In the dramatic play area, there's a doll in the crib, pans on the play stove, dishes for a tea party set out on the child-size table. In the science area, there may be growing plants, an assortment of shells on a table, perhaps a gerbil in a cage. In the reading corner, soft pillows are on the floor and new books with attractive covers are on display.

Program has been planned　The *program* for the first day has been carefully planned, to allow for a mix of the new and intriguing and the introduction of a few routines that will help the children settle in.

Learning names　The wise teacher will not start the day by trying to teach all the names, but will work on name recognition more subtly. "Teddy, you may sit here by Pedro." "Look, Maria, Sandy has a blue dress, and so do you." By afternoon, the children *may* be ready to play a simple game such as *Rolling-a-Name* (Vol. 2, p. 4).

A fun activity　An activity that is really fun makes a good beginning. Weather permitting—that is, no rain or high wind—take the children outside for a new experience in bubble blowing: *Table Bubbles* (Vol. 2, p. 195).

Not too much　Do not plan too many activities for the first day. Resist the temptation to make sure every child is doing something all the time. Some children need to stand back and watch for a while.

Winding down   Winding-down activities for the end of the day could include making a game of putting toys away (Vol. 2, p. 87), putting the dolls to bed, or hearing a story. Playing with soapsuds at the sink sends the children home with clean hands (have plastic aprons so they will also go home with dry clothes). If they play a game, choose one that can continue even as the children leave one by one, such as *Guess Who?* (Vol. 2, p. 4).

Final check   As the pilot of a plane uses a checklist to be certain that everything is ready for takeoff, so a director makes one last check of people, environment, and program. It's possible that Monday will run so smoothly that a visitor would never know it was the first day.

Chapter 13   **ADJUSTMENT TO SEPARATION**

First day feelings   If the parents have taken advantage of the plan offered in Chapter 11, *Orientation Day*, the first day should not be a problem. However, if that has not happened, a child's first experience away from home is as earth-shaking to him as the first trip across the ocean is to an adult. Feelings of anticipation and excitement are mingled with fear and apprehension. Recognizing this, the staff will have considered every tiny detail which might pave the way for a happy experience. It is important to step into the child's skin, to try to relate to a remembered experience, such as your first day on a new job.

The crying child   You will have done everything you can to make this a happy day for the children, and for most of them it will work—but there's no guarantee. What about the child who *does* cry? Why does it happen? Sometimes all the advance preparations are not possible, as in this story:

Sudden change   *It happened:*

A father, a busy executive, called a school one night at eight o'clock. "My wife left me, and the housekeeper I hired also walked out today, leaving my son with a neighbor. I have just heard about you and your school. Can you take my boy tomorrow?"

The director explained the usual procedure, expressing sympathy for his problem but stressing the fact that this boy must also be feeling very insecure and deserted. "Yes, I agree," replied the father, "and I will be able to spend some time at the school soon, but tomorrow I have an important meeting, one which I just can't postpone." "Then I suggest," replied the director, "that you bring your son at seven o'clock and stay until you have to leave. I hope by then he will be willing to let you go. If he isn't ready, I think it would be better for you to take him with you and let your secretary take care of him in the next office than to let him feel deserted again." Because he had no alternative, the father reluctantly agreed. The staff were advised about this child's special needs and made every effort to make the boy feel welcome and to interest him in some activity. He was a bright, alert child. At nine-thirty he smiled at his father and said, "OK, Dad, you can go now." A grateful and relieved father left, saying, "Please call me at work if you need me. I can see how important this was, and I must say I feel very comfortable about leaving my son in your care."

The mother who can't let go A less dramatic, more common reason for a child who cries the first day may be the mother who finds it hard to let go of the apron strings. She may treat the child like a yo-yo, letting go but holding on, saying goodbye but not leaving, saying "Mommy wants you to be happy—you don't have to stay unless you want to." This behavior puts an impossible burden of choice upon the child, and the teacher must be able to explain this to an anxious parent. A teacher will *never* allow the parent to slip away from the child when he has been distracted.

Fourth-day-itis Most baffling of all is Fourth-day-itis, the sudden, emphatic statement that "I am not going!" It occurs in a child who has been looking forward to going to school, who has sat on the doorstep waiting for the school bus for the first few days, who has come home with exciting accounts of events and new friends at school during these first days. The immediate and obvious reaction is to say, "Something must have happened yesterday." But when the anxious parent calls the school and is told that all had apparently been fine, distrust creeps in. "They must be keeping something from me."

Parents, when they are forewarned, are better able to cope with this problem when it arises. Simply stated, the child wants to be grown-up, to venture out of the nest, but isn't quite ready to cut the umbilical cord. He needs help in taking this decisive step. It may not necessarily be in his conscious thought, but the doubt and hesitation are very real.

This is for real Gradually the child has come to realize that this is different —this is the way it is going to be every day. For this child the following suggestions, which apply to any child having difficulty with the transition from home to school, may serve as the bridge which brings his two worlds together.

Helping the child adjust
• Ask the parent to come in and spend time reassuring and working along with the child.
• Ask working parents who cannot leave work to come for breakfast. Or ask whether there is a close relative, neighbor, or friend who might come.
• Encourage the child to bring objects from home. Vic began his first school experience in an all-day program at a time when things were quite mixed up at home. His father had had a heart attack and mother had gone to work to support the family. Vic carried with him his father's necktie, his sister's scarf, and an old silk blouse of his mother's. One by one, as he became more comfortable, he relinquished these symbols of home and family.
• Use "homework" assignments to bring home and school together. For example, "Bring something blue from your bedroom." (Pin a note to the child explaining such assignments and inform parents of their significance.)
• Help children feel important by giving them notes and bulletins to deliver to their homes.

• Suggest that an insecure child bring a carrot to feed the rabbit, diverting his attention from his anxiety. Holding the guinea pig, something smaller than he is, soft and cuddly, may help allay fears and homesickness.

• Use water play: it is a great relaxer. A child can spend a whole morning playing at a sink full of soapy water, blowing bubbles through a straw and pouring water from one container to another.

• Invite the parents to drop by the school on the weekend and let the child show "my school" to brother, sister, or grandparents.

It happened:

Gene had carried on for three weeks. His mother was ready to make the break. She could see that all was well in school and that Gene needed to be a part of it, not clinging to her. The teacher suggested that she say to the child, "I will take you to school, but when we get there, I am going to go home. Daddy and I have decided that it's good for you to go to school. I know it's a good place, and I know you have fun there. I know the teachers are kind—they all like you. I know the children are your friends. So I will go home."

As expected, he did cry. The teacher put her arms around him and held him firmly while his mother walked away. Then, in a voice so soft he had to stop crying to hear her, she asked, "Have you ever seen purple noodles?" He looked at her in astonishment. Taking his hand, she led him to where the children were coloring uncooked noodles with paint and then gluing them on paper in various shapes and designs. After watching for a few minutes, he joined them. He went home at noon, proudly bearing his paper. He did not give in immediately, but each day he fussed with less vigor and soon was one of the group.

No single answer There is no single answer to the problem of separation. Teachers must follow their intuition and keep in close communication with the parent. The parent must *trust* the teachers — the child must *trust* the teachers — and the teachers must *trust* that the parents really want what is best for the child.

When the parent has to stay In rare cases the parent may have to come and stay until the child is ready to make the break. When that is the only solution, the teacher should try to put the parent to work. "Would you please get the juice from the kitchen?" or "Could you sit at the table with these children?" The child can stand nearby but should not feel the full force of parental attention, anxiety, or impatience. The parent can break away gradually: "Your teacher wants me to go out and get some crackers. I *will* be back in a few minutes." or "I'm going to the store. I *will* come back to take you home." The time will come when the child will say, "You can go home now." Reassure the parents that this will eventually happen and keep reassuring the child that the parent *will* come. Above all, avoid any suggestion of criticism, such as "You are a big boy now, why don't you stop crying and come and play?"

It happened:

    A supervisor observing in a nursery one morning noticed a cry-ing child. "Why is that little boy in the corner crying?" she asked. "Oh, he wants to sit in my lap," was the reply. "Did you leave your lap at home today?" the supervisor asked. "If I let him sit in my lap, every child will want to," was the answer. "Every child doesn't need your lap, but he does!" advised the supervisor.

Don't give up   A word of encouragement. Just when parent and teacher are about to give up in despair, the problem disappears. The child settles in as if he had been going for years, and all is well. Not infrequently this change comes about when another new child enters, and the once insecure child sees himself as a veteran.

Who is she? The young child comes to the teacher as a puzzle, holding the promise of a beautiful picture when "completed." At times the teacher will feel frustrated, unable to find a missing piece, always careful not to make assumptions when an important bit of information, a piece of the puzzle, seems to be a perfect fit but will not fall smoothly into place. The child, unlike the puzzle, will never be seen in totality by her teachers. The separate bits of information or pieces of the puzzle will only aid in the solution, perhaps completing the outer borders into which her life-long growth will blend the final picture.

The early years of childhood are a time of sorting out the many pieces of this human puzzle—the wobbly edges of social awakening, the rounded shapes of physical progress, the straight edges of intellectual growth, the bright and subtle shades of emotional color.

Learn to observe Teachers of the very young are among the first *important* outside influences who will begin to work on this puzzle. How? Where are the clues? One of the most valuable tools will be *observation,* sometimes by standing off to gain an impression of the total developing picture, this growing child; at other times, by careful and close scrutiny of a single facet, a tiny puzzle piece. First, the teacher must understand the full scope of the developmental patterns of the growing child: How does she grow? Where? The individual child must be placed against this background and accepted as she is. Facts, beginning with her name, age, physical makeup, family setting, experiences, cultural heritage, neighborhood, have all contributed to her "I AM." A teacher learns as much as possible about her before she comes into the classroom and can determine that one child came from a world she has learned to trust and another from an environment which has taught her to be wary and suspicious.

Study the facts What are the facts?
Dick is the youngest of five children.
Frances is an only child.
Consuelo is the middle child of five.
Lurene's mother is pregnant.
José speaks Spanish, very little English.
Bill has had one year in a highly structured nursery school.
Steve recently moved from far away.
David was in a car accident and is still having nightmares.
Hans's mother is dead and he has had to adjust to the chaos of a
    succession of housekeepers while coping with his loss.
Kathie is confused by the impending divorce of her parents and the
    relationship of her mother and a new boyfriend.

What do you see?   If the children have visited the school, as suggested, the teacher can add visual observations to the facts he has gathered.

> A physical being—short, tall, fat, agile, clumsy, pale, ruddy, freckle-faced, blue-eyed, elfin brunette, pixie blond.
>
> An emotional being—screaming, stamping a foot in anger, dictating demands to a mother, whining, silent, cowering, whimpering, or happy, exuberant, calm, interested.
>
> A social being—darting from people to things, sampling all with enthusiasm and interest, or a shy, scared child, clinging to a mother.
>
> An intellectual being—unusual vocabulary, loves books, asks questions about classroom materials, recognizes and writes letters and numerals, responds to directions, or one who shows no interest in these areas.

This background information is merely the outer frame for the puzzle; much more is needed. The teacher will never know all of the facts and must be cautious not to jump to conclusions, based on circumstantial evidence.

At first it is enough for the teacher just to be there, comforting, caring, keeping the child close for as long as the security of his presence is needed. During the year, he will seek to understand behavior, needs, and growth patterns through careful observations, and will plan his program around all he learns about the children.

Chapter 15   OBSERVATION AND RECORDING

How can you be sure that no child is being overlooked? That the child who is neither good enough nor bad enough to attract attention is not slipping through the cracks? The teacher can keep records based on observation of the child. The method of record-keeping described here, developed during the 1950's at Green Acres School, not only measures the growth and development of the child but also provides valuable information about the staff and the program.

What the records tell the director

The information the teachers record tells you something about their ability to interact with the children, and even about the quality of their programs.

Using cards

After experimenting with written reports kept in file folders, we decided that everything that needs to be said can be kept on five inch by eight inch cards. In most cases one card per child per school year is enough. Both the cards and boxes to hold them are readily available.

Who writes them?

At the beginning of the year, each teacher is given cards for all the children in her group. She will either take pictures of the children or ask parents to provide pictures to attach to the cards. (It is much easier to bring the child back into memory if you have a picture as well as recorded notes.)

Until a new teacher has been indoctrinated in the procedure, she may need to write out her comments on paper and talk about them with her supervisor. Learning how to condense important information into small segments is a skill which takes some practice.

How often?

Each teacher is expected to record three or four entries during a school year. Each entry should give some information on all four areas of growth and development. Each entry must be dated—it is important to know whether the information comes from the beginning, middle, or end of the school year.

Who reads them?

The cards are first read by the lead teacher, then by the director. In a large center, that may seem like an impossible task for an already overburdened director, but the information will provide a handle on everything that is going on in the center.

Reports are confidential, and should never be left lying about.

It happened:
    A parent glanced through the cards, which had been on top of the cubbies. She created havoc by discussing what she had seen with other parents.

Observing Observing goes beyond *watching* children to be sure they are physically safe and not being disruptive; observing means *thinking about* what can be seen. A very good teacher will relate that thinking to the four sides of the developmental square.

- Sally needs the soothing motion of this swing now, while she is adjusting to new surroundings.
- Cappy has been watching something near that tree for more than fifteen minutes. I must go over and see what it is.
- Today is the first time Gretchen has listened through an entire story. I'll have to remember to tell her mother.

Recording Observing and recording are so interwoven that it is hard to separate them. The following examples of things you might *record* is also a guide to the kinds of things you should *observe*. You will want a pad of paper and a pencil at hand at all times, in a pocket or on a nearby shelf. The time to record is immediately after the conversation or incident—the flavor will be diluted if too much time elapses between seeing and recording.

Improves teaching Accurate recording about a child is a very difficult, yet a very important, function of a teacher. These reports do not just provide a permanent record—they also improve the quality of teaching. The difference between a good teacher and an excellent one can be equated with the gap between observation and perception. The necessity for accurate recording will constantly send the teacher back for another look.

- Does Juan initiate activities?
- When a story is announced, who comes running?
- Is Serena the first one chosen?
- If I say Jim loses his temper easily, can I say what usually triggers an outburst?

Shows progress When a teacher writes a report half-way through the term, does the report show progress?

- Susie clung to her best friend in September. Has she changed?
- Harry was a watcher. Is he participating more now?
- Katrina was bossy. Has she learned to lead without being obnoxious?
- Is it possible that I wrote that Carmela hadn't talked? She never stops talking now!

A teacher will refer often to daily notes while writing cards. A simple description of an event is worth a paragraph of educational or psychological jargon. For example:
- Instead of "Dick is socially mature," the card could read, "Dick is the first to greet a visitor or a new child. He says, 'I'm Dick. What's your name?'"

• A card that reports that "When Delia's little brother was hurt in an accident, she was concerned, but she managed well. She talked about it freely and often" tells more about Delia's emotional stability than the dry, technical term "emotionally stable."

Physical description Writing requires a certain amount of skill, but the skill can be acquired with practice. The first entry on each card should make the child come alive for the reader. It should begin with a *physical* description, set in colorful words that create a visual image of that child. For example:

• Petite and pixieish.
• Breezes through the day like a breath of fresh air.
• Never runs out of gas.
• Gorgeous child —moves with grace and a kind of sophistication.
• Cheery, chubby, curly-headed little cherub.
• Facial expression is guarded and reserved.

Each record should include some evaluation of *physical* prowess or strength. For example:

• Dislikes rough play—is very cautious.
• Excellent stamina. Walked to the top of the hill and was not tired.
• Has no notion of how to manipulate scissors. Holds a crayon in fist, not fingers.

Social behavior Observations of *social* behavior and interaction might read:

• Usually sits by herself watching the group.
• Sweet, gentle, kind; never pushes or reprimands another child.
• Can handle only one friend at a time—gives full attention.
• Not an exhibitionist, but loves to ham for an audience.
• A giving person—offers to help me and other children.

Emotional side The *emotional* side of the square cannot be ignored. It may be picked up in other descriptions, and the language is usually less concrete:

• Boastful, but not to the point of being obnoxious.
• Will stop in the middle of a race to smell a daisy.
• An angry young man—reacts to the slightest provocation.
• Reacts with anger, argument, or avoidance, depending on his mood of the day.

Intellectual growth We are all familiar with the parent who evaluates intellectual progress in terms of papers or rote recitation of the alphabet and numbers. A teacher has many more ways of determining and recording progress.

• Wants to *do*. Made a car with wheels that turn.
• Asks questions until he has sorted something out to his own

satisfaction—then ends questions by saying "Okaaaaay" to himself.
- Enthralled with learning.
- Tries to figure out how things work: the lock on the gate, the hose.

Describing one child A teacher was having trouble writing reports, so the director asked her to "pick one child from your group and talk to me about him—right off the top of your head." She described Chan: "Chan is the kind of boy who never chatters, the way most four-year-olds do; but when we are having juice, and Chan talks, the others all stop and listen." She gave some information about Chan in three areas—social, emotional, and intellectual. Such an example will prove to be more valuable for later reference than a whole page of checklist facts.

Using the cards The cards remain on file long after the child has moved on, and the information they contain can prove to be valuable. A guidance counselor wrote to one center, "I see that John Smith was with you when he was four. What was he like?" Another event that will occur sooner than you think: Melinda applies for a position as a summer camp counselor. When you go to the files and pull out her card, you can recognize the little dynamo who loved to organize games.

The main use of these cards is immediate, not in the future—in conducting parent conferences. It is important for parents to feel that your teachers really *know* their children. Parents also have the right to demand access to any recorded information about their child.

Recording development What follows is not to be used as a checklist. The items listed may lead you to further thinking about the children in your care as you and your teachers watch them grow and develop.

Physical General appearance
    Body type
    Coloring
    Facial expression
Large-muscle coordination
    Walking
    Climbing
    Running
Small-muscle coordination
    Dressing
    Handling scissors, crayons
    Using manipulative materials
Tempo
    Fast
    Slow
    Jerky
    Hesitant

Social Leader
Watcher

Clings to adults
Can share and take turns
Respects rights of others
Resists authority

Emotional   Aggressive in behavior and language
Excessively fearful
Dependent on adults or other children
Withdrawn and shy, but can be drawn in
Easy-going
Able to cope with unexpected situations
Easily frustrated
Uncontrolled temper
Sulks
Moody
Poised
Exhibits crying, tantrums, high-pitched voice, screaming, uncontrolled
laughter, nervous tics, whining, attention-getting devices

Intellectual   Able to follow directions
Has special interests
Has imagination
Is aware of detail
Has initiative
Inventive
Work habits
     Is careless
     Is excessively neat
     Concentrates
     Completes the task
     Accepts rules about using materials

Language development   Speaks only when spoken to
Talks only when he has something to say
Talks all the time, but says little
Speaks in clearly defined sentences
Has special speech defects
Enjoys stories, listening or dictating
Enjoys poetry, listening or dictating
Has good vocabulary

Side One:

Year _____		Driver _____	
Group _____		Teacher _____	
Name _____		Date of birth _____	
Address _____		Telephone _____	
Father _____ Occupation _____		Telephone _____	
Mother _____ Occupation _____		Telephone _____	
Emergency Name _____		Telephone _____	

Names and ages of children in family _____ paste

Previous school or camp experience _____ picture

Entrance date (if other than September) _____ here

Departure date (if other than June) _____

Side Two:

Alice — age 4

September: A small, blue-eyed child with strawberry blond hair and a fair complexion. She is extremely quiet and timid. She is agreeable, entering all activities when asked. She talks when spoken to but does not initiate conversation.

December: Alice has opened up! I should put that in capital letters. We look at her with unbelieving eyes. She talked to me first, then Marcy, and now just everyone. Has a little trouble with pronunciation, calling yellow "lellow." A bright child—knows colors, can count, and knows names of all the children. The change is quite gratifying.

February: Still quiet, but has blossomed in her peer group. The school day isn't long enough to crowd in all she wants to do. But she seems somewhat frail and is very tired by the end of the morning.

June: Has suddenly opened up to all her teachers. She delights us each morning with stories of where she is going, all about her new house, etc. She loves music. Can take off and put on her shoes and socks. We have enjoyed her and been pleased with her progress.

Chapter 16   DEVELOPMENTALLY APPROPRIATE PRACTICES

What does this mean?

We speak of developmentally appropriate practices in early childhood education. This means that we plan environment and program to meet the changing needs of the growing, developing child.

We recognize that certain behavior changes go along with physical change. The poor muscular coordination of the two-year-old must certainly have some bearing on the developing "I AM! I CAN!," as does the acquisition of new physical skills at age five.

We recognize the individual growth patterns of each child. Thus we do not say to Ray, "Sammy can do it and he's six; why can't you?"

We recognize that cognitive development follows a predictable pattern, and we match our expectations to the stage in that pattern which the child has reached.

We recognize that the home environment in which the child is growing will have a direct effect on development.

Since individuals are as different as their fingerprints, we will not find a single child who is exactly on target in all four areas of development at a given point. The norms which have been developed as a result of research can be compared to the inch marks on the ruler. They give us a measuring stick, which we must constantly remind ourselves is to be used only as a guide to understanding behavior.

Finding the norm

The inquisitive teacher might ask, "Who said so? Who determined that it is 'normal' for a four-year-old to use so much silly talk?"

A simplified answer is that observations of a hundred children, identical in chronological age, will show that a given behavior will be common to about half of them, twenty-five percent will not have reached that level, and another twenty-five percent will have gone past it. Thus, the behavior of the middle group will be described as typical for that particular age.

There is some danger in attempting to allocate certain characteristics to age levels. "The book says Roberta should be able to ... by the thirty-eighth month." And so her parents either push her to make sure she doesn't fail the test when the fateful date arrives or worry because she didn't even seem interested in that particular performance. Either way, the child is vaguely aware of pressure—that she is not quite measuring up to the expectations of the adult she wants to please, be it parent or teacher—and her "I AM" suffers.

Same equipment —changing use

An observer in a school with chronological age groupings will see the same basic pieces of equipment in each class, such as blocks, paint and clay, water and sand tables. If each of these teaching tools is being used in the same way at each age level, something is wrong. But when the classroom observer can see a growth progression in the use of a toy, such as the "stacking up/knocking down" block play of the twos and the sophisticated block village of the fives, then "growth and development" becomes more than educational jargon. Developing children use the same materials in different ways at different age levels.

Let them grow at their own rate

It would be well for the teacher of young children to keep in mind the word "kindergarten"—thinking of the classroom as a "childgarden." The gardener does not try to pattern his plants, he accepts their differences in growth and design. He protects them, nurtures them, but lets them do their *own* growing. He does not poke at the seed to make it sprout more quickly, or try to pull open the first buds. Sometimes it seems as if parents and teachers are using hedge clippers to try to make a smooth, look-alike product—a group that merges into a solid blob. In a child care center we will see as many varieties of children as there are flowers, each one interesting and beautiful in its own right.

Reversals are normal

It is important for a child care worker to know that growth is not always constant. There are distinct swings in the stages of development, described by Pitcher and Ames as periods of *equilibrium* and *disequilibrium*, and by Piaget as *stability* and *change*. Advance knowledge of these reversals in behavior will enable the adult to see them as normal phases of growth rather than discouraging regression.

Know what to expect

Teachers need to know what they may expect of a child in physical development, in social skills, in ability to cope with emotional frustrations, and in cognitive development. They need a nodding acquaintance, at least, with more than one theory of learning. They need to analyze the similarities and differences, and to measure them against their own observations. They need to *think* about children, understand them, and constantly seek the perfect match, offering enough challenge to keep the child involved, but never so much as to discourage her; enough stimulation to help her reach higher, but avoiding the discouragement which results when the standards are set too high. Teachers need to recognize that when a child has ample opportunity to creep before she walks, when her experimentation with sounds is recognized as a prerequisite for speech, and when her scribbles and blobs are appreciated as a stage in development leading toward the actual representation of figures, which eventually leads to writing—the fruition of these graduated experiences will be rich and satisfying. When teachers push, prod, and accelerate this natural development, they diminish the child's "I AM!" and stifle the "I CAN!"

The following descriptions of and suggestions for each age are intentionally simplified. They will serve to give the beginning child care worker a minimal understanding of reasonable norms. The books and pamphlets listed in the bibliography are recommended for additional reading. Consulting more than one is advisable, observing that descriptions and opinions will vary. The beginning teacher will gain more from reading material when it is combined with frequent consultations with experienced staff members.

Infants When this book first appeared in 1976, infants were, for the most part, still at home with their mothers. Since that time there has been a gradual change, and today many child care centers are accepting babies, some as young as six weeks. It is the fastest growing and most sensitive aspect of child care. Providing this service is an enormous responsibility, involving much more than keeping the baby fed, warm, and dry. These tiny human beings are developing in all four areas of growth. Starting when they emerge from the safety of the womb and draw their first breath in the real world, they are changing physically, as social and emotional beings, and they are learning how to adapt to and live in that world.

Physical Infants need space in which to grow, and freedom to move within that space. They should be confined to a crib *only* when sleeping. In addition to the time when they are being held, they should be placed in a variety of supporting chairs, such as infant seats or baby totes, which allow them to stay in a partially upright position. Putting infants on a blanket or pad away from the crib makes them part of the environment and allows for growing interaction with teachers and other infants as the weeks go by.

Social A child's understanding of a world in which there are creatures separate and apart from himself comes when he is held and cared for. Much has been said and written about the importance of "bonding" in the first few months. Ideally the infant finds that relationship with his mother, but when that is not possible, it is essential for him to form an attachment to another adult. If your center has more than one caregiver for the infants, try to have the same person consistently hold, feed, and change each child.

Emotional The emotional side of the infant's growth stems from the way in which his basic needs are met. If he has to cry himself purple to get food when he is hungry or a blanket when he is cold, or if he is left to lie in a wet or soiled diaper for long periods of time, he will come to know the world as a harsh, uncomfortable place. On the other hand, if his needs are cared for promptly, with warm, loving attention, he will come to find the world a good, safe place to be. Who is to say how much his future "I AM!" is influenced at this crucial time?

Intellectual What can a little baby learn? Cognitive growth begins with language. From the very beginning, the way a primary caregiver responds to an infant—talking to him as she changes his diaper, responding to his babbling—is *teaching* him the art of communication.

Toddlers:
Physically,
on their feet

As the name suggests, the term "toddler" applies when the child gradu- ates from the crawling, creeping, or hitching stage to moving about in an upright position, which may happen anytime between six months and fifteen or eighteen months.

The toddler is an explorer. He learns about gravity when he pulls himself up and falls down, climbs over, and crawls through, under, and around.

Socially,
incapable of
sharing

Socially, the toddler is an independent, self-centered being. *His* wants, *his* needs, *his* space, *his* toys, bear no interference from others. *He is incapable of sharing!* That will come later. The parent or caregiver can *make* a child share, but cannot make him *understand why* he must re- linquish an object.

Emotionally,
tempestuous

This lack of social maturity can get toddlers into a lot of trouble, and their emotions can only keep pace with a gradual understanding of their place in society. Toddlers can be trying and tempestuous, making constant demands on the physical and emotional energy of the care- giver, but for those who enjoy sharing in the development of this emerging personality, toddlers can bring great satisfaction!

Intellectually,
testing and
exploring

As the toddler's world expands, his actions are repetitive. He fills a cart, carriage, pail, or pocketbook, moves it to another location, empties or dumps it, and then puts everything back. He is constantly testing relationships of space and volume as he plays with toys that fit together and come apart, nest, and stack.

The important thing for the caregiver to understand is that this testing and exploring is *program*. Her job is to talk about his efforts and his surroundings, encourage him, and interfere only when neces- sary. This is learning at its best. The worst possible image is of tod- dlers sitting at a table, painfully trying to write the letter B on a piece of yellow lined paper.

Grace Mitchell writes:

"I saw a beautiful example of a good toddler program in a center in the Midwest. The teacher sat on the floor with a copy of a well- known magazine. One child plumped down beside her and they looked at the advertisements, naming the items which were familiar. Gradually more children joined them, staying awhile and then moving on to other interests. Everything about that room said that this was a good place for toddlers to be."

Safety a major
concern

The environment must be scrutinized on a regular basis for elements of danger to inquisitive, prying hands. Remember, *everything a toddler picks up goes straight into the mouth.*

Twos:
Need gross
motor activity

In planning an environment for twos we recognize their need for gross motor activity. Indoors, they need toys to push, pull, and roll: a small climbing apparatus, some steps, places to crawl through and climb over, safe high places to let them feel big, and places to crawl in and feel small and cozy. *Twos are still nesting.*

Need a separate playground   Playgrounds for toddlers and twos should, if possible, be separated from those for threes, fours, and fives. Playgrounds should be fenced, and not too large. Older children can be invited to visit the little ones in their play yard, helping or just playing with them. At the right time, and with plenty of supervision, twos may venture into the larger areas for brief periods, and it will be an adventure! The needs for pushing and pulling are met outdoors with carts and wheelbarrows. Properly scaled climbing apparatus helps to develop large muscles.

Move from solitary to group play   Socially the two-year-old is very much an individual. He is interested in others, but has yet to learn the rules for interaction. Solitary play moves to parallel play and, as he gains the ability to tolerate interference with his wishes, he will play in small groups. At first the two-year-old cannot share, and parents are urged *not* to let him bring toys to school (not to be confused with a security blanket).

Cannot sit and wait   It is inappropriate to ask twos to sit at a table and perform as a group. Twos should not be expected to sit and wait until everyone is served, at snack or at lunch, and it is *not* advisable to keep them waiting in line for the toilet. *"Now!" is their byword.*

Need to watch from safe places   Emotionally twos need the lulling effects of swinging and rocking, which we wean older children away from just as we gradually take a pacifier away from a baby. Rocking horses or boats or chairs are safe places from which to watch and relax before venturing forth into active participation. Indoors, water play, clay, and fingerpaint provide a release which is stimulating to the imagination and also relaxing.

Inclined to be rebellious   A two-year-old may be compared to an adult with his first powerful, shiny new car, who is anxious to get out into the country and test it. Twos want to be strong, to have power, to have everything *now*—they cannot wait. They are inclined to be inflexible, rebelling against any changes in routines. This is not the best time to attempt to introduce new foods or new rules. Two-year-olds have a basic need for repetition and will want the same story, the same finger-play.

The two-year-old will frequently say "No!" and has a real need to bump against adult reactions to find the limits within which he can safely operate. Twos are negative, but once their "I AM!" begins to take root and emerge, this negativism starts to subside, a healthy and welcome sign to frustrated parents and teachers.

Doing leads to learning   We set the stage for later learning when we give these young children toys that enable them to *do*, to act on the environment rather than placidly observing it. Children who, at an early age, gain satisfaction from success in manipulating objects, are less likely later on to be content to sit before the television set. They are too busy, too involved.

"Do it myself" is a common response, and adults should provide clothing, toys, challenges which enable the child to satisfy this urge and develop the "I CAN!"

Need limits For twos the world is frighteningly big and so they need fences, physical limitations, and the security of a solid "home base." A wise teacher builds trust in the two-year-old by giving him freedom and at the same time holding him close with the apron strings of love. (Read: *The Runaway Bunny*, by Margaret Wise Brown [Harper].)

Twos need warm loving adults with quiet voices, comfortable laps always ready when needed, welcoming yet not coming on too strong, attending but not smothering with attention. There must be enough adults for each child to identify with one person, "*my* teacher." The classroom and teacher of twos provide a warm extension of the home.

Threes   Certain ages seem to represent plateaus in development. Threes and sevens fall into this category. They are not periods of rapid change or violent struggle, but of quiet maturing and even growth. Returning to the analogy of the plants, they might be compared with the time of blooming—lovely to look at and pleasant to have around. Twos love to resist. Threes want to conform. They use "yes" as frequently as "no." Twos take—threes can give.

New physical skills   Three-year-olds stand between the physical and social "lumbering" of twos and the gusty exuberance of fours. They have advanced enough in physical coordination to gain satisfaction in climbing to new heights and are able to sit down for periods of time to develop manipulative skills. They can dress themselves, with a little help, and they like to help others.

Cooperative play   Threes have gained quite a bit of self-control and will conform to reasonable rules. Cooperative and easy-going, they are secure in relationships with others. At this age they are able to enjoy cooperative play with other children, can wait for turns and share toys, and can often carry their social techniques into helping others. "Emil will give you the bike after he has a turn" or "Jin is the father and I am the mother, but you could be the baby." They often go to great lengths to please peers in order to have a friend and become very upset when told "I won't be your friend." Threes are capable of sympathy.

Emerging initiative   Initiative emerges during the third year. Their "I can do it myself!" is an expression of a new sense of power and should be encouraged, but at the same time they are inclined to dawdle, requiring infinite patience. Many a conflict at home is brought on when a parent, in a rush, says, "I can't wait for you to do it yourself." School is the place, sometimes even the haven, where time and patience are afforded this young plant needing room to grow, allowing each new leaf to open by itself.

Readiness for work   Threes are beginning to recognize and pick out letters of the alphabet. Many recognize their names—some will want to try to write them. They are beginning to know colors, to remember the words to songs, and to count one, two, three. In the block area, they are starting to build with a purpose. They remember stories—and know if you leave something out. Threes are ready—and eager—to work.

Three-and-a-half turnabout   Threes at first are eager and responsive—a pleasant interlude before they reach the next stage of disequilibrium, which occurs sometime in the latter part of this year. Many then do a complete turnabout. They are in a state of disequilibrium, caused mainly by growth factors.

Some of these are poor coordination, stumbling, falling, fear of heights, stuttering, tics, crying, and whining. They make demands such as "Don't look!" "Don't talk!" "Don't laugh!"

Because they are socially insecure, threes go about making friends in a backwards manner by excluding others. Their group life is stormy and so it is a time when imaginary companions emerge. When the truly delightful three-year-old disintegrates into an insecure, disagreeable bundle of problems, her bewildered parents often send her off to a pediatrician or ask themselves where they have gone wrong. This is a time to keep in mind that "this too will pass," to give extra doses of love and understanding, equal doses of attention, and as much patience as one human being can muster. Often being forewarned makes acceptance of these changes possible and helps to avoid confrontation over the less desirable traits.

In the child care center, the doors between threes and twos should be opened as soon as both groups have had a chance to settle in; at first for a short period of time, gradually expanding the time until doors are open most of the day, allowing threes to go back to be little again or to feel "bigger than." At the same time the twos who mature quickly and are ready for more activities and new experiences are not held back by their less adventurous peers. They can venture into the new world, returning when they have had enough.

Fours:
Whirlwinds of activity

Fours seem to be bursting at the seams in all four sides of our developmental square. They are restless, whirlwinds of activity, constantly out-of-bounds! There are times when we wish their "I AMs" and their "I CANs" were not so positive. It is at this age that the physical part of the circle within the square bulges. Fours have great need to use their large muscles, and they do, in running, leaping, and jumping, climbing, hanging, and swinging, pushing, pulling, and tugging. They will roll, tumble, hit, punch, wrestle, chase each other, fall down, ending up in a heap of arms and legs. The teacher of fours accepts this hard-working play as a vital need and makes provision for it.

Socially uninhibited

The social behavior of a four-year-old is likely to be quite uninhibited —bold, aggressive, noisy, swaggering, swearing, and out of bounds with adult relationships. Fours may kick, bite, snatch, and grab, and they express their feelings in very explicit terms, both to their peers and to adults. "I hate you," "You stink," and name-calling are a part of their social patterns. It can almost be guaranteed that at some time during this year they will engage in bathroom talk, and worse. Despite acceptance in today's culture, four-letter words still sound inappropriate when they come from the mouth of a child, and even though the meaning may be hazy, fours soon learn how to use such language as a manipulative tool. They know and appreciate inappropriateness, and will be as defiant as they dare. Punishment has little chastening effect.

Less sensitive

On an emotional level, fours are learning to get along better with other children and to be less sensitive, less vulnerable, less demanding.

Never stopping for a breath, gusty fours accompany action with verbal outbursts and threats.

Sorting fact from fiction

Imagination knows no reasonable limits at this age. There is a thin line between fact and fiction and at times fours may be very silly. A four-year-old is most creative and shows understanding of real life. Fours are interested in what people do and how adult roles are learned.

Intellectually, a four-year-old tries to sort out real from unreal. She makes real drawings of airplanes. She may be confused about what she sees on television, and what is real, or near, and how quickly it might affect her or her security. At this time, her coordination begins to improve, as do her skills. This is often a catching-up time.

There may seem to be a wider span in the interest of fours than at some other ages. Some have an urgent need to play—hard, active play—and absolutely cannot be persuaded to sit down and work at table activities. Others are so eager to learn to read and write that they need to be encouraged to expand their interests to physical and creative activities. Fours need materials which enable them to try out their own ideas, rather than mechanical gadgets.

Discovering maleness and femaleness

Fours are discovering maleness and femaleness and are greatly interested in trying on many new roles in their dramatic play. However, it is well for teachers to remember that in this fourth year the same fathers who were able to look the other way when their three-year-old sons played with dolls may begin to impose different standards, with pressure to "be a man" or engage in what have traditionally been considered male sports. Little girls are often envious of maleness and will go to great lengths to be like boys in appearance and behavior. Parents may have to live with a tomboy for a time!

Need unlimited patience

Parents and teachers of fours need to hold the reins loosely, but be sure to pull up tight when necessary. They need unlimited patience and the ability to stand noise. Fours are fascinating, frightening, and fun.

Fives

At this age, the child enjoys life. It is a period of stable equilibrium. Gone is the out-of-bounds exuberance. The five-year-old is secure, calm, friendly, and not too demanding, exuding self-assuredness.

Aware of differences

Five is a year of awareness. Suddenly it seems that the light breaks through. At four, it seems that children literally do not see differences. At five, they see them and talk about them quite openly.

It happened:
 Ellie, who was blind, had been in nursery school for two years when she asked her mother, "Am I blind?"
 "You know, Ellie, I have always told you that you are," replied her mother. "Why do you ask?"
 "Today in school Marty said, 'You can't play with us because you are blind.' What is blind?"

Her mother, who thought she had succeeded in helping Ellie to adjust to her difference, started all over again to explain what it means to "see with your hands instead of your eyes."

Developing better coordination

The lusty exuberance of the four-year-old is nature's way of preparing for the well-coordinated five. Children who have been denied the freedom to live through the physical outbursts typical of fours will have difficulty fitting in with their more fortunate peers.

Fives are ready for simple tasks requiring hand-eye coordination: holding a pencil, using scissors, tying their shoes, throwing a ball, and creating designs. Most fives can print their own names and many are attempting to write them. Left- or right-handedness is well established, and adults should not attempt to change that which comes naturally. Fives have achieved balance, which leads to organized rhythmic activities and simple dances.

Influenced by television

Television opens doors which fives are more ready to walk through. Fives need to talk about the alarming things they see—riots and violence. A riot in New York is frightening to children who do not know whether New York is just outside their own backyards or far away. News of floods and earthquakes may have a profound effect on young children. Though they realize that their own home is safe, at the same time they wonder, "Will the flood come here?" "Is the earthquake going to knock over my house?" Young children often carry burdens of worry or fear as they ponder such questions.

Work well together

Socially, five-year-olds have a sense of "We-ness" that allows them to work cooperatively on murals and to plan and coordinate projects. They can combine forces, work together, give and take leadership. Their interest in people extends to the types of work those people do. When at election time the teacher provides them with their own voting booth, fives vote with great seriousness.

Eager to learn

Fives are curious, filled with a sense of industry, their wheels humming. They have an insatiable desire to learn and may carry their interests to great lengths. Fives want to read, write, do arithmetic. Many a kindergartner has gone home at the end of the first day of school, devastated because "I didn't learn to read!"

There is a tendency for adults to think of kindergarten as a preparation for first grade. Too many five-year-olds are hushed, required to walk in a line, sit a whole morning in school, by teachers who do not appreciate these lively, active, curious, social, imaginative beings. This is sad and unnecessary. Fives are not *preschoolers* marking time and getting ready for the magical age of six. Fives are vibrant, active, learning *doers.* The best preparation any child can have for formal learning is a happy and wonderfully busy year of "five-ness."

School-age children

In some child care centers, older children will be present in the mornings until the public schools open and again at the end of the elementary school day. Some will be enrolled during public school vacations, when parents are at work or at school. Sometimes it is possible to have separate staff for these children, but often they will be under the supervision of the regular staff. A few words about age characteristics of older children may be helpful in planning appropriate activities geared to their needs.

Sixes: Period of physical change

The six-year-old child is going through a period of physical body changes which may cause fatigue. Programs should be planned carefully, allowing for alternate activity and rest. As he adjusts to school and new standards which may cause insecurity and fears, he needs reassurance.

"Best friends" important

Special friends may be very important but may also be shifted frequently. The six-year-old can have close relationships with only a few at a time. Sixes are quick to observe fairness. Good role models are extremely important. The six-year-old should be accepted *as he is* and comparison with other children, for whatever reason, should be avoided at all costs.

The self-confident five-year-old may change into a shy, anxious six, prone to fears and emotional swings. Where the fives were engaged in group activities, sixes often enter their own private dream world of make-believe and pretend. Sixes have to cope with entry into school, make friends, and live by new sets of rules. If they seem to be aloof, it is because they have a need to sort out impressions and to develop their own style of coping with the world around them.

Adjusting to formal learning

During the sixth year public school systems decree that all children shall learn to read. Of course, many children are reading when they enter first grade, while others are not ready, and are still floundering at the end of the year. However, for the majority, this is the year when the mysteries of the printed word are revealed and children discover the joy of opening a book and being able to read it themselves.

Sixes are also being introduced to a more formal program of math and the language skills of spelling, composition, and penmanship. In most school systems, this all takes place in a fairly structured day, with not many choices about when and how they do their work. When these children come to the child care center after a school day, they do not need more structure. Interesting activities suited to their age should be available, but not required.

Sixes enjoy stories and drama and respond enthusiastically to music when it is shared in a spontaneous, voluntary way. They will participate in a joyous manner when it is not a regimented activity. They should be encouraged to make up poems, patterns, and rhythms and to compose their own songs, expressing their own creativity.

Six-year-olds are building a set of values. In the child care center, they need space, materials, and time for imaginative play, free from the imposition of adult standards, but with adult help close at hand when needed.

Sevens:
Gain fine-muscle control

This age group is very similar to the threes. Both seem to be settling in as they quiet down, and are less noisy and violent. They are more cautious and purposeful. Physically there is an increase in fine-muscle control. For example, they can tie a shoelace tightly enough to stay tied. Sevens can sit still longer as they enter this period of perfecting skills. Once accomplished in a skill, sevens will add extra hazards and fancy approaches to the feat. Large constructions will often be well planned and built.

Enjoy working with others

Socially, the seven-year-old is changing. His "I" turns more to "We" and he truly enjoys working and playing with other children, but he works better with small groups.

The seven-year-old is more in competition with himself than with his peers, and this is not a good time for a teacher or parent to present competitive sports or new social or mental activities. *Seven should be allowed to set his own pace.*

Sensitive to failure

Emotionally, seven is very critical of his own work; rather than have it criticized by others, he will beat them to the punch by saying, "That's crazy" or "This stinks!" He is very sensitive to ridicule, failure, or loss of prestige. When the going gets tough, sevens will tend to withdraw, using statements such as, "OK, stupid, do it your own way. I'm quitting!"

Good listeners, good talkers

On an intellectual basis, sevens are good listeners and good talkers. They like to make up plays to perform for audiences. Memorizing is possible, but they prefer making up characters with their own words and gestures, and they are more apt to take time with costumes and properties than with dialogue.

Enjoy creative writing

Sevens enjoy stories, poems, riddles, and limericks and can understand the moral of a fable. Stories with plots and suspense intrigue them. They relish the opportunity to use swearwords and vulgarities and love rhymes and couplets that are tinged with off-color connotations. This is a good year for creative writing, and, if physical effort is standing in the way of setting down their own thoughts, the use of a tape recorder for taking dictation and a willing "secretary" to type these thoughts will help to encourage this creativity.

Eights:
Well coordinated

Age eight has similarities to age four. Eights are well coordinated, smooth, quick on their feet, as the physical side of their developmental square becomes predominant. They have not yet reached the awkwardness of preadolescence; their reactions are sure and secure. This is a good age to be taught simple, rhythmic dances and games. Eights have bursts of energy which are like gusts of wind but can also stay with an idea or project. They are most cooperative, especially when they help to initiate a plan.

Want to be liked These youngsters want to be liked socially and are willing to work at it and make some concessions. While a seven-year-old might walk away from problems, an eight-year-old will stand his ground and muddle through. Even though it may involve some fighting and tears, he can accept the consequences and learn from them. During this year, the child begins to acquire social aptitude and insights, learning best from his peer group.

Eights are strong on clubs, especially the secret type. They become very conscious of *in* and *out* groups. Eight-year-olds form crushes and choose adult models. They like being with adults and enjoy conversations with them.

Industrious and Eights are industrious, curious, and matter-of-fact. Imagination often
curious gives way to reality. They have a keen sense of fairness and want rules, although they may change them daily. Eights can engage in some competition—they like to be right or best. Adults should avoid imposing standards that are out of reach and should be generous with praise for each new achievement. Between the placidity of sevens and the concerns of the nine-year-olds, eights can be delightful company and cooperative pupils.

Emotional development at this age is delightful to behold. The physical exuberance, wide-ranging curiosity, and awakening knowledge of self offer rich rewards to adults who accept and understand the eight-year-old's flair for bravado and enthusiasm.

The early years are important years for learning for *all* children, but especially for those with special needs.

Grace Mitchell tells this story:

"In 1949, the mother of a totally blind boy wanted to enroll him in our nursery school at Green Acres. I refused, feeling that my staff and I were not properly trained for this responsibility. A few months later, I attended a meeting of nursery-kindergarten teachers, where the speaker was from the Division of the Blind. She urged us to integrate blind children into our schools. This was during the period when a frightening number of cases of retrolental fibroplasia were emerging, and before the cause had been discovered. She tried to allay our fears, saying, 'You need not be afraid of a blind child running in front of the swings. A blind child *will not run* until he is thoroughly familiar with the environment.' Before I left that night I assured the speaker that we would be willing to accept a blind child, and would offer a scholarship, if necessary. A few weeks later, Joy came to us, a beautiful three-year-old with a sparkling personality and no vision. Joy not only brought *joy* to our school, but also opened the way for hundreds of other children who had physical or emotional handicaps."

Early years especially important   Now it has been recognized that these early years in a child's life are important years for learning for *all* children, but especially for those with special needs. Their education has been mandated by law. We encourage you to open your doors to these children, but understand what such a course involves. Read carefully the following information.

What is normal?   When considering the child with a physical or emotional difference, think first about what might be termed *normal*. Some people have 20/20 vision, some need glasses, others distinguish only light and dark, some are blind. Some people hear the tiniest sound, some have partial hearing loss, others need hearing aids, some receive only vibrations, others are totally deaf. One person has a well-built, beautifully coordinated body, another is awkward and clumsy, still another, deformed. Visual and auditory perception are matters of degree; perfection and norms can only be determined in the context of each person's life.

Everyone is more or less   Who then can say what is *normal?* Everyone is *more* or *less*, in many ways. Everyone is entitled to live in a so-called normal world, in as nearly a normal way as possible. The way a child is accepted in that world, her way of functioning in it *before* she is five years old, plays a large part in determining her future.

Acceptance by peers   Children take differences in their stride; often they seem not to notice them. The exceptional child who is able to attend school before she is five has a distinct advantage. Though her family may coddle and protect her, she will have to "earn her way" with her peers. A four-year-old classmate will not give in to her demands. On the other hand, the young child *does* develop a casual consideration which is not at all like the maudlin sympathy of an adult, which is so degrading to a person who is different.

Children are not cruel

Contrary to the often-voiced opinion, young children are *not* deliberately cruel. The life of a so-called normal child is enriched by an encounter with one less fortunate. In the following examples, it would be hard to say which children received the most benefit.

It happened:

Steve was an aggressive, active four-year-old, always pushing to be first and not above using his strength to get what he wanted. One day when the teacher said, "Time to go in for juice now," Steve started off at a run as usual, stopped suddenly, went back to the sandbox, and walked quietly beside Cindy, who was totally blind. He did not take her hand, but talked to her as they walked along, leading her with the sound of his voice.

Lenny was severely disabled, a victim of cerebral palsy. His gait was loose and distorted, his speech almost unintelligible, and facial grimaces which he could not control contributed to an appearance which was, at first sight, shocking. But Lenny had a good mind and an indomitable spirit. He earned the respect of his seven- and eight-year-old campmates.

Richie was everything Lenny was not: strong, agile, well-coordinated, handsome, and popular. As they lined up one day for relay races, the counselor noticed an act which was so carefully disguised he had to see it himself several times to be sure. In each race, Richie carefully aligned himself opposite Lenny and, when their turn came, he slowed down just enough to give Lenny a fair chance, but not enough to be noticeable to the other contestants.

Acceptance by adults

Most children accept differences casually, and that is the greatest gift they can give to the child with special needs. But what about adults? Can they give the same kind of casual acceptance? Not always. It takes a new kind of courage. A physically disadvantaged child cannot be helped to independence by a teacher who insists on holding her hand. She must be allowed to fall, to find her own limits, to develop her own patterns for daily living. Certainly, the adult needs to watch over the safety of the deaf or blind child who may not be aware of danger, but without being overprotective or unduly solicitous.

Before enrollment

Before the special child is enrolled, at least one, and probably several, visits should be made to the school, allowing everyone who may be concerned with her care to observe her. There is much to learn about previous experiences, habits, and special needs before a decision is made. It is cruel to accept a child and decide later that it was a mistake. The exceptional child will be "put down" many times throughout life. The weakening of the "I AM" should not start at this early age.

Criteria for eligibility   What criteria should be used in determining eligibility?
• It should be agreed by *all* concerned that this particular school will be right for this child, and that this child will be good for the school.
• The child should be able to function without demanding more time and attention from an adult than is fair to the other children.
• If a child must be lifted or carried, or is incontinent and has to be changed frequently, one extra adult should be available to help. If it is the child's parent, he or she should be willing to take the training offered to volunteers.
• A professional referral should be required, with the promise of continued communication and help from the doctor, clinic, guidance counselor, or social worker. This is particularly important when the problem is emotional. Often when behavior is becoming intolerable, the professional can give information or advice to the staff which makes it possible for them to continue.

It happened:
  Jay, aged six, refused to take part in any activity. After a reasonable length of time, his mother was called and she disclosed that he was seeing a psychiatrist, information she had not previously shared. The doctor came to school and explained Jay's problem to the staff. "This little boy needs to have a detailed description of each part of your program before it happens. Take time before each change to explain what will happen next." With the cooperative efforts of a concerned staff, his parents, and the doctor, Jay made great strides in that year.

When to let go   Even when the greatest care is taken before the child is enrolled, there will be cases in which it becomes necessary to "let go." It is very hard for a teacher, who has invested so much time, effort, and heart, to make this decision. When the director observes that a child is draining the extra reserves of a teacher, it is time to step in and seek out an alternative plan. Sometimes complete withdrawal is not necessary, but instead the hours can be reduced or additional help provided.

Any activity that brings parents into the classroom in a casual but meaningful way is a good beginning.

PEOPLE: THE PARENTS

Chapter 21   **CREATING THE PARTNERSHIP**

A working partnership must be just that—working together in every possible way.

We begin by having the welcome mat out. When parents do not feel welcome early in the year, they may begin to draw back, leaving things to the school. In very subtle ways, the school must keep the mat out:

"Good morning! Do you have just five minutes to see our baby gerbils?"

"Come in and see what happened when we put out three colors of paint for the first time."

"You're early today—why don't you hear our story before you take Phan home?"

"If you have an extra half hour some morning, come and have juice and watch the children cleaning up. Your daughter has the whole crew organized."

These casual comments make a parent want to come a little early or stop in for brief visits.

Parent involvement   It is one thing to talk about parents as partners. What do you do if they don't choose to dance with you?

In single-parent families, or in families where both parents are employed, it is difficult for them to be actively involved in the child-care program. Any participation which brings them into the classroom in a casual but meaningful way is a good beginning. For those who are willing and able, the following actual experiences may spark some ideas.

Ways parents have helped   •   Charlie's father set up a calling team to notify parents of special events.

•   Debbie's mother stopped in once a week to straighten out the books on the library shelf.

•   Abe's mother picked up a list of books to supplement the curriculum, located them at the public library, and brought them in.

•   Some parents came in at noon to eat with the children and supervise nap time so the staff could have a meeting.

•   One parent visited industrial plants and stores, gathering materials for the resource center. Another helped devise a system for keeping creative materials in order and making them accessible to the children.

- A parent who sews volunteered to alter clothing from the dress-up corner to fit the children.
- Some parents took time off to accompany the children on field trips.
- Parents with experience on newspapers or magazines, as well as former English teachers, helped publish a school newspaper.
- A parent with social work training gave a course in parenting and a psychiatrist conducted a discussion on explaining death to children.

Visits that enrich program Parents enrich programs when they talk to the children about their work. *No work is ordinary to a child*, be it office work, gardening, truck driving, or plumbing (*Parent's Occupations*, Vol. 2, p. 100).

- Carmen's mother came once a week to teach Spanish. The children learned rapidly and looked forward to her visits.
- A father who gave performances as a clown came to entertain. He applied his makeup in front of the children—the best part of the visit!
- Tony's father made musical instruments out of funnels and hoses. He also played the trumpet. He demonstrated both, taking time to let the children experience with all their senses, ask questions, enjoy.
- Dr. Smith, an ophthalmologist, brought in specialized medical equipment and explained how it was used and what could be learned from it, as she tested the children's eyes.
- Van's mother told a class about computers and gave the children a chance to experiment with statistical research. They made choices between pink ice cream cones and pony rides as they put a needle through punched cards—a real life experiment.
- An artist set up her easel and painted in a corner of the room. The children observed, admired, and were allowed to use her brush to add some small bit to the work of art. Painting at their own easels took on new dimensions after that day.
- Arturo's father was a chef in a large hotel. Wearing his tall white hat and crisp white uniform, he gave a demonstration of bread-making to the kindergarten which was the forerunner of a variety of baking experiences, and a scientific discussion of leavening.
- A doctor and a nurse put on operating room garb and explained procedures, with children volunteering as patients. Their presentations led to much role playing and opened the door for some very informative discussions about hospitals.

The resources are there, and parents are willing, *but* they seldom respond to a request in a bulletin. It is up to you or the teacher to issue a personal invitation and then to follow through with a cordial welcome, set the stage for the activity, and send written notes of thanks, including some of the children's comments.

Special events for parents: Speaker meetings There was a time when parent meetings meant speakers—speakers who dropped their pearls of wisdom on the tired ears of parents who were made to feel unworthy and guilty. It is unrealistic to expect a parent who has worked all day to pick up a child, feed and bathe him, hire a sitter, and go back to the center for a meeting. If the request for an outstanding speaker or a seminar series covering a particular phase of child rearing comes from the parents, and if they are involved in all stages of planning, it is your place to be supportive.

Curriculum meetings These include a very specific description of goals and methods in the curriculum, with suggestions for ways parents can extend them into the home. Stress the value of enrichment experiences such as stimulation of language through family discussion as well as reading to children.

It may be assumed that parents are primarily interested in knowing what is going on at school. At the first curriculum meeting of the year, label interest centers with explanatory signs outlining the goals. Display some work, explaining its purpose and motivation. Parents should be able to roam about and capture some of the atmosphere of the school. Teachers should be free to visit informally and answer questions about curriculum.

Later in the year, hold another curriculum meeting. Have other staff members talk about the areas of activity, demonstrating with pictures, slides, and the children's work.

Back-to-school nights This is a chance for the parents to see what the children are doing during the day and to understand how painting, singing, building with blocks, and playing games contribute to learning. Most important is that teachers have a chance to *de-emphasize the importance of the product and stress the importance of the process.* This is a good time to ask the parents not to pressure their children to bring home a paper every day.

Parent-teacher workshops Workshops might focus on a wide variety of topics—games, science, holidays (how to plan parties and make simple gifts with children), projects to do at home with the young child, learning simple songs and games, choosing the right books and music for a child, and so on. Every school has staff members gifted in these various areas. A series of workshops led by individual staff members and focusing on a special topic can greatly enhance parents' "I AM - I CAN" as they relate more effectively with their children at home. "Come find out about unusual ways to make valentines with your child!"—this was the invitation extended by a teacher.

Special events for the family More and more directors are finding that events which include the whole family will be well attended. Some which we have found successful include:

Picnics Held at a time when the entire family could come, picnics need no special program. Teachers were free to move about, introduce themselves, and chat with family members. (It should be made clear in advance that this is *not* the time for a conference about an individual child.) It was extremely helpful for the teachers to see a child in the context of the family.

Pot-luck suppers These were held at the end of the day and were particularly appealing to parents who could go home afterward without having to think about preparing a meal. The food was provided by parents, paper goods and beverages by the center. Parents seemed to enjoy sitting at small tables, meeting their children's friends and their parents, sharing their problems and joys in a casual environment. A popular feature was slides of the children engaged in daily activities, set up on an automatic projector, to be viewed at will.

Holiday parties A most successful party was held in December in the evening (from 6:30 to 7:45). The children made the invitations, decorated the rooms, and helped prepare the refreshments. This event required minimum effort and was applauded as one of their most successful school functions.

Grandparents' This is a delightful way to reassure grandparents that, even though
Day both parents may be working, the needs of the child are being fulfilled.

Two invitations were sent home, to be addressed to both sets of grandparents. As much as possible, the day was normal, so grand-parents could see what actually happens. Children prepared for the visit by making pictures of their grandparents. (One child used red yarn to create his Nana's hair and, when the woman arrived, it was startlingly accurate. Another made a lovely picture and then covered it with black paint, saying, "This is my Nanny sitting in a dark room.") They were encouraged to write stories about grandparents and talk about what it means to be a good host or hostess.

How often have you found yourself blaming a bad situation on poor communication or lack of communication? You must constantly check all the lines to be sure they are open and clear.

Bulletins to parents   When the child is first enrolled, make a point of telling the parents that dated and numbered bulletins will be coming home every so often. Suggest that the parents watch for the bulletins and keep them in one place, such as a folder. Explain that you will use them for important announcements—notice of a field trip, a reminder that your center will be closed a certain day, a lost-and-found list, and so on. Tell the children that the bulletins are important, and say it again to the parents as you hand them out.

Some parents will *not* read their bulletins, and it is important for you to be able to say, "I'm sorry you didn't know there was no school yesterday, but it was announced in bulletins 2, 3, and 4, which were dated Sept. 10, Oct. 15, and Nov. 5. The bulletins are our means for telling parents about these things. Would you check the numbers on yours, now, and let me know if any are missing? I can send you extra copies."

It is a good idea to include calendar reminders in every bulletin. It is also wise to spread out over the year requests for special items to supplement the curriculum, such as small boxes, egg cartons, sewing trims, toilet-paper tubes, or frozen food dishes. One long sheet, with a hundred or more requests, may be tossed aside. A few specifics in each bulletin seem to bring better results.

Newsletters   These are after-the-fact reports on special activities related to curriculum, parent meetings, family picnics, and so on. They may include comments or dictated stories from the children and suggestions for home activities.

School newspapers   These may be more sophisticated, printed pieces. They are intended to tell more about the people in the center and may have interviews with anyone—the director, custodian, visiting teachers, students, parents. They are an extension of the educational tools employed by the school. They may include reviews of books for children or for adults, suggestions for places to take children on weekends, and recipes and other suggestions for activities parents can share with children in the home. Properly done, a school newspaper can serve as a valuable promotion piece, but it does require much time and a fair amount of expertise. You could provide an editorial with thoughts on current issues in education and child care.

What we did today   Sometime before the first child is due to leave, each teacher should prepare a list of things the group did that day. It does not have to be a long list, nor does it have to cover every single thing the group did, but it should mention the highlights. "We went to a farm and saw the baby pigs." "Kelli's grandmother came and told us a story." "We looked for things that are red." "We had a triangle hunt." "We made muffins and had them at snack time." These are the kinds of things that show parents that there is learning going on.

These notices should be clearly printed in large letters and posted on the bulletin board near the pick-up area. Each one should indicate which group it is for (color coding might help) and should always be in the same place, so parents know just where to look for it. This not only gives parents a clue to your program, but also gives them something to talk about on the way home. Instead of the frustrating "What did you do today?"—"Nothing" routine, the parent can say, "You went to see some baby pigs today. What kinds of noises do baby pigs make?" or "What kind of muffins did you make? Blueberry muffins?"

Infant checklists   If you have infants in your center, you should have duplicated checklists you send home with the child each day. Report on the sheet all the things the parent needs to know, such as the time when the child had a bowel movement, when and how much she ate, and when and how long she slept. Allow room at the bottom of the page for a few words if something of special note occurred.

Teacher newsletters   In some centers each teacher composes a newsletter for the parents, telling what is going on in his group. A director should edit such newsletters for content and style.

Bulletin boards   You should have an attractively arranged bulletin board near the entrance of the center and remind parents to look at it daily. It might include current articles from a magazine or newspaper, notices of meetings in the community which might be of interest, special events planned for children, Lost and Found—the content is unlimited. Some directors allow parents to advertise their services by placing business cards on the bulletin boards, or to place "For Sale" notices.

You may ask staff members to take on the responsibility of arranging the bulletin board. It is an artistic task as well as a source of interesting information. Learning how to do it well is a valuable experience.

Parent conferences   There are two kinds of parent conferences, the first when a child's behavior is disturbing, the second a routine, scheduled conference to discuss a child's progress.

About behavior   It is hard to say when is the best time to ask for a conference about behavior. In the morning, giving the parent a worry to take to work? At night, when the parent picks up the child, and is already feeling pressured? We suggest telephoning the home about 8:30 in the evening, after the children have had their meal and are probably in bed. Be tactful, taking the attitude that you want the parent to work with you to solve a problem that concerns both of you. Offer as many options as you can for a time, but do not hang up until you have set a time. If the matter is serious enough for you to call the home, then there has to be a meeting.

Never call on Friday with a request for a meeting, leaving the parent a whole weekend to worry about the reason.

Be specific Prepare well and be very specific. Never say such general things as "Joel is aggressive" or "Steve uses bad language." Instead, give details that spell out what you mean: "On Tuesday Joel hit Danny when he wouldn't let him have the truck." "Steve called John a stupid bastard and had poor Gail in tears when he called her a dumb fatso."

Be prepared for a certain amount of belligerence. *Listen* and try not to be resentful or defensive. Do not let a parent go away feeling guilty, ashamed, or hopeless. Be supportive, not judgmental.

Follow up If you have been discussing a problem, say, "We should talk again in two weeks. In the meantime, we can both try the strategies we have discussed." Wrap up the discussion with "This has been very helpful. Let's plan to meet again on ...." Set the date and put it on your calendar. Bring things to a conclusion with a pleasant "Thank you for coming in." Your facial expression and body language should indicate that the conference is over.

Keep notes Make some notes about your discussion and any promises you may have made. However, *never* record, even for your own eyes only, anything the parent may have told you in strict confidence.

Finally, as in any conversation, try to *listen* more than you *talk*.

Progress reports At least twice a year it is good to schedule a conference between the teacher and the parents to discuss the progress of the child. (Some states have laws requiring such meetings.) At these conferences, you should be able to give the parent specifics about the ways in which the child has developed since the last report. These reports should deal with all four areas of growth, not just the intellectual. Of course you will report that Carlos has learned to recognize his own name or has learned to count to ten—but you will also mention that Carlos is now able to catch a large ball, that he is making friends more easily, that he is now putting toys away neatly, and so on. After a conference, the parent should be aware that you know Carlos very well and that you are spending time and thought in helping him develop. However, communication is not one-way, and you must be ready to listen to parents, as well as talk to them. Let them express their concerns, and treat them with respect.

Have something to show A progress report will not be successful unless the teacher has been aware of the child's growth and development and has kept written notes. Starting with the first week, it is wise to keep a folder for each child with such items as samples of her work, her ability to print or write her name, depending on age, and some of her drawings. Visual evidence of progress is far more effective than educational jargon.

If it is necessary to introduce a negative, it should be accompanied by concrete suggestions for ways to help the child at home.

Set a convenient time It is important to schedule these conferences at a time which is convenient for the parent. Some will want to stay when they drop off the child in the morning, some may come during their lunch hour, and others will ask for time at the end of the day. The director should make every effort to free the teacher for a reasonable period of time.

An organized group of parents who wish to participate actively can be a great source of help and support for you as director. It is important that leadership be enthusiastic, energetic, and consistent, and such leadership may take time to emerge. In a new school, it might be wise to wait until the children, staff, and environment have jelled.

You might introduce the idea initially at the time of enrollment, saying, "We will be inviting all parents to participate in a Parent Advisory Council. When our children and staff have had time to settle in, you will receive a notice about the first organizational meeting." It would be advisable to plan at least one social occasion first—simply an opportunity for parents to get acquainted. In a large center, such a meeting might be for the parents of one group or one class at a time.

Parent participation is a requirement in all Head Start programs and is usually found in other agency-operated centers. The private owner-director may be reluctant to encourage such an organized group, lest it tries to take over management, hiring and firing staff, and making decisions about curriculum. A tactful director can explain that the administration will make final decisions, but will welcome suggestions and give them due consideration.

Aside from establishing a friendly, cooperative climate, why would you open the door to parent participation? Consider how a special event at the center might be organized. If you initiate it, putting the onus on the staff to help, members of the staff may work very hard (with some resentment), only to have four or five parents show up, because *they* didn't want that event in the first place. If members of the council plan an event, it is because they have decided that it is appropriate to their needs. They will shoulder responsibility for the program and provide refreshments.

A Parent Council can help with fund-raising. Your budget may be so limited that there is no possibility of buying an expensive piece of equipment or sending teachers to a workshop unless you raise additional money. But, if you raise that money, it is considered income, and a hefty chunk of it will go out in taxes. There is another way:

It happened:
   Members of a Parent Council set up a non-profit (and therefore tax-exempt) corporation to raise funds for new audio-visual equipment. They were so successful, they went on to raise funds for new playground equipment.

An active Parent Council can be a tremendous source of support in a crisis—and, in these troubled times, the next crisis is always lurking around the corner. When tough decisions have to be made, it is good to have people standing by, ready to share the burden.

It happened:

In a northern town an unusually bad winter resulted in seven "no school" days over a two-week period. Parents who normally did not complain about paying for such days were having to stay home from work, and tension was rising. The director was sympathetic, but at the same time had to meet a payroll and other fixed expenses. The facts were laid before an emergency meeting of the Parent Council. After a lengthy discussion, it reached a reasonable compromise. The director announced the decision, and it helped to be able to say that the decision had been made with the assistance of the council.

Meetings should be held often enough to develop some spirit and give the members the feeling that they are serving a useful function. You will have to help a new council set up a system for electing leaders. A governing board can help to ensure that the council will continue from year to year.

Chapter 24   **THE DIRECTOR, LEAD TEACHER, AND TEACHER**

The Director:
Personal
qualifications

A director is a special being, first and foremost a people-oriented person whose most important task is to establish relationships of mutual trust with parents, children, and staff.

A director has feelings. Directors who believe that self-confidence can be instilled in children must be able to *trust,* believe in, and rely on their own competence. Each day in the life of a director presents new challenges which will demand the ability to cope, to accept crises as they come, and to deal with them without losing emotional and physical stability.

A director has physical limitations. Child care is a demanding, exhausting task which requires constant and boundless stamina. The "I CAN!" means literally that a director can trust the body to rise to any occasion when it is demanded, while also knowing how to alternate activity with sufficient rest to renew energy.

A director must know the field. Degrees in education are certainly an asset, but they should not rank highest on the list of qualifications. What is more important is an attitude toward education as a continuing process and a desire for growth in the profession. The director must be the one who reads the articles in professional magazines, scans the book reviews and the education pages of newspapers, and belongs to professional organizations, participating in their activities to assure knowledge of what is going on in the field. A director needs to attend conferences, seminars, and workshops and relay all of this enrichment to the staff.

Responsibilities

A director must maintain morale. The breakdown of morale in an organization can be so subtle, so insidious, that even the perpetrator may not be aware of the seriousness of the act. "I never gossip. If I have anything to say, I say it to a person's face," he says, self-righteously, and yet, with a shrug of the shoulders or a facial grimace or a sly wink, he sets the wheels in motion which can carry the morale of the team to destruction.

The positive
grapevine

"Today we are going to talk about tattling," the director announced. Her expression indicated the seriousness of the topic, and the teachers assembled for a staff meeting began to nod knowingly. "I am not referring to the children," she went on. "I am talking about you, and asking for your cooperation." By this time she had the full attention of everyone present, their amazement clearly registering on their faces. "Is she really asking us to snitch on each other?" they were thinking.

Before anyone had time to express indignation, she continued, this time with a smile, "There are so many great things going on in this center—and I can't begin to see half of them. One of you will be having a terrific program experience, or diverting a potential behavior explosion smoothly into something else. You all quietly lend a hand to help one another. You are usually too modest to tell me about your own successes—you may not even think them worthy of mention—so I am asking you to tattle on each other. When you see something good happening, come and tell me, or leave a note on my desk. At our next staff meeting, I am going to ask each of you to come prepared to tell about such an incident We all know how an ugly rumor can get into the grapevine and break down morale. A positive rumor is just as contagious as gossip. When you start really *looking* for some good thing to report, you will be surprised at how much more you will *see*."

The positive grapevine is an effective way to maintain morale.

A director is a catalyst. The director can share ideas and enthusiasm in such simple ways as dropping into a classroom with a bird's nest and showing it to the children, following up with, "There are books in our library about birds and how they build their nests." Such sharing might well be the spark that fires up a teacher who has become a little stale, yet it does not come as a directive.

The director senses when teachers need revitalization and will try to help them in various ways: arranging for them to visit another school or browse in a recycling center, sending them to workshops, or encouraging them to join professional organizations.

A director is a public relations expert. As the first representative of a school, the director will influence the attitudes of the community about the school while dealing with neighbors, service people, business leaders, and the personnel of other schools, public and private. The task of presenting a positive image to the public never ceases.

A director is a salesperson. A child care center, whether publicly or privately funded, has a service to sell, and the director is chief of sales and service. The need to *sell* the school to the customers—the parents who will pay for the service—will continue to exist, even though the school may reach the point where it has children on a waiting list.

A director is a housekeeper. The custodian handles most cleaning, but every center has daily chores that cannot wait for attention. The director will see that these tasks are fairly assigned, but will never feel it demeaning to carry a fair share. It is healthy for members of the staff to see the boss pick up papers, wet a paper towel and wipe sticky hand-prints off the door, or wipe out the bathroom bowl. The director will be wise to consider the toilet plunger one of the tools of the trade.

A director is a decision-maker. Some directors find it hard to strike a balance between democracy and leadership. They start by telling and assigning, trusting that as soon as members of the staff know what is expected of them, they will be able to share in problem-solving and decision-making. But, as a strong leader, the director realizes that rap sessions over details which should be routine create a general feeling of instability. An effective director will sense when strength and conviction are required and be forceful and explicit.

Lead Teacher In team teaching, the prototype advocated in this book, every member of a team is a teacher and is expected to contribute to the education of the child. However, some one person has to make decisions and accept responsibility for these decisions. When the lead teacher is absent, *one* other person must always be designated to assume this responsibility. Such an assignment cannot be left to chance, to a casual "Sue is out today, so you take over, Todd," but should be planned in advance.

The leadership role In addition to the qualifications for a teacher, a lead teacher has an additional challenge—accepting responsibility for the combined efforts of the members of the team. When morale begins to break down, the lead teacher must bolster it. When one team member does not carry his share of the program or help with routine chores, the lead teacher has to get him back in line. When parents complain about the program, the lead teacher needs to be able to respond by asking first himself and then other members of the team whether the complaints are justified.

In a team relationship, each member is important and respected and feels free to contribute ideas and suggestions. The members support one another; if one has a bad day, the rest are willing to extend themselves, and know they can expect the same help when they need it.

Responsibilities to the child *To see every child in the group as an individual,* respecting her right to be herself. A teacher will recognize that the child's experience is limited and that the forces which have made an impression on her life may have differed greatly from those affecting every other child.

To be completely fair to every child, whatever her physical or personal limitations may be, and to make an honest effort to find something to love in each one, scrupulously avoiding favoritism.

To be sympathetic, friendly, and alert to the physical and emotional needs of each child.

To be aware of the growing needs of each child, offering new and enriched experiences as she reaches new levels of development.

To avoid speaking critically about the child in her presence.

To the parents *To protect the health and safety of each child* as parents would their own children.

To learn as much about the family and home life as will be helpful in working with the child.

To be careful not to jump to any conclusions about parents' methods of training without knowing the facts.

To respect the privacy of parents by overlooking any family secrets the child may divulge.

To respect the parents' right to decide what is best for the child. When their choice is in direct conflict with school policy, to explain as tactfully as possible and, if there is still disagreement, to refer the matter to the director.

To know each child well enough to be able to give the parent a reasonably accurate and concise verbal report when it is requested.

To confine such reports to information about the child, taking care not to make comparisons or talk about other children.

To establish a system for the care of clothing which will keep damage or loss to a minimum.

To call the parents to report any incidents, falls, scratches, or emotional experiences.

To the members of the team

To respect each member's right to share in making daily and long-range plans.

To provide opportunities for them to ask questions, disagree with policies or procedures, and offer suggestions.

To divide chores such as housekeeping, playground supervision, or dressing the children, assuming a fair share.

To look for and draw out every talent of team members, encouraging and aiding them to enjoy satisfying teaching experiences.

To schedule regular conferences for purposes of evaluation.

The Teacher

Many of the responsibilities listed under Lead Teacher apply to any teacher on the staff. Added to them are the following criteria, which also apply to assistant teachers and aides. They are put in the form of questions with the idea that a director might give this list to teachers. They would then have guidelines as to what is expected of them.

Guidelines for self-evaluation

• Do you maintain at all times a pleasing, neat, professional appearance which will be a credit to the school?
• Do you consistently exhibit warmth toward the children, parents, and your fellow workers?
• Have you a sense of humor, even when the joke is on you?
• Can you keep the tone of irritation out of your voice and keep your face pleasant when your nerves are strained?
• Are you free from touchiness, so that others do not have to handle you with kid gloves?
• Do you refrain from listening to and repeating gossip?
• Can you accept criticism without anger or hurt?
• Are you dependable? Do you do what you say you will *when* you say you will?
• Can you easily adapt to changes in programs, weather, plans?
• Can you weigh facts and exercise judgment in making decisions?
• Are you curious? Do you have interests in a wide variety of fields?
• Have you initiative? Ability to get started without prodding?
• Are you careful not to judge parents?

What makes a good teacher? Enthusiasm is the secret ingredient. Teachers have to be excited about what they are doing. *Teaching cannot be a duty—it has to be a love.*

A teacher is a classroom companion who, because of age and experience, can extend the value of activities a little further each week.

A teacher has twenty eyes all around the head—they see everything; two enormous ears—they hear everything; one smiling mouth—used often; one frown—used sparingly; two India rubber legs; two India rubber arms; gentle voice, sense of humor, sense of fair play, and trust.

A teacher has a sense of beauty, is open to new experiences, and has a relish for new tastes.

A teacher is an adequate, fully functioning person with a positive view of self, and the ability to identify with others.

A teacher will be on guard against using a child to satisfy personal needs.

A teacher will resist the temptation to be center-stage, overusing feltboards or playing the role of actor/magician.

A teacher will be involved in the children's activities, not just a bystander.

A teacher will make a conscious effort to plan a program which will strengthen a child's "I AM! I CAN!"

Resource files: *Saving and sharing* A teacher is an inveterate scrounger who sees possibilities in everything, one who can never walk through a dime store or past a hardware counter without looking for some new item. Visits to yard sales and second-hand stores are commonplace. One teacher confessed, "I have to control myself when I walk down the street on rubbish day!"

In keeping with this resourcefulness, we have a most important piece of advice for teachers—whether beginners or ones long in the profession—who feel disorganized. Set up a system, *now*, for recording and storing the ideas you glean from others, the things you read, the results of your teachable moments. Make the system simple, easy to use, and accessible. Otherwise you will find yourself saying, on too many occasions, "I remember something that speaker said—it would be just right for what I'm doing now. Or did I read it in that book? Or was it in that video we saw at the last staff meeting? If only I could remember where to find it!"

These suggestions are the results of years of such frustration:

Idea file • Buy a five-inch by eight-inch file box and a generous supply of cards. If you are a copious saver, you may want to start out with the two-drawer type that can grow—upward.

• Set up your system by topics to begin with. As you use your file, you may decide to change the organization later on, but the material will be there.

• As you read, or as you transcribe your notes from a conference, course, or workshop, get into the habit of selecting the nuggets of line, phrase, or thought which condense the idea, jog your own thoughts, or stir your memory. File them away, recording the source. You may want to go back and put the quotation into context, reading what came before or after it in the book or article, or to find the person who said it and ask for elaboration.

• Make a simple diagram or sketch of an idea. Use both sides of your cards when necessary.

• Go through your file at least once a year, lest a good idea gets buried. Clean out the deadwood.

Library files • Set up a file for your own personal library, using three-inch by five-inch cards. You will save money and great annoyance if, in addition to labeling your books, you make a card for each one. Record the date and borrower's name *every* time you loan a book. Do not assume that the label will ensure your book's return—check your file cards regularly and ask for any book that has been away a reasonable time.

• Save pamphlets, magazine articles, papers you have written, and speeches you have given in a letter-size file. Depending on how much you save, you may want a filing cabinet with drawers or doors.

Picture files • Provide special storage for sets of slides, which also need some kind of cross-reference files. The same slide might be used in talking about integration of the exceptional child, use of new equipment, or a good day with the fours.

• Make photo albums throughout the school year. You can use them to illustrate program and its progress, reflected through actual children and events. You can also use them with parents at conference time and with individual children, showing their growth and recalling happy times.

• File pictures from magazines, calendars, and posters in folders large enough so you will not damage them. Sort them by subjects, by seasons, or by whatever key ideas will make them most useful to you.

Stay loose A teacher has a philosophy, a set of beliefs about what he is doing, but usually it is in his head and heart. Confronted with a request to spell it out, he may find it difficult to express. It is a healthy exercise in self-discipline to try to express one's convictions in words.

The philosophy stated in this book is only a beginning. The very nature of the "I AM!" and "I CAN!" theory carries with it the implication that each teacher is also a four-sided individual with strengths and weaknesses. It is expected that some will be strong in one area of interest and weak in another. It is hoped that each teacher will contribute generously of enthusiasm and talents and special interests and make an effort to grow in those which are less appealing.

As a teacher grows, an individual teaching style will develop. Our advice to the neophyte teacher is, "Do your own thing!" but also "Never let your convictions become encased in cement. Leave the doors of your mind open to new ideas. Let your 'I AM' develop to the point where you can experiment with enthusiasm, succeed with satisfaction, and fall flat on your face without frustration or a sense of overwhelming failure." In other words, "Stay loose!"

Chapter 25   STUDENT TEACHERS, SUBSTITUTES, VOLUNTEERS

Student teachers

A good student teacher program enhances the educational image and scope of a school. You should find out what teacher training programs exist in nearby colleges and junior colleges and invite the department heads to visit the school and discuss the possibilities for mutual service. Join the team educating the new teachers. The teacher to whom the student is assigned also becomes a member of that team, and will be a model for that student, sharing philosophy and attitudes towards children and teaching.

The way a teacher feels as an individual and about the profession will influence the student. A person who is rigid or uncompromising, implying that there is only *one* way, may turn off a potentially good teacher. On the other hand, the person who creates an exciting learning experience that meets the needs of the children in her care may inspire a young student to go on to become a great teacher. At the same time, she will see this relationship as a two-way street and will reach out for the fresh ideas and additional resources the student can bring to enrich the program. Helping the professional student become a teacher is an extension of one's self.

Helping the student teacher

The following suggestions will guide you in making this a valuable experience:

• Try to have the names of student teachers before they arrive—and, when they come, greet them by name.

• Plan to sit down in the staff room with students on the first day to explain the background and philosophy of the school.

• Try to give students some choices in making group assignments. Talk about which age they really want to work with. A student who has just finished a semester with threes may desire some experience with fives.

• Take the students on a tour around the school. Give it as much time and enthusiasm as you would if you were showing it to a prospective parent.

• Introduce the student to the lead teacher and other team members.

• Explain that the student will be encouraged to work directly with the children and to bring in materials and ideas, but that she should try to make these fit into the current curriculum themes.

• Suggest that when observing something she does not understand or approve of, the student should make a note of it and find an opportunity to ask the teacher about it later.

• Make sure that time is allowed for conferences with the supervising teacher and director, and for an occasional break in the staff room.

• Suggest that the student try to attend weekly team meetings and, if possible, a parent meeting.

• Explain at the first meeting that the student will be asked to write a letter at the end of the practice session evaluating the experience and offering constructive criticisms. The supervising teacher will also write an evaluation, and these two documents will be consulted if references are requested at a later date.

Substitutes A list of good substitutes is like money in the bank for you. It never fails—when one teacher calls in sick, there is almost sure to be another. The director who cannot find a substitute may end up in the classroom. This, in itself, is not all bad: directors should go back to the classroom occasionally, but it is not always convenient.

An ad in the paper offering free training to people who are interested only in part-time work will usually bring applicants. Before they can go into the classroom, they must be screened as carefully as any teacher, and that takes time. A training program will give them an opportunity to discover whether this is something they really want to do. At the same time, it will help you and your staff to determine whether the trainees are competent.

A substitute who enjoys working with children may apply for a full-time position, which can be a valuable resource when a vacancy occurs.

Volunteers In many centers there will be individuals who, for various reasons, of-
Set standards fer their services. This can be enormously helpful, but also calls for a word of caution. More than one director or teacher who eagerly entered into a situation which turned out to be undesirable has found it difficult to back away. It is best to look at the volunteer with the same care you use when employing a staff member. They will be with your children, and the fact that they are not paid does not enhance or limit the relationship. Motivation is a consideration. Is this to fulfill a need of their own, and is it compatible with your goals and philosophy? Will they make a definite commitment and expect to be conscientious and prompt in adhering to that promise, or will they feel, "I'm not getting paid, so I come when I feel like it."

Would you employ this person if you had a vacancy? If not, would your objection be based on the individual's personality, appearance, speech, or education? Is it a negative quality, serious enough to be detrimental to your school?

Will this person agree to volunteer and then feel put upon when she finds she is performing much the same work as the teachers, but not being paid for it?

Should be Remember, the parent or visitor cannot always distinguish the student
easy to identify teacher or volunteer from employed personnel. One director solved this problem by asking volunteers, student teachers, and substitutes to wear colored arm badges to indicate their status.

We do not intend to negate the value of these additional people to your program, only to suggest that such a relationship needs to be given careful thought.

Who are they?   Who are volunteers? Where do they come from?

A retired schoolteacher was delighted when a child care center opened across the street from her home. She called on the director as a neighbor and when they had established a friendly relationship she explained that she missed daily exposure to little children and offered her services. "It would be wonderful if you could help us at noon, and through nap time, because that is when we have team meetings," the director replied.

It was a happy situation for both sides. Living alone, the teacher welcomed the opportunity to eat one meal a day with company, and she was able to make that her main meal of the day. The children enjoyed her grandmotherly presence and looked forward to her coming during the day. When she could attend meetings, she was able to make contributions based on her long experience. Some of her methods were more traditional than those of the center, but she was open to suggestions and receptive to new ideas.

In another school, a half-day nursery in a church, a senior citizens group used a classroom twice a month for lunch and a meeting. One elderly gentleman, who happened to arrive early, was thrilled when the children flocked around him and asked, "Are you a grandpa?" His arrival time became earlier and earlier, and finally the director asked him if he would like to volunteer on a regular basis. That, too, turned out to be a happy arrangement.

Arrange training   A caution: With the growing interest in child care, the proliferation of extra adults in a classroom becomes a serious problem. High school teachers are introducing courses in child care and may request training opportunities for their students. Managers of government programs designed to furnish employment which may lead to training for a career will often seek placements in a center. You must steer a careful course between the desire to be helpful and responsibility to the children. Basic rules should be determined—and discussed—in advance. Minimum ongoing training should be required, which in itself may serve as a deterrent to the insincere applicant. There will be many fine, sensitive people, who can add to and enrich programs, but their selection and approval is not to be taken lightly.

Training for substitutes and volunteers   If an emergency situation means sending a substitute or volunteer into a classroom before you have been able to give them any instructions or training, you will have to rely on their common sense, which can be totally *unreliable*. It is best to have a training program in place and to have enough trained extras on call so that you will never be caught in this predicament. (Paying applicants to attend would be a worthwhile investment.)

You can use the following program to prepare substitutes or volunteers before they come into the classroom. We have outlined it as five two-hour sessions, but you could condense it into a single day. In that case, give participants written summaries of the main points to study at home.

If you own the videotaped training program, "Early Childhood Staff Training," described more fully in Chapter 44, you can help your substitutes and volunteers to continue to learn by letting them use, on their own time, the sessions you feel would be most helpful to them.

Session I   *History and philosophy of the school*
Using the diagram, explain the educational philosophy of the school. Tour the center, pointing out examples of how the philosophy is carried out in curriculum and behavior management. Show where materials and supplies are kept and offer guidelines for their use. Explain housekeeping responsibilities.

Session II   *Physical development of the child*
Cover large-muscle development, eye-hand control, and small-muscle development.
Health
Cover procedures for toileting, hand-washing, and preparing snacks.
Safety
Cover indoor and playground supervision and fire drills.

Session III   *Intellectual development*
Cover how to read a story, how to encourage conversation among children, how to develop math and block play.

Session IV   *Creativity*
In art, provide a list of various painting activities. Remind trainees never to lay a hand on the child's work. Explain what to do with "elegant junk" such as sewing trims, pipe cleaners, Popsicle sticks, and pieces of material.. In music, sing familiar songs and make up new words to familiar tunes. Display a few home-made instruments.

Session V   *Social and emotional development*
Cover behavior management, also known as discipline. Study together Grace Mitchell's *Ten Commandments for Teachers* (which appears on page 132). Stress respecting children's feelings.

At the conclusion of the program, you should give participants a certificate or some other form of recognition. Often this is the first step toward a career in education.

One final note: you should have on file for any substitute or volunteer—as for any member of the staff—a completed medical history and health screening report, as well as the phone number of the person's doctor and someone to call in an emergency. You should ask for and check references, even for volunteers.

Chapter 26   **NON-TEACHING STAFF**

Some members of your staff are not teachers, but are essential to a smooth-running operation. Though they may not be "educators," they are role models who do influence children. They should be aware of their importance as such.

The Secretary-receptionist
Very often the first impression of a center is conveyed by the person who answers the phone. Training, specific to *this* job in *this* center, is essential, including role-playing with simulated questions and situations. The secretary-receptionist must be able to maintain confidentiality in regard to a knowledge of the people (parents and staff), the business (salaries and income), and mistakes that happen in every organization. Professional attire and appearance, speech, and smile are important. Finally, the secretary-receptionist must like people and enjoy children.

Daily duties
• Greet visitors promptly and courteously. Screen them before calling the director and make them comfortable while they wait.
• Answer phones. Give information on class schedules and tuition, but refer all questions on curriculum or philosophy to the director. Keep notes when interviewing callers. Respond to complaints with courtesy: "Thank you for reporting this. Our director will look into the situation and call you back." Record all incoming and outgoing calls in a *log book* (time-consuming, but important).
• Discuss any special plans for the day with the director and make calls prearranging trips or outside activities. Check *permission slips* in the file to make sure every child can go on field trips.
• Keep the director's calendar up to date, calling attention to daily appointments. Take care of incoming and outgoing mail.
• Record extra hours or services provided *for* children and *by* staff.
• Help prepare and distribute copies of newsletters or bulletins to parents and staff, making sure no one is omitted.
• Receive applications and send out acceptances. Check for the return of health cards, emergency cards, and trip permission slips, and file them for easy access. When a child is withdrawn, be sure to get a final statement from the teacher, have the director approve it, and put it in the permanent file.
• Accept and record payments and follow up delinquent accounts.
• Fill in whenever or wherever needed if an emergency arises!

The Cook
In a child care center, the kitchen should not be hidden, but placed in view of the classrooms. A cook who likes and enjoys being with children is an important addition to the staff. The cook need not be a professionally trained chef, but needs to know about simple food preparation, nutrition, and dietary rules. The cook should wear a

uniform, smock, or other cover-up. It need not necessarily be white, but it must be spotless. The same rules that apply to a nurse and doctor for cleanliness should be considered for all who prepare food. If hairnets are not required, at least hair should be secured away from the face. The cook will keep the kitchen spotless and shining, track expenses, make reasonable requests to update or replace equipment, and use accepted forms and procedures.

The Nurse When the school budget does not allow for this extra service, the director may find a person who will be glad to give part-time service in exchange for tuition. It would be unusual to have a full-time nurse, except in a very large child care center. When a nurse is not available, licensing regulations usually require that at least one person trained in first aid be on the premises at all times. In some cases a nurse who lives or works close by the school can be "on call."

The Custodian Maintenance is one of the most difficult problems a director has to deal with. Child care is a *messy* business, and the materials that are important to creative programs are not only difficult to keep in order but also in direct contradiction to the need for cleanliness. Teachers should expect to share this responsibility. They cannot wait for a custodian to clean up a spill or keep their tables and counters clean. When children are taught how to clean up after messy activities, they are learning responsibility—and *that is program!* Since the buildings have to be cleaned when the children are not present, the teachers and custodian seldom meet face to face. They can exchange notes (both of direction and appreciation), but a meeting with real conversation may be necessary at times to avoid confrontation.

Where do you find cleaning personnel? An ad in the classified section of the newspaper may bring responses from people seeking part-time work. Occasionally someone will be attracted by an opportunity to exchange service for tuition. Ideally the same person who keeps your building sparkling clean will also be able to handle minor repairs. In a large center, maintenance may be provided by the establishment that houses it, such as a factory, office building, or hospital. In a small proprietary center, it is usually the owner and members of the family.

A custodian who enjoys children and understands the goals of the center may contribute to the curriculum.

It happened:
   When the teacher asked Henry to shorten the legs of a painting easel, he did it right in the classroom and, at the same time, conducted a class in problem-solving with the four-year-olds. "How shall we do it?" he asked. Cutting one leg at a time, he stood the easel up after each cut and asked, "Is it right now? What's wrong? What shall I do next?

A sound | The director who helps staff members climb the ladder of professional
investment | growth is making a sound investment. When a teacher learns some-
thing new, improves his teaching skills, or finds a way to share his
ideas with others, his "I AM!" expands, and when he can see visible evidence of success, his "I CAN!" knows no bounds.

Many states now have at least minimal requirements for in-
service training, and that is a small step in the right direction, but the
quality of that training often rests on your shoulders.

In-service staff | In-service training can be defined as everything taking place within
training | the school that is planned and designed to contribute to the profes-
sional growth of each individual staff member. A well planned program of in-service training can go far to narrow the gap between
lethargy and excitement. Often it makes the difference between mediocrity and excellence in the curriculum. Present a workable plan
(based on the size of the school, the hours open, and the daily schedule)
in detail to each staff member. Make it very clear that full attendance
is a condition of employment.

An effective program will serve to *stimulate, educate,* and *inspire.*
Every teacher, no matter how well qualified, needs to expand his scope
of activities, improve skills, refresh knowledge of proven methods, and
keep an open mind to new approaches to learning. The classroom
teacher who is not afforded this opportunity has a lonely job, always
wondering what may be happening in the educational milieu which is
new and exciting or even controversial. This person gets stuck in ruts,
using the same methods and materials in the same way, year after
year, and becomes a teacher who starts looking forward to Friday on
Monday morning and who counts the years to retirement. This lack of
enthusiasm is contagious, and the children begin to dread school.
They, too, live for the next vacation.

Teachers applying for and anxious to secure a position will agree
to comply with the in-service training program schedule with genuine
sincerity, but as the weeks pass and the responsibilities of a teaching
job become more demanding, enthusiasm may wear thin for putting in
extra hours, especially to attend meetings. You need to stress the possibility of sacrifice before the contingency arises. "There are certain responsibilities which are part of our profession. Are you sure your
family understands this and will not stand in your way when your attendance calls for some sacrifice on their part?" You need to be firm
and at times even hard-hearted on the first occasion when staff members begin to make excuses for missing meetings: "I can't come, it's my
wife's birthday." "I need Saturday for my housework and shopping. I
can't attend the conference." When one excuse is accepted, the domino
theory goes into effect—each person certain that his excuse is of equal

importance. To help avoid this problem, establish all training schedules and special conference dates well in advance.

Staff meetings   Regularly scheduled staff meetings give all members of the staff an opportunity to maintain a sense of unity; review past achievements, current procedures, and the need for new ones; problem-solve and share techniques; develop teamwork among staff members; help individual staff members develop and maintain self-confidence and assist them in building their professional skills; help one another function comfortably within the framework of center policy and regulations; be prepared to handle emergency situations; and maintain an in-service training program that will help keep everyone up to date on current trends in child development and early childhood education.

Procedures for   Set a regular time for staff meetings and stick to it. Remind each per-
staff meetings   son about the meeting on the preceding Friday. Post a general outline of the topics to be discussed and allow staff members an opportunity to suggest any additional subjects they may want to discuss.

Scheduling   In a hypothetical school with four groups or teams, a meeting schedule
staff meetings   might include the following:
* The director meets with lead teachers once each week.
* The lead teachers meet with their teams once a week.
* The full staff meets at least once a month. This meeting may have to take place in the evening, but it is an important link in the chain that connects the total structure.

    In addition, we recommend the following meetings:
* The director meets with directors of neighboring schools.
* The teachers meet with the teachers in neighboring schools.

Once you establish a schedule, see that nothing interferes with it. Often it seems impossible! "It's foolish to have a meeting today. Miss Smith is sick, and we don't want to meet without her." "Sorry, I have some important visitors coming—we'll have to postpone our meeting." "I just couldn't get a substitute for Marge, so I'm afraid you'll have to miss your meeting and cover for her." All legitimate reasons, but they start a pattern that will snowball. If the rule is, "You *must* find a way," and if you are consistent, meetings will attain an importance that makes postponement or omission a major catastrophe.

    Timing is always a problem. Usually it is best in a full-day child care center to take advantage of nap time, when fewer people are required to sit with sleeping children. Some teams prefer to meet early in the morning, between 7:45 and 8:45; some during the lunch hour; and some late in the afternoon, between 4:00 and 6:00.

    When a full staff meeting is held in the evening, there should be some time for socializing. The expense of providing a supper is justified when it leads to a relaxed atmosphere and open communication. All of these meetings, if handled properly, do constitute staff training. To see how, let us look at them more carefully.

Director and lead teachers You and the lead teachers may eat your lunch together in the office. The topics should cover matters relating to the over-all management of the center. They may follow the pattern of people, environment, program, as in this sample agenda:

• *People*—"Mary Jane is leaving April first. If you know anyone who might be a desirable candidate, please let me know." "This week someone from the fire department will come to talk about safety. How do you feel about including the toddlers and twos?" "Let's talk once more about what it does to the rest of us when one of you comes in late or calls me too late for me to find a substitute." "Does anyone need to ask for help with a problem with a child?"

• *Environment*—"This is the list of workjobs for the next two weeks. Wendy will check the kitchen, bathrooms, and staff room twice a day. Wu Li will be responsible for supplies and storage. Naomi will keep track of books—both adults' and children's—putting out new ones each week relating to curriculum. Rosa will arrange and update the bulletin boards."

• *Program*—Since planning takes place in each team meeting, some of the good things you have observed can be mentioned here.

Team members The lead teacher should assign a day for their meeting, usually held at nap time. When possible, extra staff will cover the nap. Otherwise, members of the team can meet around a table in the room after the majority of the children have gone to sleep.

The primary topic will be program. "How much of what we planned last week did we cover? Is interest still high? Should we continue or go on to a new plan? What materials will we need for next week? Have you checked out the supplies? Will you need petty cash to buy special items? Can anyone go to the library to look for related books?"

Specific problems with individual children should be discussed only if all members of the team are involved.

The full staff How can you plan for meetings? A clear, concise agenda is most important, drawing on suggestions from the whole staff. Plan it with some of the same criteria used in planning programs for young children—a balance of activity and rest, listening and participation. A change of vocal tone helps to keep an audience interested, as does alternating topics you present with reports presented by others. Remember that messages conveyed enter through all of the senses and employ visual, audial, and tactile methods of presentation.

Number the items on the agenda in order of importance, with an estimate of the time needed to present each one, a device that will keep speakers from rambling and discussions from dragging on. Designate one person to act as secretary. When possible, notes of the meeting should be distributed soon after it. Members of the staff should save these notes for later reference.

You set the stage for the meeting with notes assembled and ready. You might present notices of conferences or workshops, some new books, an idea for curriculum, an item in an equipment catalogue to introduce and discuss, or a sample of an activity observed at another school.

Finally, you must find the right mix of autocracy and democracy. There are times when you issue directives and make statements on policy. There are also times when you pose a question, present a problem, or offer a topic for discussion. Although teachers need to know that their ideas are respected and welcomed, too much "What do you think we ought to do?" can degenerate into fruitless talk while important business is neglected. The members of a staff need your leadership, inspiration, and encouragement.

A copy of the agenda and the minutes of the meeting should be kept on file. Where states require a certain number of hours of in-service training for each child care giver, staff meetings may be accepted only if it can be shown that the time was used for education and professional growth, rather than discussion of management and operations. For this reason, it is also wise to ask each participant to sign a dated attendance form.

The results will be worthwhile when you devote time and energy to providing opportunities for professional growth. When the "I AM!" of the caregivers expands, it is reflected in the quality of their work with the children.

Assignments for staff meetings
Assignments help to ensure active participation and maintain interest. The following suggestions have proven to be successful.

Stretching a story—The well-loved book *Caps for Sale*, by E. Slobodkina (Scholastic), was used to demonstrate the variety of ways a story can be extended into various aspects of program. One group developed math activities; another, music and movement; the third looked for opportunities to include language and drama; the fourth brought in suggestions for art, including a variety of ways to make the caps. (See *Monkey Business*, Vol. 2, p. 193.)

Science workshop—One group contributed ideas for water play, another for plumbing, and the third for electricity. They used the suggestions offered in the curriculum manual and either demonstrated them by assembling the equipment or made additional contributions.

Book reviews—The director distributed a number of children's books which the book committee of the Parent Council had asked staff to review for recommendations to purchase. Each team chose two books, read them to children, and reported back at a subsequent meeting.

Neighboring schools
Directors form a network with directors of nearby schools, meeting once a month to discuss mutual problems and share ideas.

Teachers at neighboring schools also meet once a month, discussing environment, curriculum development, staffing patterns, zoning throughout the day, and similar topics.

Sharing teaching skills   Another way you can help a teacher grow is to watch for a special skill or talent and suggest that it be shared in a workshop.

> *It happened:*
> *Pamela had discovered many ways to enhance her program with home-made games. The results were clearly apparent in the excitement and enthusiasm in her kindergarten group. When her director suggested that she might offer a workshop and teach her colleagues how to use easily available materials to create games, Pamela was surprised and pleased. The director sent notices to a few neighboring centers and about twenty people responded. Pamela had spent time preparing the content and materials for her workshop, but she hadn't realized that working with adults is not quite the same as working with children. Her first workshop was only partly successful, but, undiscouraged, she was determined to try it again. The experience gave her inner confidence, her "I CAN!" was enhanced, and ultimately she presented workshops at a national conference.*

Individual staff conferences   Staff meetings are essential, but cannot take the place of individual appraisal conferences, which should be scheduled at least twice a year. Experience has shown that January is a strategic time for one of them. Morale often takes a dip after the excitement of the holidays, especially in northern climates, where struggling with snowsuits and boots, and being confined indoors, can deplete a teacher's physical and emotional energy. The director who says blithely, "Oh, that isn't necessary. I see and talk to my teachers every day!" is making a mistake.

> *It happened:*
> *"I had been dragging my feet on scheduling conferences," Neil said. "We seemed to be getting along so well, I thought other matters should take priority. Imagine my surprise when Peggy, the assistant director, stormed into my office and quit. She had a long list of grievances, all of which I could have dealt with if I had given her an opportunity to talk earlier. As it happened, her problems began with personal matters at home, but by the time she reached the boiling point, it was too late—and now I'm looking for someone to replace her."*

Appraisal form   Prior to the interview, give the teacher an appraisal form, saying, "Take time to think about your answers to these questions. Make notes if you wish and bring the form with you. I will bring my copy of the form with my notes." The form should contain these questions, as well as spaces for your appraisal, the employee's appraisal, and the date:

• In order of importance, what do you feel are your three strongest points?
• In what area do you feel a continuing need for growth?
• What have you done to promote your own professional growth since our last conference?

- What are you doing to improve your job performance?
- Are there any ways in which you feel the center could give you more support?

Setting the stage   Treat this appointment with the same respect you would if it was with *your* employer. Clear your desk and calendar. Arrange for someone else to answer the telephone. Hang a "Do not disturb" sign on your door, with instructions not to interrupt you except in case of dire emergency.

Arrange two comfortable chairs away from your desk—the climate you want to establish is destroyed if you take an intimidating stance behind your desk, facing a nervous employee on the opposite side. If you can offer tea or coffee, it will help to establish a climate, but at any rate allow time for some casual conversation: "How is Sarah getting along in college?" "Is Bobby adjusting well to first grade?"

Conducting the interview   When you are both comfortable, begin a discussion of the points on the appraisal form. In addition, you might want to add such questions as:

- In your previous job, you were the only teacher in a self-contained classroom. Are you comfortable working with a team?
- What would you boast about in your program?
- If you find yourself just waiting for Friday, can you isolate the reasons?

For most directors—for most people—the hardest part of any interview is learning to *listen*.

It is up to you to draw the interview to a close. Summarize with, "I'm going to write a brief report of our meeting which I'll give to you for approval. When we agree that it is accurate, we will both sign it and it will go into your permanent file. Thank you for coming in—and please remember that you don't have to wait for our next scheduled conference to come in and talk with me!"

Allow at least an hour for each conference. If possible, schedule no more than one a day. It is disconcerting for both parties to know that there is another employee sitting outside the door, waiting his turn.

A well-planned program of in-service training can make the difference between mediocrity and excellence.

Remember, communication is a two-way street. Learn to listen with your ears and with your heart.

All members of the teaching staff will find that their days go more smoothly if they read, understand, and *use* the following material. Non-teaching staff should at least read this chapter.

Definitions   When the word *discipline* is used as a *verb*, it means "to punish or penalize in order to train and control." When we punish a child, we act upon her, because we are bigger, stronger, or more powerful. The dictionary tells us that *discipline* is also a *noun*, defined as "a set or system of regulations leading to behavior in accord with rules of conduct."

In the context of this book, we will treat *discipline* as a noun and offer the following definition: *Discipline is the slow, bit by bit, time-consuming task of helping children to see the sense in acting in a certain way.*

The key word is *sense*, and children have far more of that than we are willing to admit! They can be helped to realize that it feels better to act in a certain way, and gradually they will learn to take charge of their own actions—self-discipline.

It happened:

Hearing loud voices from the block corner, the teacher saw Jerry and Angie tussling over a truck. Taking their hands, she led them over to two small chairs and seated them, facing each other, their knees almost touching. "This is called 'negotiating,'" she said. "Angie will talk first and then you will have your turn, Jerry." As Angie began to state her case, Jerry interrupted, but the teacher intervened. "This is Angie's turn to talk," she said. "You will have your chance." When the children had expressed their feelings, she guided them to an acceptable compromise.

The next time there was an altercation, she said, "I guess we need the 'talk-it-over' chairs." Other children watched the process with interest. The next step occurred when several children came to her, saying, "We need the talk-it-over chairs." Finally, she knew her teaching had paid off when she saw two children get chairs and sit down to discuss a problem, without asking for her interference or guidance. These children were learning the art of communication, the need for negotiation and compromise, but best of all that it makes sense to act in a certain way.

Four-step plan   If we base our definition of discipline on sense, we must assume that the adult will practice common sense, but unfortunately our natural instincts sometimes get in the way, and we react without thinking. To help an adult practice self-discipline, we offer the Four-Step Plan:

Anticipate!—When you find a child is becoming "the enemy," when you wake up in the morning thinking "This could be a great day if only Ginny Jones were absent," make a plan for dealing with her when she acts out the particular behavior that is getting you down. (Have Plan B ready in case Plan A doesn't work.)

Hesitate!—Find your own best method for buying time. Turn your back. Count to ten. Walk away and get a drink of water. It does no harm to let the child see that you are disturbed. Doing nothing about it for a minute, rather than reacting with anger, may be enough of a surprise to get her full attention!

Investigate!—You will know you are a successful teacher when you are able to look at the child who has just kicked you in the shins, sunk her teeth into your hand, or blistered your ears with four-letter words and your major concern is, "I wonder what can be going on in the life of this child that could cause such anger!"

Start searching for the evidence. Learn as much as you can about her family and home life, or whether something scary is going on at home, such as sickness, pending divorce, moving, or the death of a pet.

That is one way to investigate. The other is to hold your tongue—and your actions—until you are *sure* you have all of the facts about an incident. Check them as you would for an accident report. Who was involved? What was going on just prior to the incident?

Communicate!—So many of the problems in human relationships can be attributed to lack of communication. *Talk* to the child. To your director. To the parent. Let your feelings be known. Remember, communication is a two-way street. Learn to *listen* with your ears *and* with your heart.

You are a model   The word *discipline* stems from *disciple*, and that is defined as "one who follows in the footsteps of a respected and admired leader." This definition has two messages for the teachers of young children. First, you are the model for your young charges. They will copy your mannerisms, tone of voice, and behavior.

Second, your children want very much to bask in the sunshine of your approval. This fact can serve to your advantage when used properly. Reward good behavior with justifiable praise and let it be clearly known when you are displeased. Keep your rules simple and appropriate to the ages of the children. On the other side of the coin, you abuse this admiration when you use it as a club over the child's head, withholding affection and love as a form of punishment. "No, you can't sit beside me today, because you were mean to Pedro."

A contented, busy child who has a healthy "I AM," and is able to exert her "I CAN," will not find it necessary to test herself constantly in her social environment. In the same vein, the adult who has a strong "I AM" is able to maintain a calm confidence which the child senses—and can lean against.

One of the first things a neophyte needs to learn is that it doesn't hurt to say, "I made a mistake. I was wrong to say 'No' to you—I just wasn't thinking very well." Too often adults fear that if they retract their threats, they will lose face and thus weaken all future relationships with the child. On the contrary, when they admit error, they are teaching the child one of life's most important lessons: that we all make mistakes, that we all have need of a second chance, that this need will continue to be true even when the child becomes an adult.

The second piece of wisdom for the beginning teacher is that it takes experience to become a wise and confident disciplinarian. The child knows this—and will take advantage of the insecurity of the adult. She has a great need to push against something resistant—it is only by testing each newfound strength that she can recognize her own power, that she can assess her own "I AM." In the fumbling and feeling out which must necessarily take place between teacher and pupil, the following faces may emerge:

Discipline styles   *The Queen*—Teacher reigns supreme, daring any ordinary mortal to oppose her slightest command. Everyone who reads these words will remember at least one such autocrat—one who aroused such fear that it practically erased all potential for learning. Seldom do you see such a person in a preschool, but occasionally an assistant or aide who has known school in no other terms will adopt this style.

Loudmouth Mary—Mary can be heard as you approach the school: "Jimmy Jones, get out of that sandbox!" "No, you can't take the bike from Tommy, he had it first! " "Everyone come in now—time to wash up for lunch!" She screams and bellows all day long. Unfortunately, however loud her voice may be, the children can always top it.

Nagging Ned—"How many times do I have to tell you?" "I told you not to ...." "Joyce, put on your rubbers. Put on your rubbers, Joyce. Have you got your rubbers on yet?"—all in the space of two minutes. Ned doesn't even hear his own voice, going on, and on, and on. Neither will Joyce, who soon learns to tune out that continual nagging.

Miss Anne—the Teacher, with a capital "T"—Anne is so tuned in to program that she doesn't need to worry about whether she will be able to control the children. She assumes that behavior will take care of itself if children's minds are challenged. When she does see the need for correction, she moves quietly over to the situation and sizes it up, interfering only if it seems necessary. She knows children need to learn to manage their own squabbles. She *will* step in if one child is in danger of hurting another. Then Anne gets down to his level—eyeball to eyeball—and in a *very* firm voice says, "I will not *let* you hurt Eddie" or "You may not take the bike away from Van—he had it first. When he's through with it, you'll be the very next one to have it." Anne will not humiliate a child by berating her in a loud voice before her peers. She will not hurt her already injured feelings by scolding her. She *will* offer her support, saying, "I will not *let* you do that." The child has a right to lean on her, to trust that she will be stopped before she goes too far, to know that her teacher will set reasonable limits.

Anne knows when to ignore blustering threats such as "I hate you! I'm going to chop you up!" She answers with a pleasant "I'm sorry, I do like you." She answers a defiant "I won't" with a confident and pleasant "Oh, yes, you will," at the same time holding the child's hand firmly and moving toward the action she had requested.

Anne trusts her own ability to say and do the right thing at the right time, and to back up gracefully when she goofs. She has the light touch which can sense when the healing balm of laughter may be more useful than the abrasive action of anger.

Signals What if the tempo of the room is rising? Things are getting noisy? One or two children are acting silly, and the rest are beginning to react? What can you do? One thing you will *not* do is to raise your voice and scold—you will only add more noise to the rising clamor. Nor will you clap your hands and shout "Children! Children!" nor snap your fingers, nor blow a whistle, nor say "Shhh!"

There are other methods for gaining the attention of a noisy group:

• *Play one or two notes* steadily and rhythmically on the *black* keys of the piano. If you have no piano, use two drums or two tone bells.
• *Have drum signals* with various meanings—call it drum talk. One signal means wash your hands, another means juice time or nap time.
• *Blow up a balloon* or a paper bag. Children will stop to see what you are going to do.
• *Put out the lights.* When children stop to see what has happened, talk about noise.
• *Start singing* a familiar song and, when all have joined in, tone it down, softer and softer, until it is just a whisper.
• *Start a motion,* such as tapping the top of your head. Encourage some children to copy you. As more children join in, change the motion. When all are participating, slow down the motion and then bring it to a stop.

When the children are quiet and ready to listen to you, it is better to smile and say, "That was fun. Now let's go back and finish what we were doing!" than to berate them or scold.

As the weeks progress, the group will *develop an understanding of attention signals*—how many there are, who gives them, why, and when they are used. Developing recognition and response to signals carries over into the very important area of safety. Training children to respond to signals is basic education. Talk to them about street signals and fire alarms.

If play is building up to a high pitch, try to *divert* it. For example, if the block tower is getting too high, suggest extending it sideways into a village and add some accessories.

Group control:
the "Meeting"

It happened:

It was the last week of January, the weather had kept the children in for most of the month, and it was getting noisier day by day. One morning when they came in, they found the chairs arranged theater-style.

"What's this for? What are we going to do?"

"As soon as the rest of the children come, we are going to have a meeting." All children know that word—parents are always going to a meeting. One told another as new arrivals came in, and soon all were sitting on chairs, looking very serious.

When they were ready, she began: "Things haven't been going too well around here this week. I went home with a headache last night. Does anyone know why?" The children responded with giggles and nods. She went on, "Grownup people have to have rules—they call them laws. They say things like 'Don't drive your car too fast!' or 'Don't take things that belong to others!' I wonder whether we could make some laws for our room."

The answers came freely. As the children began to make up rules, the teacher wrote them on a large sheet of paper, then numbered them. When they were through, she read them all back, then made a game of them: "What is number five? Which rule says, 'Don't run!'" Then the teacher asked, "How could we use these rules?"

"You could say 'Number four,' and we would know that means 'Don't holler!'"

"I know another way," Chan said eagerly. "You could take a number out of a box and give it to the one who was breaking the rule."

"That's a terrific idea," the teacher responded. "Can anyone think of another?" By the time they were through discussing the rules, most of the children had the numbers and rules pretty well put together in their minds. After that, they reminded each other. If Harry ran, Bess might say, "Number five," and he would slow down.

Transitions

How can teachers move a group of children from place to place without chaos?

In an open classroom there will not be many occasions when an entire group will be moving, but there are always some. For example, if meeting time is held at the beginning of each session, the children will disperse to chosen activities at the end of the meeting. The natural tendency for children, especially if they have been sitting for long, is to make a wild dash. Teachers need to develop a variety of techniques to avoid this. It is far easier to lose control of a group than it is to get them back into a mood of purposeful activity.

Some teachers use songs. Many become proficient in creating songs on the spot to fit each occasion, adding new words to familiar tunes. Other teachers dismiss a few children at a time, suggesting a way for each to go: "Miss B's children will go out like mice. ... I think it would be fun to have the fours be great big heavy elephants. How will you walk? Be careful, don't step on any of those little mice. ... I just heard a plane go over. How could you fly out of the room? ... All of the children whose names begin with *A* may go."

Send out a group at a time to rhythms you tap on sticks, a drum, or a tambourine—fast or slow, heavy or light, running or walking.

Hold up a *name card* and allow each child to leave when she recognizes her own. With fives, you might be able to say, "I will hold up a card. If that person is sitting on your *left*, you may get up, and the two of you may leave together. If you see your own name, do *not* stand right away. Wait until the person next to you has a chance to try to read it."

Only when you are experienced enough to keep your mind one step ahead of the present will these suggestions become effective. If, in a sudden burst of enthusiasm, you announce, or even suggest, a move without warning, children will react suddenly and spontaneously.

Avoiding the pitfalls

• *Don't make threats you can't carry out*—Mr. Ben digs his own hole and falls into it. "Luis, I'm tired of telling you to put on your jacket. If you aren't ready when the taxi comes, it will leave without you." So the taxi comes. Now what? Ben can't keep Luis—he knew he couldn't when he made the threat. He has no choice but to finish dressing Luis and get him into that car. *Every* adult falls into this trap sooner or later, and every adult has to find a way out.

If you find yourself sitting out on that proverbial limb, the best way off is to retract, promptly and openly. "Well! That was a silly thing for me to say. I *will* help you this time, but we had both better think of a way to keep this from happening again."

• *Don't make negative comparisons*—"Come on, Bill, you can put on your boots. See, Simon can do it, and Jill can, and they are four, just like you. Now try!" Maybe Bill *can* put on his boots, and maybe he *should* put on his boots, but the reason is not that Simon and Jill can put on their own boots. Being four does not mean that physical and manual dexterity reach a common level. Bill may very well be more advanced in some other area than Simon or Jill. Suggesting that he is lacking by setting him in competition with his peers may have the opposite of the desired effect.

• *Don't embarrass a child*—Picture yourself walking down the main street, loaded with bundles, when you trip and fall, dropping bundles, tearing your clothes, and scraping your knee. You are embarrassed and hurt. How will you feel if some wise adult comes over and says "Come on, get up, that didn't hurt!" or "Be a big boy, don't cry—everyone is looking at you!"

When a child falls, she hurts her pride *and* her body. The most you can do is to recognize this fact. "It hurts, I know. I'm sorry. We will go in and put some cold water on it. That will make it feel better." More than anything else, the child needs the assurance, through your tone of voice, that she is *not* permanently injured, that it *will* feel better in a few minutes, and that you *do* understand that it hurts.

• *Don't force children to try something if they aren't ready*—"Come on, try it, you'll like it!" says the new substitute teacher as he *puts* Linda on the slide. Linda, who is not ready for the slide, tenses up, and when she reaches the bottom her leg breaks. Exaggerated? Maybe, but not impossible. Children are better judges than we are of their readiness for new experiences. They may need help. "If you would like to try it, I'll hold you all the way down, so you won't go too fast." Or "This time why don't I hold your hands?" Gradually Linda gains the confidence that will let her clamber up and down the slide as well as her friends. *Putting a frightened child on a piece of equipment is dangerous!*

• *Do plan with the children*—Ken is starting off with ten children, going from classroom to play yard. His mind has moved ahead, considering the possible hazards. He gathers the children around him and they have a short meeting. "When we go outside, we need to remember some rules. First, wait for me. You may go as far as the big tree, but then stop and wait until we all catch up with you. Second, we will use the tree house playground. Another group is using the bikes. When they are through, perhaps we can have them."

Ken doesn't talk about the "or elses," but he knows what they are. Donna does not wait for him. He does not yell and scream after her. But when he does catch up with her, he says very quietly in her ear, "You did not listen to me. Now you will have to hold my hand for a few minutes while the others play." On the first offense he does not hold her hand very long (a minute is an eternity to a child in these circumstances), but he *must* do something to fix the idea firmly in her mind that there will *always* be consequences for infractions.

• *Do anticipate problems and have a plan*—Easier said than done, but a sign of teaching maturity. While the children are still sitting at the table having juice, the teacher is thinking of what will happen next, how he will manage the transition from one place to another. Anticipating the hazards (which may mean knowing that Johnny will take off for the block area) and thus armed with pre-planning, he will be able to keep his voice down and his face serene.

The troublemakers   It happened:

> "Why are these boys sitting in your office on such a lovely day?"
> "They are being punished," the director of a full-day center answered. "They have behaved so badly on the playground that the teachers are at their wits' end. I spoke to the parents, and they have talked to their children, but nothing seems to do any good."
> Inquiry disclosed that these bright, active four-year-olds were in the center ten hours a day, five days a week. They gave little or no trouble in the morning, when program activities kept them occupied.

Some helpful   The following suggestions were offered:
suggestions   •   Go back to the books and read everything you can find about four-year-olds. What are they like? What are their needs?

- Discuss these two boys with all the teachers who work with them at various hours of the day. What do they enjoy most? When do they perform best? What seems to set them off?
- Get them involved in an activity which has some continuity, such as building or making something which requires them to think, plan, look for materials, and bring things from home; or developing a play, which will involve making costumes, props, invitations, and so forth.
- Greet the parents each night with some positive comment. "Don helped the little ones dress today. Does he help you a lot at home?" "You would have been proud of Shawn if you had been here at clean-up time. He organized a crew and they all worked very hard for him." In watching for positive acts to relate, members of the staff will find their own negative attitudes toward these two boys changing.

Asking parents who have worked all day to scold or lecture a recalcitrant child is not helpful. In the first place, the parents are going to be anxious about whether the center might exclude the child, jeopardizing their jobs. Secondly, they are not in a position to handle punishments for deeds which they have not seen. In either case, the relationship between child and parent is disturbed. The objective of the staff should be to strengthen the family, not to weaken it.

When emotions run high   Adults have varied ways of releasing their own strong emotions. Some vent their feelings on others, leaving behind them a chain of bruised feelings. The boss gets a memo from the president, so he chews out the foreman. The worker gets the backlash, so he vents his frustration on his wife or child when he gets home. The dog, recognizing the signs, hides under the bed.

Some find more acceptable means. One woman weeds her garden, letting her irritation drain out into the soil as she yanks and pulls weeds out of the dirt. Another puts the energy generated by anger to practical use and washes the kitchen floor. Some adults find it soothing to take a long walk alone; others can look at the mountains or the ocean and put their problems into perspective.

Releasing feelings   Children need help in finding acceptable ways of releasing their feelings. First, they need to know that it is *all right* to be angry or sad. *All* people have such feelings. We *cannot* hurt other people, but there are things we *can* do.

- *Working with clay*
- *Hammering nails into wood*
- *Tackling a dummy* or *punching a punching bag*
- *Tearing cloth or paper*
- *Throwing things* at a legitimate target

Water diverts a child before the crisis is full-blown, although we do not recommend it for a child who is having a tantrum.

Verbalizing strong feelings often relieves the tensions within.

It happened:

"Let's go in here," said the teacher, walking into the staff room with a firm grip on Amy's hand. They sat down at the table. When she stopped crying long enough to listen, he said, "Why don't you tell me about your angry feelings. I will write them down." Faster than he could write, she vented her anger and frustrations. When she was through, he read back to her what she had said. She listened with great interest. "What shall I do with this now?" he asked. "Keep it," was her reply. "I might need it again."

Teacher—are you listening? Children have a second language! Long before they have acquired verbal skills, they express what they are feeling and thinking through their actions. A sensitive teacher will attempt to read the message a child is trying to convey through behavior.

Children have a built-in radar that tells them how adults feel about them. They are not fooled by sweet tones or forced pleasantries. Sensitivity to the unspoken language of a child can be developed only with experience. Adults need to think constantly, "What is going on inside this child that makes her need to behave this way? How can I help her communicate her needs? Set limits for her that will protect the other children and still allow her to get rid of bad feelings?"

It is very hard for a parent, in the midst of the pressures and tensions of twenty-four-hour-a-day living, to respond in this way. We cannot condone a quick reaction, such as slapping, yelling, or shaming, but we can appreciate it because, as teachers, we too want to react with anger when we hear a defiant "I won't," "You stink," or "I hate you." But we are teachers, and our profession has taught us to stop, look, and listen to the messages children try so hard to convey.

Discipline should strengthen the "I AM! I CAN!" As with every other facet of our teaching, we go back to our basic philosophy and apply it to behavior management. Punishment which embarrasses, humiliates, or destroys the child's self-image will stand in the way of our ultimate goal, self-discipline. Turn the page to read Grace Mitchell's *Ten Commandments for Teachers.*

TEN COMMANDMENTS FOR TEACHERS

I   Thou shalt pay honor and respect to the children in thy care, treating them with the same courtesy thou wouldst accord a guest in thy home.

II   Never, never, never in all the days of thy employment wilt thou strike, shake, or physically manhandle a child.

III   Thou shalt not embarass, ridicule, or humiliate a child with words or actions.

IV   Thou shalt not raise thy voice to call across the room or playground to a child or colleague, but shalt instead walk over and speak directly to him.

V   Order and cleanliness are refreshing to the spirit; therefore, thou shalt make clean-up a part of the children's daily program.

VI   Respect for property is a lesson to be learned at an early age; therefore, thou shalt not dump dress-up clothes, musical instruments, blocks, or toys in cartons, but shalt teach "a place for everything and everything in its place."

VII   Thou shalt not decorate thy walls with cute look-alike art projects.

VIII   Music and singing soothe the spirit and bring joy into daily living, but singing is not shouting; therefore, thou shalt not be heard saying "Louder! I can't hear you! Sing louder!"

IX   Not by so much as the lifting of an eyebrow, the shrug of a shoulder, or a snide remark shalt thou express contempt for a fellow worker, but when angered or annoyed thou shalt seek to know him better or start a positive rumor about him.

X   Consider carefully the image thou projectest to children, for they look upon thee with respect and will seek to copy thy speech, mannerisms, walk, and dress.

Grace L. Mitchell

Chapter 29   **WHAT IS ENVIRONMENT?**

Environment is an all-encompassing term. It comprises everything within the four walls of the child care facility that contributes to the living and learning that takes place inside, as well as the playground, which is also a laboratory for growth and development.

As the gardener chooses the location for his plants with care, seeking the right balance of sun and shade, as well as protection from the elements, traffic, and animals, so we, who nurture the growth of young children, are concerned with safe and convenient access to our buildings, a balance of sun and shaded areas, and traffic patterns within the school and on the playground which achieve a smooth flow of movement.

Voice control   Environment is more than space and equipment. It is the ambience that children, parents, and staff sense upon entering a center. Just one harsh, strident, overbearing voice will destroy the atmosphere of purposeful activity and serenity that children need and deserve if they are at the center for six to eight hours a day, sometimes five days a week and fifty weeks of the year.

You should stress this point during pre-opening staff training, but that will not be enough. Throughout the year, you will need to be alert and to speak immediately to the offender. It happens so easily—a teacher speaks across the room to a colleague, or calls out directions to a child, and instinctively all within the vicinity raise their voices to match. Within minutes, the whole tone of the center will jump several decibels.

Repeat over and over again the admonition, "*Walk* to the person you wish to *talk* to," whether inside or on the playground. A visitor's first impression of your center should not be one of adults shouting at children.

It happened:

"*Something will have to be done about the acoustics in this building!*" *the director complained to a visiting supervisor. While they stood talking, the fours came bursting through the door. Boisterous and still filled with the vigor of outdoor play, they were noisy enough —but the voice of their teacher rose above the din. "Peter, stop fooling around and hang up your things! All you people who are ready line up over here to wash your hands! Ramona, your mother is com-*

ing for you. Stand here by the door." She went on and on, shouting, directing, filling the room with her importance. The children's voices followed the same pattern.

"Do you see what I mean?" the director asked in plaintive tones.

"I certainly do," the supervisor replied, "and before I come back a week from today, I will expect you to have held a meeting with all of your staff to discuss voice control. You will find it hard to get people to change their habits. You'll have to be creative in thinking of ways to help. You may want to use a tape recorder to detect the worst offenders and persuade them. But, when you get the message across, you'll find that every other aspect of your daily program will improve.

Learning happens best in an environment of purposeful activity, not chaotic, noisy confusion.

Planning the environment In Part I we offered suggestions for all directors who have the luxury of planning before a building is erected. The following questions can be used by the owner-director who wants to make the best possible use of a property that already exists. Referring once more to the four sides of the developmental square, we will want to ask whether the space and equipment offer opportunities for growth in each area.

•   Are there places where children can run and climb to release excess energy? Are there ways for large muscles to stretch?

•   Does the equipment encourage development of hand-eye coordination?

•   On the social side, does the space provide cozy places where a child can be alone, or play with one or two friends, as well as areas for group activities such as meetings, circle, and music and creative movement sessions?

• On the emotional side, does the center give the child the sense that it is his second home? He often spends more waking hours in it than in his own house. The arrangement of space will have much to do with his emotional reaction to it. Is it too controlled? Too open? Has every possible effort been made to create a homelike environment? Curtains and rugs in some areas? Pictures at the child's eye level? A dramatic play area where activities that take place in the home can be acted out? Lights which can be lowered for quiet activities?

•   Do the space and equipment encourage children to explore and discover, to seek answers to questions by asking and testing hypotheses, to carry a project through to completion, and, above all, to achieve success? The saddest sight in a child care center is to see children's normal curiosity and spontaneity stifled while they sit at a table and carry out adult-planned projects.

Here is an account of an imaginary tour of a school. The conversation between the director and the parents may be hypothetical, but it is real in that it poses and answers questions which parents do ask.

As Mr. and Mrs. Jackson entered the child care center, bright red geraniums in window boxes seemed to offer a cheery welcome. An attractive foyer extended the message; one wall bore mounted silhouettes of children—children with pigtails and ponytails, snub noses and chubby cheeks. (See Self-portraits and Silhouettes, *Vol. 2, p. 94.)*

Parent: "Are they real?"

Receptionist: "Oh, yes, they are our own children. They love to look at them and name their friends."

In one corner was a large, gaily painted papier-mâché ostrich.

Parent: "Surely the children couldn't have made that!"

Receptionist: "The fours had a lot of fun putting that together. The frame is chicken wire. Last month we had a dinosaur created by the kindergarten."

She invited the parents to sit in a cozy alcove to wait for the director. Several comfortable chairs were grouped around a coffee table, and a coffee urn was on a side table. A rack on one wall held pamphlets of interest to parents. Standing at the entrance was a bulletin board with notices to parents, some newspaper stories, and an announcement of a forthcoming lecture.

Receptionist: "While you are waiting, you may want to look at a recent copy of our school paper. It is written and printed by our parents' group."

At this point the director appeared and invited them into her office. She did not conduct an interview from behind her desk, but sat with them in comfortable chairs.

Director: "Let's talk a bit about you and what you are looking for in child care and the needs of your child. Then we will walk around the school. I'll explain our philosophy in the classroom, where you can see it in action."

The director's office was cheerful and inviting. A small table and two chairs stood beside a low shelf on which a few toys and books were arranged. A divider set off one corner, shielding a cot. Seeing the parents looking at it, the director explained, "We do not plan to keep children here if they are sick. Until a parent can come or send someone to take him home, a sick child will stay in here with me. Sometimes they can play with the toys, but if they are really sick they use the cot. I like to have them in here, where I can keep an eye on the situation."

After a very brief explanation of the basic organization of the school, they moved into the school itself—one large room (about forty by ninety feet), separated by movable dividers into areas of interest and age groupings. The director paused at a carpeted space (about twenty by thirty feet).

Director: "We call this the meeting area. It's where the children who arrive early stay until their teachers come, and where they wait for their parents at the end of the day. Two teachers are there to open the center and others come as needed to maintain the required teacher-pupil ratios. During the day, this is a place for meetings, for using audio-visual equipment, and for other special programs. We do have a television set, and the early and late children may watch children's programs, but more often than not they find other things more interesting."

Parent: "I've heard of child care centers where the children sit in front of television for most of the day."

Director: "Oh, yes, so have I, but I can assure you *that* doesn't happen here. Our television set can also be used for videotapes. We make tapes for staff training, and occasionally the children like to see themselves on television. If there is an outstanding program we feel the children should see, we might use television during the day, but that seldom happens. In any case, it would not be a command performance—it would be one choice among many."

Parent: "Do you mean the children can just do anything they want?"

Director: "If you are thinking of the stereotype image of the so-called progressive school, where children are jumping on the furniture and climbing the walls, the answer is 'no.' We are trying to teach children to live comfortably within the limitations of their own society. At certain times of the day we offer a choice of activities, but when it comes to routines, such as eating, napping, washing, and dressing, they are not given much latitude. We *teach* them how to care for their own needs and try to establish routines which will become good habits. We also expect them to respect the rights and property of others."

Parent: "What do they do besides watch television when they arrive early?"

Director: "It's all very low-key. We try to think what a child might be doing at home at that time of day and create a similar environment. The reading corner and dramatic play area are close by, and we usually have one or two table activities available. The children do not wait to be entertained. They quickly form friendships and carry on their own ideas from one day to the next. When their teachers arrive, they move to their own areas, and when all in a class are present, they have a meeting."

Parent: "What kind of meeting?"

Director: "Sometimes it includes some singing, some conversation, but it is really a planning session. At first, the teachers will have set up activities and the children are given choices. As the year progresses, the children participate more and more in deciding the program. We have a curriculum, which I will be glad to show you when we get back to the office, but it is intended as a guide, not a rigid plan. Cues come from individual children or from the nature and direction of the group activity at a given moment."

Parent: "Suppose a child chooses to do the same thing every day?"

Director: "We let it go on for a while. Some children need time to absorb, enjoy, or test ideas and materials. An experienced teacher knows when it is time for diversion. He controls activities by changing the environment. For example, if a child stays too long with trucks and blocks, he simply closes off the block area for a few days."

Parent: "Won't they all choose to play outdoors most often?"

Director: "No. It's like a smorgasbord: at first they may choose all desserts, but eventually our experience shows that they will level off and choose a balanced diet. Now, this area is for fours. They have most of the same activity centers, except for blocks, which they share with the kindergarten. We have the large building blocks here and the unit blocks on the other side of the divider."

As they moved to the other end of the building, they saw that the bathrooms had been installed in a walled room in the center. On the outside of one wall, to take advantage of the plumbing, was a low sink.

Director: "This is the painting area. It has a floor drain—we do some pretty messy activities, and we need to wash up often."

Parent: "Where did you find these little mops?"

Director: "They are adult size, with the handles cut down so the children can help. *Cleanup is program, just as important and just as much fun!*"

A sign bearing the words "Elegant Junk" stood above a bank of large plastic crates, each filled with items for creative activities, such as yarn, ribbons, feathers, and string.

Director: "We want a variety of materials to be available all the time to stimulate the child's imagination, but storage of these materials is always a problem. The way in which a teacher displays such items can be compared to merchandising. People are trained in stores to set out merchandise so customers will want to buy. A teacher wants children to be so intrigued by materials that they will want to explore and examine them, use them, and create with them."

Parent: "I see many signs. Can they read them?"

Director: "Quite a few, by the end of the year. We believe that children learn to read when they want to know, so we put up signs that have some special message for them: 'Entrance' and 'Exit,' 'Go around' and 'No blocks today' (Vol. 2, p. 79). We change them often. Children are quick to ask, 'What does that say?' and will pick out the letters they know. They learn that important information is conveyed through symbols. Sometimes the teachers will mix up the signs—for example, putting 'Door' on the 'Piano'—to see how quickly someone will notice."

As they passed a science area, they saw a table with shelves on both sides on which were seeds, dried beans, rice, measuring cups, and scales for weighing.

Director: "Sometimes a science area includes plants and animals, but we prefer to scatter ours about the building. We try to avoid large groups of children around an animal. We also think this is a nice way for a child to be solitary occasionally."

She called attention to a rabbit cage, set up on legs, with a small rocker beside it and several books about rabbits on a table nearby.

Director: "At this end of the building we have threes in the back and the twos over here, nearest the kitchen. We feel that they need to be apart, to have a room of their own, and so you will see that we have six-foot dividers around them. The rest of the dividers are four feet high, which is a wall to the children but enables the teachers to see over them. As time goes on, we open a space between the twos and threes for a part of each day. By mid-year, there is quite a bit of going back and forth."

Parent: "Do the kindergartners ever mix with the twos?"

Director: "Yes, as the teachers get to know their children, and the children settle into their environment, the fives are invited to help the little ones dress, to eat with them, and sometimes to nap beside them. It's good for some of our children to be chosen for this kind of responsibility. It stretches their "I AM!" and often they can communicate with a little one when the teacher can't. In fact, as the year goes on, the whole building opens up more and more. It's fascinating to see children working in mixed age groups of their own choice."

Parent: "When you said the school was one big room, I thought 'How awful!' I expected it to be much noisier."

Director: "If we tried to function in that way at first, it would be chaotic. Children need time to adjust to the necessary rules of society, the fore-runners of adult laws. This is May, and what you see now is quite dif-ferent from what you might have seen last November. We have done a lot of stretching, growing, and changing since then. Did you notice as we walked about that several children were alone? We deliberately plan for small private spaces, and we talk about respect for privacy, that it is all right to like to be alone and have time to think or day-dream, or just relax. Jessie was in that big tire with a soft pillow in the middle, looking at books. One of our staff made a cloth cover to fit over a rectangular table like a tent. She put a clear plastic window in it to let in light. Jean has been working with those design blocks for almost an hour. The majority of young children prefer some companionship most of the time, but *everyone* needs to be alone for some time."

Parent: "Mmmm, I smell something good!"

Director: "It's almost lunchtime. The children who are going home will take their things to the meeting area, and those who stay will be getting ready for lunch. If you would like to stay and watch, you are welcome. But you must excuse me—I like to be there to say goodbye to the chil-dren and to speak to the parents."

Parent: "No, thank you, we'll be on our way, but we'll be back!'

Coming back the next day to enroll their child, these parents gave this enthusiastic report:

"We sensed something very special when we came into your school. It was bright and cheery, but, more than that, it was the faces of the chil-dren and teachers. They looked interested and involved. Everyone seemed busy, and yet it wasn't noisy or chaotic. In thinking about our visit after we left, we couldn't recall hearing a single teacher's voice raised above the children's. The other thing we noticed was that every child did not seem to be doing something every minute: some were just watching. We saw two children by themselves, playing a game. One little girl was lolling on a big, soft cushion, looking at books. She was all by herself there for half an hour, and no one seemed to feel the need to interfere. The children were *living* while they were learning."

These work areas are called by various names, such as activity centers, learning centers, or play areas. They are designed and equipped in a way that enables a child to explore and master his world through the medium of play. They should be clearly defined and, in most instances, separated with dividers.

How established Interest centers are established on the basis of the children's interests and needs, their level of development, and available materials and resources. Children learn through play and first-hand experiences, and many opportunities for exploring real items should be provided. It is important to have a variety of activities available for children to use to manipulate their environment.

Considerations to keep in mind when arranging interest centers in the classroom include:

• *Classroom traffic*—it should be minimal, and the traffic that does exist should flow freely. The major concerns are safety and efficiency. A central area should be kept open for traffic flow and whole-group activities.

• *Noise level*—the typical amount of noise one interest center will generate should be taken into account in determining its location.

• *Monitoring*—teachers should face the room, so they can monitor activities other than those with which they are working.

• *Storage and cleanup*—storage facilities and cleanup equipment should be located for maximum efficiency, independence, and safety.

• *Lighting*—the amount and type available should be appropriate for a particular activity.

• *Flooring*—carpeted areas and tiled areas should be appropriate for the activity and should ensure safety and quiet.

• *Boundaries*—equipment should be used to define where one interest center stops and another begins.

• *Equipment*—it should be of appropriate size for safety and independence.

• *Number of children*—the size of the interest center and the amount of active play in it should determine the number of children allowed in it at any given time.

Art area This is the one activity common to all nursery schools, often to the exclusion of other learning which might take place if the environment were better planned. The art area should be accessible to sinks, and should have a floor surface which can be cleaned easily. A floor drain is a great advantage. There should be some provision for painting, either at easels, on large tables, or on the floor. Wall easels permit children to paint side by side, thus enjoying a social experience. They also conserve space. Out of doors, look for the possibility of placing wall easels against a fence or against the side of a building on the playground. There are many days when painting is enjoyed out of doors.

Crayons and a plentiful supply of blank paper for coloring and drawing should be kept on a low shelf, accessible to the children. Magic markers are more exciting than crayons and easier to use than paints. Only the washable kind should be used, and only children old enough to put the caps on and put them back in the right containers should be allowed to use them.

Materials for what we call creative activities should be on low shelves or in containers accessible to children. In the beginning, materials will be limited, but as rules are established and learned, the variety can increase. Shelf space or plastic bins should be provided for crayons, paste, white glue, scissors, staplers, paper punches, paper fasteners, and paper of varied sizes and textures, including pieces of cardboard and wallpaper. In addition there should be storage for a generous supply of items such as yarn, string, ribbon, thread, scraps of dress trims, pieces of cloth, feathers, artificial flowers, beads and sequins, spools, scraps of wood, and ice cream sticks.

An ingenious teacher will find other interesting and unusual items and inviting ways to display them that will motivate children to creativity. Creativity cannot flourish when children are limited to the one or two materials a teacher chooses to put out, or when cluttered storage or difficult access to materials discourages their use.

Block area The value of block play cannot be overestimated. Given an adequate supply and a well planned place to use them, blocks are an important tool in providing growth on all four sides of the developmental square. The block area should be located out of the main stream of traffic. There should be room to spread out, to create a whole city or farm or zoo, and, ideally, a space where a large building project can be held over for a couple of days.

Wooden unit blocks and large building blocks offer two separate activities and, while they may be back to back, they should *not* be combined. *Unit blocks* should be on low shelves, divided according to sizes. Replacing them after use becomes a part of the learning experience. Some teachers prefer to start with one or two sizes, and add new shapes gradually as skills increase. Accessories, such as people, small cars and trucks, and materials for tracks (including cardboard, paper, or masking tape), add to the variety of the play. Large trucks and riding toys may be used nearby if they are supervised carefully so that they do not provide distraction and disruption of good block play. Pulleys, ropes, trolleys, and dollies are stimulating to block activities.

The large *building blocks* can be next to the family center or dramatic play area. Housekeeping equipment can be shared when a store, hospital, office, or some other building is constructed.

Learning games This is a place for manipulatives such as Lego, small table blocks,
and puzzles learning games, puzzles, and a host of fascinating items which can be

found in the educational catalogues, all designed to increase hand-eye coordination and stimulate mental activity. They should be on low shelves with easy access, but not everything needs to be available all the time. A few items may be put out at a time, and the selection changed each week.

Dramatic play area This is often called a housekeeping center, and as such should never be limited to a child's stove, sink, and table, devoid of accessories for play. It should offer some semblance of four walls, with window cut-outs and a door. Inside one would expect to find a table (with table cloth) and at least two small chairs, dishes in a cabinet or on shelves (never thrown into a box!), cooking equipment, a bed for the dolls (clothed) with clean sheets, blankets, and a pillow, possibly a small rocking chair, a broom and dustpan, and dress-up clothing and accessories. Each item is kept in its own place—and telephones are a must!

Dress-up clothing and accessories are an important part of dramatic play. Clothing is sized to fit reasonably well and kept clean and in good repair. Extras might include a dressing table and mirror, equipped with razor (minus blades), jars, bottles, and fancy containers from men's and women's vanity tables. Hooks and shelves are provided for dress-ups—a full-length mirror is excellent.

In this area, much play relating to family life will take place. However, the same space should be converted at times to another focus, such as a post office, a hospital, or a store.

Science center A science center may provide a good buffer zone between the noisy activity of the block area and the quiet of a reading corner or learning center. To many teachers "science" suggests only animals or plants, and both are important in the nursery school as samples of living and growing, but they need not be confined to one place. Plants will add a pleasant touch to any part of the building.

In one school, the teacher brought in a large cut-leaf philodendron from home. The plant became a palm tree and was the incentive for jungle play. It was moved with pride to various areas of the room and was treated with care and respect. After it served its purpose, it was returned to the teacher's home.

Animals should be in cages—where little ones cannot hurt them, or risk nipped fingers. Some teachers prefer to use glass aquariums, with wire screening over the top.

The science center should provide space, equipment, and work areas for things to look at and act upon. It should have a counter or table space to accommodate two to four children at a time and shelves for equipment and display of materials. Exhibits should be changed often. One week it might be stones, another shells or seeds.

The science center should arouse curiosity and give children a chance to solve problems, experiment, and test. Scales, rulers and tape measures, magnets, and magnifying glasses are necessary equipment, and books which elaborate on the central theme should be accessible.

Woodworking area Carpentry is an activity which calls for careful instruction in the use of tools. It should be limited to a small number of children at one time, with adequate supervision and strict adherence to rules. It should be located away from any activity which might interfere with safety and concentration. Tools can be hung on a pegboard. Shapes painted on the pegboard will help the children replace the tools properly.

Reading corner Every effort should be made to create an environment which is inviting, quiet, and cozy. Dividers might be formed by the bookshelves. A rug on the floor (a piece of real soft shag is nice), a small rocking chair, a table with two small chairs, or a child's recliner chair add to the atmosphere. We have seen cozy places made by placing a large soft pillow in the center of a tire, lining an old-fashioned bathtub with carpeting, using a seat from a station wagon as a couch, and making a sofa by covering a sheet of plywood with rug samples, setting it across concrete blocks, and adding pillows. The books in a reading corner should be attractively displayed and should be changed often. Good lighting is essential.

Soft area In one school a platform was covered with a soft shag rug. Draperies were hung around three sides and colorful pillows of varied sizes and shapes were stacked on the floor. The soft area was used for small group activities and sensory games and activities. It also served as a reading area, a story carpet, and even, on occasion, a place to allow two angry children to work out their aggression with a pillow fight! (Vol. 2, p. 88.)

Music center This should be located where furniture can be pushed back to allow movement. Instruments are displayed on shelves or hanging on a board. Children are taught to use them with respect. Storage for instruments can be constructed, using cardboard cylinders or boxes attractively painted. Extra materials which invite creative experiences, such as scarves, hoops, and rug squares, will be close by.

Water play area This is one aspect of science which needs its own place. An industrial hand-washing fountain is ideal. Because it is round, it encourages social interaction and stimulates creative use of the materials provided. These should include articles for pouring, measuring, straining, funneling, sailing, and whipping or beating. Waterproof smocks are essential: children cannot be allowed to get their clothing wet and stay wet all day. A raincoat, worn backwards, may be used.

Sinks, water tables, or large tubs are all acceptable vehicles for water play. It is one of the most important (and least expensive) activities offered in a preschool curriculum.

Space Playground space must be carefully arranged. A minimum of 75 square feet per child is the usual requirement, but in urban areas this is not always possible. In the city, rooftops or tiny vacant lots can be designed to provide ingenious uses of space and materials, and supplemented with visits to nearby parks. Fenced-in areas, cozy nooks, and divisions are needed for control and safety.

Design In designing a playground, we look once more at the four sides of the developmental square and attempt to provide opportunity for growth in each area. It helps when we take the stance that the playground is *not* just a place for children to let off steam, as it was in the traditional recess; it is *an outdoor classroom.*

On the physical side, we will want to create opportunities for what we call the *ing* words: climbing, hanging, running, swinging, pushing, pulling, dancing, crawling, sliding, digging, and throwing.

The social side of development is enhanced when safe places for small groups are set apart and there are cozy niches where one or two children can play quietly.

It happened:
The men doing major construction on a nearby highway were persuaded to give the center a section of cement pipe, five feet across, which was cracked and therefore useless to them. It was expected to be a climbing piece, but actually turned out to be a clubhouse where three or four children would gather for cozy conversations.

On the emotional side, the chance to glide back and forth on a swing may be excellent therapy for a child who is having a hard time for one reason or another. For another, a throwing place where she can vigorously throw balls, beanbags, or rubber-tipped darts against a hard surface may be an outlet.

On the intellectual side, interest centers can be set up outdoors as well as inside. A shelf attached to a fence or wall can hold science objects. A special corner, sometimes called the Magic Circle, provides space for music, movement, stories, and dramatic play, undisturbed by activity games. Boxes, boards, and packing cases take the place of blocks for building, and easels attached to the fence can enable children to paint outside.

Children are learning wherever they are, and the playground, however small or inadequate, can be a laboratory for that learning.

Equipment: In a new center, designing and purchasing outdoor equipment is a
Swings and slide major expense that calls for careful consideration. The tendency is to start with swings and a slide. There is nothing wrong with these, so long as they are not the only selections made. Swings, though they are

relaxing, offer minimal opportunity for imaginative play or a variety of uses. A slide, if it is just a slide, is expensive in relation to its value as a means of physical satisfaction, social growth, emotional release, and intellectual stimulation. The money might be better spent for building blocks and boards, balance boards, and climbing ropes. In one school, the directors had given serious thought to every piece of equipment. The slide was incorporated into a total climbing configuration. The child climbed a ladder, walked a plank—with guide ropes for those who needed them—and then chose between going down the steps (a new experience for many children who live in ranch-style homes or apartments with elevators) or sliding down a slide on the other side. A similar structure in another school had a firefighter's pole in the middle for sliding down.

Jungle gyms   Jungle gyms are good for climbing, but again very expensive, and in a very small playground they take up a large proportion of valuable space. Climbing poles with dowels on the sides are an alternative.

Picnic tables   Tables are necessary for snacks, picnics, and some art projects. Older children will need full size tables; toddlers and twos can use small indoor-outdoor tables.

Sandbox   The sandbox is as necessary to the child as the kitchen is to the home-maker. It is the focal point of the yard, the social center and work area. In a sandbox, engineers and cooks can work side by side. Sensory and social experiences are stimulated. The sandbox should be first on the essentials list, and would be justified even if it occupied a fairly large proportion of limited space.

Some teachers look upon the sandbox as a television-watching type of babysitting service. Children are left to content themselves with a continuous program of sifting and pouring. Sand, to be effective, must be combined with water, enough to make it adhere. Sandbox toys need to be carefully selected (eliminate tin shovels and toys with sharp corners in favor of wooden spoons and plastic shovels), and they should be stored at the end of every day on shelves, in a box or closet, out of the weather. Rusty coffee cans, broken plastic dishes, trucks and cars minus wheels are not good teaching toys for children, and they are hazardous. Motivation through new toys and planned projects relating to curriculum activities are as necessary here as in the block corner. How long has it been since you really looked at your sandbox? (See *Sandbox Trails and Settlements*, Vol. 2, p. 167.)

Other items   The variety of things children can play with is limited only by your imagination. For example, automobile tires are light enough for fours and fives to move from their intended exercise path into many other playground configurations. Giant tractor tires, sunk upright firmly into the ground with most of the center exposed, give children places to crawl through. A wooden boat (with any lead paint removed and the surfaces sanded and weatherproofed) offers endless hours of imaginative play. With a pole for a mast and a piece of vinyl or cloth for a sail, or with long boards for oars, it can be as real as any child might want.

On a playground where the terrain was flat, an ingenious director had contractors deliver two large piles of dirt. They quickly became mountains and led to many imaginative experiences. A director whose playground enclosed a steep hill about ten feet high embedded a metal ring in the top and fastened a rope to the ring, letting it hang down the side. Children used the rope for mountain climbing and as a way to get to the top of the hill. This center also had a tri-level climbing structure that extended from the top to the bottom of the hill, with steps from one level to the next. In this playground, ingenuity turned an apparent handicap into an asset.

Multiple use Each piece of equipment should enhance at least three of the four sides of the developmental square. Whenever possible, it should serve more than one purpose. For example, a playhouse can double as storage for sand toys, riding equipment, and wagons.

Traffic patterns Traffic patterns on the playground require careful thought. Is there room to move from one space to another without encroaching on the rights of others? Is there space for building with blocks, cartons, or planks, without having efforts knocked down by the runners? Are there safety zones—islands where the watchers can be near and yet not into the action until they are ready? Can the total area be adequately supervised by the number of teachers available at any given time? If there are spaces obscured around corners, can they be closed off when supervision is limited? Does the arrangement of space and equipment make possible learning in the areas of music, movement, science, dramatic play, art, building, and water play?

Shade Lucky the director whose playground has natural shade. Even in the north, an unshaded playground can limit the amount of time children can be outside. Consider shade in your planning; if possible, budget money for putting up a roofed, open-sided structure of some kind, especially over the sandbox.

Outdoors every day Children belong outdoors unless the weather is too cold, wet, or hot. The decision of when to go out should not be based upon whether the teacher is comfortably dressed for the activity. It is a common sight to see a teacher huddled, with arms crossed, shivering miserably, while watching children getting their outside quota. Some teachers will stand and scold the child who has no rubber boots, and yet will not be wearing their own on the playground. Professional attire for a nursery school teacher is whatever is practical and comfortable. Waterproof rain gear, boots, warm hats and mittens—these are as much the uniform of the teacher as the white uniform is for the nurse or the hard hat for the construction worker. When, for medical reasons, it is not sensible for a teacher to go out, the children should not be sacrificed—an exchange with another willing teacher must be arranged.

Supervision Many teachers who are professionally excellent in the classroom deteriorate into child minders when they go outside on the playground. What are some of the reasons? Perhaps they think it offers a chance to exchange bits of gossip and to chat with other staff members. Some teachers are unprepared for and uncomfortable with outdoor programs, assuming that they must be nature- or science-oriented and so must be taught by specialists. Some are lacking in imagination, a basic ingredient for all good program.

Some teachers may just be tired, or may look upon this time as an old-fashioned recess. Every teacher needs interludes of complete relaxation and relief from responsibility, especially those who teach full days, but such relaxation should be completely isolated from the children. Teachers cannot turn off their switches when they go out of doors. Whatever else it may be, a playground is *never* a place for a coffee or smoking break.

When teachers are on the playground, they must be observant and sensitive to what is happening with each child. Outdoor learning is as closely related to the development of the child as indoor activities.

Chapter 33   **DAILY SCHEDULE AND ROUTINES**

So now we have the *people* and we have created an *environment* in which they can come together. What will happen in our model child care center?

Zoning   Let us start with *zoning*, a technique so simple and logical, we might suppose such a plan would just happen. Zoning enables a director to say, "My teachers have time to teach! My staff is not harried, frazzled, exhausted. I'm always ready and proud to have people come to visit."

What is zoning? Zoning is ensuring that each adult is in specific places at specific times throughout the day. Zoning is moving children easily from place to place. Those places are zones, whether for teachers or for children. When zoning is a smooth, well-established procedure, children can move alone and in groups without the guidance of adults.

Zoning does not just happen. Each center presents its own set of zoning needs. You must spend time analyzing:

- *Zones* in the building and on the playground. Give each a name.
- *Daily schedules* of staff.
- *Workloads* of teams and of individual staff members.
- *Numbers of children* present in the center throughout each hourly time block during the day. Chart the schedules of staff and children for easy reference and correlation.
- *Transitions* and *activity periods* when children are moving from one zone to another.
- *Traffic patterns.*

Zoning within each team allows one teacher to stay with a last slow child while the other children move on. The teacher can quietly listen and talk to him without hurrying him along. For example, at lunch time, one adult can stay with the child who cleans the table and sweeps up crumbs. A second adult stands by the bathroom to supervise and guide toileting and hand-washing. Another is waiting in the napping area, settling and quieting the children on their cots.

Zoning is an ongoing process, changing as the numbers of children change and extending in scope as children and staff mature and become more responsible. You will need to change zoning patterns as programs and routines change throughout the year.

In the beginning, you initiate zoning procedures, assigning the staff at strategic points. As the staff and children settle in, suggestions for changes and improvements will come from the staff. Also at the beginning, team leaders zone within their teams. Adults, like children, need the security of knowing what is expected of them. When routines become a natural sequence of events, the school day will begin to flow. As the teams become secure, participation in planning will be a group effort.

One teacher described zoning this way: "It is like the coach of a football team who stands at a chalkboard and draws a diagram for each play. He assigns each player a number and a position, and he gives each play a number. Each player has a special job to do and every play fits into a special place in the game. As players memorize these plays and perfect their individual skills, the team plays games with greater precision and success. When a player forgets a strategy or does not use his particular skill successfully, the team loses the game."

Daily schedule A daily schedule should be posted in each classroom and near the entrance to the center. (Some states require that the schedule be posted.) It should be tailored to fit the particular center, but the following suggested schedule can be used as a starting point.

Opening This segment runs from the time your center opens until your morning program begins. Teacher arrives (pick someone who can be cheerful in the early hours!) and does whatever is necessary to make the environment say "welcome!" When the first children arrive, there should be two people in the building (see your state's regulations). As more children come in, there must be staff to supervise and to meet required teacher/pupil ratio. Children go to the meeting area.
A lead teacher or the assistant director stands near the door to greet children and speak to parents or drivers who bring them.
Director arrives and greets and inspects all children who are present and then takes over at the door (see *Health*, chapter 42). As teachers arrive, they take children to their own home base.

Breakfast In some centers, breakfast (either brought by the children or served by the center) will be included in this time period.

Morning Meeting time to discuss plans and choices for the morning.
Activity time.
Snack time (see *Eating with Children* in this chapter, p. 151).
Stories, music, outdoor play
Morning children get ready to go home. The rest get ready for lunch, wash, set tables, and so on.

Lunch Lunch (see *Mealtime*, p. 152).

Quiet time An interlude between lunch and nap helps the children settle down— with story, records, or movement session, ending up on cots. Nap time.

Afternoon Afternoon children arrive. Teachers are ready to greet them and have activities planned outdoors or as far as possible from the full-day children, who are still sleeping.
Teachers repeat the morning program for afternoon children.
When possible, full-day children function as a separate group with a

separate staff. When they get up, they have a snack and go outside or have activities inside.

Afternoon children get ready to go home.

End of day Full-day children have special programs.

Closing Teachers set up their projects and materials for the next day. The custodian comes in and begins work.

Daily routines The daily schedule takes care of the *what* and *when*. Daily routines deal with the *how*.

Early arrivals The teachers who work from 6 or 7 to 9 in the morning (and those who work from 4 to 6 in the afternoon) take on a different kind of responsibility. If they feel put upon because they must work these hours, they can hardly expect to generate a good feeling in the children.

The atmosphere is all-important. In the morning a sunny room is a real asset, and on a dark day lighting should be as bright and cheery as the smile on the teacher's face. The room needs to *look* ready, which means that the last one there the night before should have left things picked up and neat. A very imaginative teacher will keep some special things to be used only at this time of day, such as a tiny treasure box, a toy or game, a little tea set, a big rag doll, or a stuffed animal.

Some children will not have had time for *breakfast*. Cereal, milk, and juice may be offered to those who really need it.

At first children may need some *table activities*, but as they settle in they will form their own friendships and develop their own plans. Some children may head for the *dramatic play area* and take up where they left off the day before. Mike may look forward to this time when he can have the *wood-working* bench to himself. *Rules* will have to be established: "We will not take the unit blocks off the shelves, but you may build with the big blocks."

There should be a designated group area for early arrivals, and in some cases *television* will be available for those who want to watch their favorite programs. This is also a restrictive precaution, keeping two-year-old Jason from darting into the team areas and scooping all the toys off the shelves! A row of coat hooks in this area can be used until the teacher arrives, so the children need not go into other rooms to their cubbies. This may be the time when a teacher can supervise the use of the *tape recorder* and *slide projector*, while there are only a few children to watch. A five-year-old who has been taught how to use the machine can help to entertain the little ones with special stories on the *film-strip machine*. Older children can be encouraged to help the little ones with their clothing and to play with them, but should not be required to do so.

The teacher should bear in mind that some people are slow starters in the morning. Children who just want to sit or who seem apathetic may be reacting to their own metabolism and need not be urged to be actively engaged in group activities.

The goal is to create a comfortable, relaxed, homelike atmosphere.

Toileting Toileting is a time when the greatest teaching skills are needed. The teachers, however advanced their thinking about bathroom techniques and language, must understand that some education has already gone on in the home. Pepe may have already stumbled up against attitudes toward doing what comes naturally. His parent's wrinkled up nose and the vigor of hands during the cleaning and changing procedures have told him something about bowel movements and how grownups feel about them. His first impression of "bad" and "naughty" may be associated with his bodily functions. The child may have the feeling that this necessary function is associated with dirt, shame, or rejection, to be taken care of as quickly as possible. He may have discovered by now that withholding his movements is his most effective method for gaining approval, or that defecating at the wrong time and in the wrong place is one way of punishing his parents.

When a child is ready for school in all respects except for toilet training, the teacher cooperates with the parent in completing the training process. In fact, this new environment is often just the extra boost a child needs.

Although some schools may accept only children who are bowel trained, teachers must still expect them to have an occasional accident, especially during the adjustment period. All children are apt to regress in the first weeks or at times of emotional strain and illness.

We believe that it is important for twos to wear training pants. If they come in diapers and plastic pants, they are set apart and different. At first, when a child is wet, the teacher will go with him to the bathroom and change him. Gradually, he can take more and more responsibility for changing himself, finally reaching the point where the teacher can say, "Oh, you have had an accident. Well, you know what to do. Get your bag from your cubby and go into the bathroom and change. Be sure to put your wet panties into a bag and take them home." Of course, she will keep a watchful eye on the situation, making sure that the child is thoroughly clean and has washed his hands.

The teacher should accept "accidents" casually, without scolding, embarrassing, or punishing. When the child sees others using the toilet, he will conform, accepting the rules of this new school society.

Note: If there is an accident on carpeting, it must be cleaned up immediately. Use paper towels to soak up the urine and then sponge the spot with warm, soapy water. It is a good idea to let the child help, or at least to show him what was done and explain why. If you do not take care of it at once, your carpet will be disfigured with permanent stains and will soon acquire an unpleasant odor.

Hand washing There is some teaching involved in the routine hand washing before all snacks and lunchtime. The ritual-like steps described by Montessori are appropriate. Small children *need* to be taught *how* to wash both front and back and to dry between the fingers. It is inappropriate for a teacher to tell children to wash their hands and sit down without washing her own hands. (See *Hand Washing*, Vol 2, p. 6.)

Extreme care must also be taken in handling all food and materials. For example, a package of paper cups is opened from the *bottom;* otherwise fingers will go inside the cups when they are pulled out.

Eating with children:
Snack time

Little children use up a lot of energy as they live and learn. For Jari, who has barely taken his foot off the gas since the moment of his arrival, snack time is for refueling. For Ruby, it is the *kaffee klatsch* of the neighborhood, and for Lois and Jane it is the adult coffee break. The issue of formal versus informal juice time has long been debated. Some teachers like to gather their flocks around them at a table for a few songs and finger play, or for quiet conversation. Others prefer to set juice out on a tray, where the children can help themselves without interrupting their play. Both methods have their merits. Actually, there is no one right way for snack time. Whatever suits the mood of the moment or the expedience of the program makes more sense than following the same rigid pattern day after day.

Manners are better *caught* than *taught.* The teacher who relies on "Say the magic word" or "You can't have another cracker because you forgot to say 'please'" will find herself more effective if she serves as a role model—and avoids calling attention to the transgressor.

The preparation of snacks and cleanup afterward are an important part of the procedure. Counting the children and the right number of napkins or crackers is a way of learning numbers because you *have a need to know.* Children should be permitted to pour their own juice from small pitchers which they can handle easily. Two-cup plastic measures work well. The child must be taught how to hold the pitcher, with one hand on the handle and the other on the front, and to pour very carefully. The teacher says, "Fill your cup half full" and the idea of fractions has been introduced! Certainly it takes longer than if the cups had been filled beforehand, or the teacher had done the pouring, but such routine activities are *program.*

Snacks should not always consist of juice and crackers. Raw vegetables, peeled and sliced, accompanied at times by a dip, or pieces of fruit make a good change. For toddlers, raw vegetables should be briefly cooked to prevent choking.

When the snack is to be different—especially in child care centers where nutritional values are figured carefully—a teacher will communicate this intent to the cook, director, or nutritionist in advance.

The daily snack sometimes becomes whatever the magic of the child's imagination can produce. "I am eating a mushroom pizza and drinking root beer," a child announced as he munched his crackers and drank his juice.

Snack time is a daily routine, but it can also be an adventure. A picnic, with a treat such as peanut butter, jelly, or cheese spread on the crackers, carried to a corner of the room or playground, makes snack time special. Snack crackers served from a picnic basket take on a new identity. Pudding or gelatin made by the children can be served in tiny paper containers as a snack. In one school, the kindergarten children took an imaginary six-week tour through various countries, and snacks were appropriate to the country visited.

Mealtime   Mealtime in the child care center should be a pleasant, leisurely experience. There is much learning taking place in a carefully planned mealtime. It is important for adults to have spent time thinking out procedures that will be reasonable and routines that will be feasible. Once the procedures and routines are in place, they should be maintained with consistency (see *Zoning*, p. 147).

A suggested plan is offered here. It will not work in every center. The distance from the kitchen to the tables, the ages of the children, and the number of adults who can sit with the children are all variables which will have to be taken into account.

As the children are washed and ready, they may help:
- Set tables with place mats, forks, spoons (if needed), napkins, and cups.
- Put finger foods on the table.
- Pass bread around when the teacher is ready.

The main course is placed before the teacher, who will serve. Give *very* small helpings. After a few days, you will be able to judge the capacity of each child. It is better psychologically to have a child come back for seconds and thirds than to leave food on the plate.

Avoid scenes and the discussion of dislikes. If a child says, "I don't want any," just say, "I'm going to put just a tiny bit on your plate. I hope you will taste it," and let it go at that. (Be fair, and keep your word. Put just two carrot slices, or three green beans, on the plate.) Eating should be casual and *taken for granted.*

Procedures for clearing tables and serving desserts will vary. Do not withhold desserts until a child eats all of his meal—they are, or should be, an important part of his nutritional needs. *Never* withhold dessert as a punishment.

Manners are acquired gradually. Base them on consideration of others: "If you talk with your mouth full, we can't understand you." "When you take two pieces, there may not be enough for everyone to have one." "You don't have to snatch. There will be enough for all." "Please take the first one you touch."

Try never to send a child away from the table. If you know he is going to be troublesome, let him sit beside you.

If you treat your children with the same respect you would accord a guest at a dinner party, they will surprise you with their response!

Nap time: Licensing in most states requires that children in a child care facility
Attitude of adults   rest for at least one hour, and we believe that children really do need this rest. Many of the children who come to the center will have given up naps at home. For some, the idea of nap time will imply that they are still babies and may incite rebellion. You must have sympathy and understanding for their feelings if your rest time is to succeed.

A good rest begins with the teacher who sees this as a chance to relax briefly and talks about "How good it is just to *take it easy for a while,* so we'll all be able to *have fun* later." Link their naps to their other experiences: "Animals know it's important to rest. Look at your dog or kitty—they take naps in the daytime." Remind them of the behavior they have experienced: "When we get tired, we get crabby and whiny and want to argue."

Set the stage In a center which offers double sessions, lunch should be served early enough so that most of the full-day children are sound asleep before the afternoon children arrive. Arrange the cots with a space of at least one foot between children. When children rest head to foot, they have less temptation to talk or play. Some children must be separated, because otherwise they excite each other and disturb the rest.

Blankets and cots must be marked, and it is preferable not to allow one child to use another's. If cots must be interchangeable, they must be sprayed with a disinfectant after each use. If a child is accustomed to having a blanket or soft toy at home, it would be foolish not to let him use it at school for as long as needed. He will break the dependency himself, when he is ready. (See *Goodbye Kit,* Vol. 2, p. 5.)

Books or quiet conversations may be allowed until all are ready. It is important to remove shoes, unless this is frightening to the child. Then the teacher makes a definite announcement: "Now it is time to rest," and collects the books. The room should be darkened, the teacher should assume an attitude of rest, and all are expected to be quiet.

Inducing sleep There are various techniques for inducing sleep. Some start by using quiet music. Sitting or lying beside a child, rubbing backs, whispering quietly for a few minutes in serious one-to-one conversation, shaking imaginary sleep dust—whatever methods prove effective are acceptable. The main object is to achieve a quiet rest without policing action. (A child cannot relax when an adult barks commands such as "Lie down, Glenn! No, Lena, you can't go to the bathroom! I told you to go before rest time!") When all else fails, try yawning. It is contagious!

Length of nap The length of nap should be discussed with parents. Some children would sleep for two or more hours, but if this means they will not go to bed until ten o'clock that night, parents may want you to awaken them. Suggest that the child be given a few days to adjust to new life patterns before any radical changes are employed.

Afternoon programs There may be three or more separate groups occupying a child care center in the afternoon, and their needs are quite different. Determining how space and program can accommodate those needs often takes the skill of a juggler and the wisdom of Solomon!

Full-day children First there are the children who come for the full day, often a very long day. They have had a typical preschool enrichment program in the morning and are settled in for their naps. When they wake up, they need to see the same faces. They need to be allowed to "come to" at their own speed. Some will bounce off their cots, full of energy, but most will mope around, dawdle over their snack, and take their own time getting into an activity. For these children, the afternoon program should be low key, offering several choices but without pressure to participate. This is a good time to set out materials for an activity offered in the morning, for those who might enjoy more of the same. When weather permits, these children should be taken outside.

Afternoon preschool A second group will be children who are enrolled for an afternoon session of preschool education. Their parents expect them to have an enrichment program comparable to the one offered in the morning.

Straight from morning kindergarten Then there are those who attended half-day kindergarten in the public schools in the morning and are coming to the child care center for the rest of the day. Some of them will need time to relax and slow down. Others may choose to join the children who have come for enrichment, but they should make the choice themselves. Too often they are not offered a choice—their activities will be determined to accommodate the space and staffing of the center, rather than their particular needs.

Older school-age children Offering care for school-age children is one of the fastest-growing areas of child care. It is an important service. These children should not be going home to an empty house, but often when they are thrust into a setting where a building was planned, equipment purchased, and staff hired to teach the very young, chaos sets in. This is too complicated a problem to deal with in this book, but we offer a few basic suggestions:

•   The staff should spend some time discussing what these children would be doing if they lived in a traditional home where their mother was waiting for them with cookies and milk. Would they be hustled onto another bus to be taken to a park? Every effort should be made to create a natural environment and to offer choices.

•   A child's first need is for a listening ear—someone who will let him pour out his excitement over a good day or listen sympathetically to a tale of woe.

•   These school-agers should be free to choose their own activities. Some will opt to do their homework, so they can watch a favorite television program at night. Others will want to go outside and work off energy. Some will want to settle down with a book or play a quiet game with a friend. Others will elect to dabble with arts and crafts.

•   Children of this age are club-minded. The composition, purpose, name, and officers of the club may change daily, but the children should be allowed to decide these matters themselves.

•   Children like responsibility, such as taking care of plants or animals or repairing books. Some will enjoy helping with the younger children. In one center, two ten-year-old girls took on the role of teachers, planning an activity for each day. The younger children eagerly waited for them to come and afforded them great respect.

•   Older children must have some space they can call their own, with a closet or high shelves where they can keep equipment and projects out of the reach of little hands.

•   Children who have been sitting at desks all day, living with the pressure of restricted and directed educational activities, should have a teacher who will try to make this part of the day fulfill their needs.

Now that the daily schedule and routines are firmly established, we can focus our attention on learning.

Philosophy In every profession, training and experience are the basic working tools, the first becoming refined and cultivated by the second. There is a third ingredient, however, which is needed to add the polish and a special magic quality: the philosophy, the sense of value, the belief in what is right. The "I AM! I CAN!" philosophy is the yardstick by which we have measured the contents of this program.

Basic premises In our planning, we use these basic premises about learning:

- *We learn best, and retain knowledge longer, when we have a need and/or a desire to know.*

- *Rote learning creates robots.* Learning by rote satisfies adults, but means little to children except the pleasure they gain from the adults' reactions to their recitations. When we train children to recite the alphabet or count to a hundred, we dilute the excitement of learning. *Excitement* is the key word here. Learning *is* exciting. The child who can add "I KNOW" to his "I AM!" and "I CAN!" senses fulfillment—the ultimate satisfaction of need.

- *Learning comes through involvement.* Learning takes place as children interact with their world and become part of the action. They explore the world through their senses, through discovery and curiosity. The traditional "Sit still!" "Keep still!" and "Do as you're told!" practice takes all the fun out of learning. Children gain satisfaction from solving problems, finding out, testing, and achieving.

- *Children want the approval of adults.* For years we have given children credit and status for good behavior: "George is such a good boy" or "April is my nice little helper." How much better to give credit for *ideas*: "Did you all hear that? What a terrific *idea!* Now, can someone think of another way?" A climate is established where thinking is *in,* and when children start competing with each other for good *ideas,* creativity walks through an open door.

- *Learning begins where the child is.* It starts with the familiar and progresses to new understandings from that which she knows. Thus it is essential for the teacher to know each child and something about her home, her family, and her experiences prior to attending school in order to know where to begin.

• *Children learn through play.* Play is the *business* of childhood. When they build with blocks, explore their environment with all their senses, create with art materials, listen to stories and communicate ideas and feelings, children are working, just as surely as any adult who goes to work.

Play is the process, the means to education. Through play children (1) experience, (2) relate the new to the familiar, (3) make their own inferences, (4) test their new knowledge, and (5) assimilate it— making it a part of their being. Play and learning are inseparable companions.

Goals and objectives

By goals we mean generalized, long-range expectations of growth. Objectives are the specific daily or weekly results we look for as we work with the children. For example, a teacher may concentrate on *red, round, over,* and *under* for a few weeks. These are *objectives* leading to the long-range *goals* of *recognizing colors, recognizing shapes,* and *understanding spatial relationships.* As teachers plan, they align activities with goals. A well-planned activity will often be developing several goals at once.

As we began to make up lists of goals, we tried to categorize them into *intellectual, emotional, physical,* and *social* areas of development, but we soon found we were bogged down in cross relationships. The child develops in just this way. His physical "I CAN!" often becomes tangled up with his social "I AM!;" his emotional "I AM!" relates constantly to his intellectual "I CAN!"

In planning to meet goals and objectives, you need to choose activities which are developmentally appropriate. In Volume 2, *A Preschool Curriculum,* each activity is given an age range to help you.

What is curriculum?

Curriculum is a formal plan leading through specific activities to stated goals, usually associated with cognitive learning and the arts. Many people think of curriculum as the only learning that is taking place, but that is clearly not so.

What is program?

Program is everything that happens to the child throughout the day. Children do not distinguish between learning to put on jackets or boots and learning to recognize shapes. Cleaning up a spill is learning, as well as writing your name. Sweeping up the crumbs under the table after lunch is program, as is meticulous hand-washing.

The curriculum offered in Volume 2 provides monthly themes, sequential development, and a multitude of activities from which teachers may choose in meeting goals and objectives. It is based on the "I AM! I CAN!" philosophy, and the foundation on which it rests is described in this volume.

Traditional vs. interest-centered

In the following paragraphs about these two teaching styles, *traditional* would relate to the common perception of *curriculum,* and *interest-centered* to *program.*

• In a traditional classroom, the teacher directs the group; in an interest-centered classroom, the teacher facilitates the group.

• In a traditional classroom, everyone does the same thing at the same time; in an interest-centered classroom, children have the opportunity to make choices regarding their activities and to work in small groups.

• In a traditional classroom, most of the communication flows from the teacher to the child; in an interest-centered classroom, communication flows from teacher to child, from child to child, and from child to teacher.

• In a traditional classroom, materials are put away until they are required for an activity; in an interest-centered classroom, materials are placed on low shelves where children have full access.

• In a traditional classroom, the teacher decides what the children will learn; in an interest-centered classroom, there are more opportunities for discovery learning and incidental learning.

The brief descriptions of the interest centers in the classroom in Chapter 31 gave hints of the kinds of activities that can take place in a stimulating program. What follows is a more detailed explanation of the way we like to see it happening. It is also an answer to parents who ask plaintively, "But what do you *teach* them?"

Many teachers of young children fall silent when music or science are mentioned, but beam and relax when the art program is discussed. It would be nice to think that daily activities were equally divided among the major areas of interest and skills, but, in practice, art-related activities take up about fifty percent or more of the program, limiting the child's introduction to a wide variety of other experiences.

Why this heavy concentration on art activities? Perhaps it is because we are more comfortable using our hands than our voices or bodies and even, at times, our minds. Part of the problem also relates to the fact that teachers feel they do not have to "explain" their art projects. They call everything "creative," seldom taking the time to question the value of their projects. Art then becomes so much busy-work, keeping the children happy. It is easier to put out paints, crayons, and paper than to plan an integrated day in which art fits into the total program.

Encouraging creativity
The teacher who really wants to encourage creativity will throw away all of her patterns and models, replacing them with a wide variety of materials—many of them rarely if ever considered art materials—that invite experimentation. She will have available easel paint and finger paint; crayons, chalk, and magic markers; clay, plasticene, and play dough; boxes, tubes, and egg cartons; yarn, string, gimp, and feathers; pieces of material, trims, buttons, beads, and bows; and a multitude of found materials scrounged from industries, print-shops, wordworking shops, and offices.

Experimenting
When we offer this variety, letting each child respond in his own way, we help them work their way through the developmental stages which follow in a natural sequence. Just as the child creeps before he walks and experiments with sounds before he talks, so also he goes through many stages of experiencing with all of his senses the materials which he can later use to represent his thoughts and emotions.

Adults find it difficult to appreciate the scribbling or blobs of paint on paper—applied with brushes, fingers, and sponges—which children proudly carry home. Admiring relatives exclaim over these creations, ascribing unwarranted values to them. At the other extreme is the adult who disdainfully tosses the creation into the wastebasket.

"But if we don't send papers home, the parents think their child isn't learning anything."

A teacher who has goals and values firmly established will be able to explain the purpose behind all the experimentation. Conversations with the parents will satisfy them that she knows what she is doing—that the emphasis is on the process, not the product.

"What is it?"   Whether a child is painting at the easel, fingerpainting, modeling clay, making a collage, or building a structure, his right to just do it should not be challenged. When we ask "What is it?" we often put on him the burden of making it *be* something, because he wants to please us or thinks we expect it. A teacher can show interest by commenting on some aspect of the work, such as its color, not just its "subject."

> *It happened:*
>
> *A kindergarten teacher had been watching Mario play with blocks and trucks through all of September and October. He refused any suggestion that he might want to paint. One day she said to him cheerfully, as she tied a smock around his waist, "Today it's your turn to paint." Mario went dutifully to work, applying one color after another until the paper was nearly covered. His teacher came back to stand and watch him for a short time, then commented, "That's a very pretty shade of blue." Mario looked up at her with an engaging grin and replied, "I don't know what it is either!"*

"Show me!"   "Teacher, will you make me a rabbit?" How would you respond to such a request without refusing to help? Here are some suggestions: Discuss what rabbits look like, how they feel, what colors they are, what shape. If you have a real classroom bunny, go look at it. Talk about "round" body, "round" head, and long pointed ears. Make suggestions to lead the child in the right direction. "Here are some cloth scraps and some cotton balls." Lay out scissors, glue, and stapler. Ask questions which will stimulate his ideas but leave room for discovery.

Suppose the child has come to you with a picture of a rabbit, saying, "I want to make one just like this." Explain to him that "Everyone doesn't make a rabbit in the same way. You have your own way, and it is the very best way for you. Your bunny may not look exactly like the one in this picture, but it will be very special, because *you* made it."

Displaying   While we encourage displaying children's work, it should be seen as a
children's art   means to self-development, not an end, and never as visual evidence of the teacher's proficiency in her profession. Her classroom walls tell that story. A visitor who sees Halloween drawings on the wall after Thanksgiving or dusty paintings with torn or curled corners tacked to the walls in haphazard fashion must wonder about the teacher's attitude and ability.

Displays in a school should be as carefully planned as interior decorating in the home. Pictures are hung straight, with an eye to grouping. Sculptures and other constructions are set off to advantage when placed on cloth or colored paper. A cardboard box or carton, painted inside and upended, makes a satisfactory shadow box for exhibiting works of art. Mobiles are hung where they are free to turn and catch the light. Transparencies are hung in windows. Sometimes it is possible to hang a picture where it will be reflected in a mirror.

Finger paintings and string, spatter, or blot paintings can be enhanced when mounted on construction paper that draws out their colors. To conserve paper, cut out the center portion of the backing and place the outer piece over the painting as a frame. Other frames can be made from corrugated cardboard, box covers, or cardboard painted or covered with cloth. Clear plastic or contact paper stretched over a painting preserves it and adds a finished look.

Where there are attics, garages, cellars, and second-hand furniture shops, there are usually old picture frames which can be cleaned up, painted, and hung in a special place to display a child's painting. These works can be changed frequently so every child can have his picture in this place of honor at some time. Children are encouraged to reach new levels in their painting when they see them attractively displayed.

"How can you get the pictures away from the children to display them? My children insist on taking everything home," teachers will protest. The teacher should establish a rule during the first weeks of school that papers do not always go home. Samples of each child's work will be kept in folders to show progress, interests, creativity, and manual dexterity during parent conferences. Though every paper may have some significance in the developmental process, it is not necessarily a work of art deserving of praise or display by parents. The child acquires a false sense of the worth of his work when it is treated as if it were another Picasso. *He* knows it was just paint on paper, and he was content with the process. When adults whom he respects give it the rave treatment, his self-respect may turn into self-adulation.

Even more detrimental to children's feelings about themselves is the tendency for some teachers to feel that they must touch up their work before it can leave the school. This practice says very clearly to them, "Your work is not good enough." They may translate this into "You are not good enough," and may be discouraged from further effort. Laying hands on a child's work to fix it up, complete it, or make it more realistic is an absolute *no-no* for all teachers, students, volunteers, *and* parents!

Why no coloring books? A coloring book destroys the "I AM! I CAN!" instead of building and strengthening it. Outlines to be filled in say to the child, "This is the way it should look." They teach the child to be passive and take orders, to lose confidence in himself and *his* ideas. As he fills in the outlines, he need not think, be original, or be creative. Coloring books stress the point of view of one person, emphasize a *right* and *wrong* way, and inhibit creative activity. When they are given to children in a nursery school or child care center, it suggests a clear example of goofing off on the part of the caregiver.

Music through-　"Music is fun and music is as much a part of everyday living as breath-
out the day　ing and talking, as block building and sand cooking, as dressing and
　　　　　　eating, as running and resting, as looking at clouds and feeling grass,
　　　　　　as crying and laughing." (Emma Sheehy, *Living Music with Children.*)

　　　　　　In planning a curriculum for young children, music is woven into
the fabric of the entire day. Each interest center provides some opportunity for musical expression, from the child crooning to a doll in the
dramatic play center to the children experimenting with tuning water
glasses in the science center. The teacher watches and listens for cues
for the *teachable moment.*

Finding rhythm　As a group of children chant or sing spontaneously, the teacher picks
up the beat of a movement with a drum or stick and makes it a shared
experience. Four children playing with clay begin to pound it in uni-
son—and their teacher uses a drum to accentuate their physical patterns.

　　　　　　Children who are happy and content will sing. Mimi and Joan,
swinging side by side, combine the joy of movement through space
with the satisfaction of having a friend as they sing "up, up, up" and
"down, down, down." Their voices climb up and down with the musical
chanting. Robbie discovers a bounciness in the balance board and
jumps, chanting "bounce, bounce, bounce." The teacher joins his
chanting and may add a new idea with "Bounce, bounce, bounce, and
jump!" Mark joins in the fun. Soon a line forms, with each child taking a turn and all chanting "Bounce, bounce, bounce, and jump!" The
game becomes much more dramatic when the teacher gets the cymbals
and accents the "Jump!" with a crash.

　　　　　　"It all sounds so easy," sighs the self-described non-musical
teacher. It *is* easy for the teacher who is prepared to believe he is capable of *some* simple musical experience. He starts where *he* is and grows
with the children, working in a climate of freedom and fun.

Singing　Singing and childhood go hand in hand. Singing is not reserved for
special time slots, it is woven throughout the entire day. We sing as we
go through necessary routines such as dressing, napping, or washing;
we sing as we move from one activity to another or one place to another; we sing as we travel to and from school; and we sing as we walk
out on a field trip or hike. We sing to convey and reinforce ideas, we
sing for sheer exuberance, and we sing to express our moods. And as we
sing together, the seeds of harmony and unity are sown.

Starting with　When choosing songs to sing with young children, we turn first to the
the familiar　familiar folk tunes which have been passed on from one generation to
　　　　　　another. They are easy to learn, lie within easy voice ranges, and have

a simple basic rhythm. They have lasted because they came from the heart: they grew out of real life experiences.

Sea chanties were sung by sailors who led a very monotonous life. Confined to ships for months at a time, far away from home and loved ones, they were overworked, often badly treated, and underfed. As they hauled on the ropes, climbed the rigging, or swabbed the decks, they sang to keep up their spirits. The rhythms of the chanties were a vital force in many shipboard tasks.

The cowboy riding the expanses of the great western ranges sang to himself, to his dog, and to his herds to dispel the loneliness and to calm the restless animals. As we sing his songs, we feel the rhythm of his horse as it lopes along. (Play "On the Trail" from the *Grand Canyon Suite* of Ferde Grofé.)

The men who built railroads across the continent and the blacks who picked cotton under southern skies sang of the physical hardships they endured. Their folk songs are a priceless part of our heritage. As we introduce children to them with brief explanations of their origin and uses, our children begin to have an awareness of history.

Introducing a new song
Though some teachers still advocate teaching a song by rote, we are most emphatic in our objections to this method. It is unnecessary. It squeezes the joy out of singing. It takes music out of the natural flow of events and sets it apart as a lesson to be learned. When the leader says, "Now I will *say* the words, and you *say* them after me, one line at a time," children and adults tune music out.

A new song should be offered as if it were a surprise package, wrapped in bright paper. "I know a song about a clown, all funny and fat, with a feather in his hat. Listen, I will sing it to you." The teacher sings it through once, then says, "Now this time, if you remember some of the words, you help me," or indicates with a gesture that her listeners may join in. If there is a recurrent phrase (such as "a-HUM, a-HUM" in "Froggie Would a-Courtin' Go"), the children will quickly sing that part and soon will know the whole song.

Some teachers, out of nervousness, preface their songs with much clapping of hands, calling to attention, and explanation: "Okay, now, everyone, I have a new song. Now everyone listen. Matt, you aren't listening! Okay, now, here it is." If, instead of all this preamble, she simply starts singing, looking into the faces of those nearest her, some of them will join her and the rest will follow.

One teacher who could play the piano introduced each new song by playing it for several days while the children were resting. They absorbed the melody and, when the words were added, they learned the song quickly because of their previous exposure.

Key and tempo
Tempo and tone are as important as the tune. Groups tend to drag out a song, like the half chant of the playground, and if a song is intended to be light and gay, like "Hey, Betty Martin," it destroys the quality. Children sing most comfortably in the keys of C and F and most adults can sing there as well, but, again, through nervousness, have a ten-

dency to start all songs an octave lower. It is a good idea to have a tone bar, or even a bell, tuned to middle C, to help in starting a song, until the range comes naturally.

Songs to fit the moment — A teacher needs to carry some songs in his head, songs to suit many different moods and events, so he can respond to special moments with a spontaneous outburst of song. Such moments are lost if he has to hunt frantically for the right book and page. Knowing five or six songs will greatly enhance a teacher's use of classroom musical experiences.

The unmusical teacher — What of the teacher who says, "But I'm not musical. I can't carry a tune. I can't sing or read a note!" Fiddlesticks! Everyone can sing or chant the songs we all sang on the playground as children. Everyone has sung "We won't get home until morning" or "Farmer in the dell," and those familiar tunes are a starting place for the most unmusical teacher. Those who really cannot recognize or carry a tune can tape a few songs and use the tapes until the children learn. Then *they* will carry the tunes. There are many fine recordings by well-known folk singers, and children can sing along with them until they learn the songs. However, we believe that it is better for children to sing with the most inept leader—and risk learning a few tunes inaccurately—than to be denied the fun of singing.

No rhythm bands — Rhythm bands are inappropriate for young children. The noises they produce are a cacophony of distorted sounds. Some music books and records suggest that we arrange children according to the instruments and conduct them as if they were in an orchestra, each section playing at an appointed time or all together at others. While this kind of performance *may* have value for children seven or eight years old, it is not good musical training for young children. It is fatiguing, over-stimulating, and, in general, uncreative. Children have a lot of experimenting to do before they are ready for such directed music.

What *do* we do with rhythm instruments?

Introducing instruments — Begin by presenting them one at a time, each with the dignity and importance of a precious Stradivarius violin. Pass them around for the children to touch, listen to, and experiment with. For example, if you rub sand blocks together very lightly, they call to mind lightly falling rain. If you start rubbing them slowly and increase the speed, they have the sound of a train.

Coconut halves clapped together are a galloping horse. They are a fun surprise to add to a song about cowboys or ponies. Bells might be introduced two or three at a time, each with a different tone. Collect a group of bells, such as an elephant bell, a cow bell, sleigh bells, bells of Sarna, a dinner bell, and an old-fashioned teacher's desk bell.

As each instrument has been presented, display the growing assortment on a table and discuss likenesses, differences, and individual characteristics: "Which ones do you shake? Which ones are made of metal? Which make more than one sound?"

Experimenting When using instruments, expect children (and adults) to test them and try them out. To say, "Hold your bell very still until we're all ready," asks the impossible when children are given instruments for the first time. They must be allowed to experiment and find out what they can do. Anticipate this process with, "When I give you these sticks, I know you will want to try them. See how many different sounds you can make with them. Then, when I hold my sticks way up high like this, please *stop* and *listen* to find out what I am going to tell you." If this stop signal is played as a game a few times, the children will take pride in not being caught when the signal is given. It is better to anticipate the need than to try to get attention by shouting over the din.

Try using instruments for sound effects with stories and poems. Use them to add drama to creative movement and to underscore counting patterns in math. Find combinations of sound and beat that will create harmony.

Caring for instruments If we want children to treat instruments with respect, we must give attention to proper care and storage. How many times have you seen a basket or carton filled with a jumbled assortment of bells, sticks, cymbals, and drums? Have you ever searched in frustration through such a collection, seeking the hanger for the triangle, or shuffled to the bottom for the striker?

Sticks should be arranged by sizes in attractive containers. Triangles can be hung on hooks; finger cymbals placed in dainty little boxes which suit their delicate sounds; anklets or wrist bells kept in a separate bag or box; and drums stored in a special place on a shelf. Until rules are established and learned, most of these instruments will be out of reach, with just two or three at a time laid out on a low shelf.

Teachers and children can construct their own shakers, drums, and anklets. In one school each child made his own complete set of sticks, claves, sand blocks, bells, and maracas. The children could use the instruments whenever they wished, and they did so frequently. They took an extra pride in caring for them because they had made them. (See *Instruments to Make* listed in the *Index* to Vol. 2.)

Creative movement Movement, *the sixth sense*, is best developed in the *context and rhythm* of daily living. The development of movement, the body's language, into an active, vital, creative sense, should become a part of every classroom activity. Stories, games, songs, clean-up, playground antics, painting, dramatic play—all involve body language. Watchful, sensitive adults can translate such language into creative movement.

Creative movement is used to *follow up, expand,* and *reinforce* concepts throughout the daily program. Spatial concepts (such as *on, through, around, over,* and *behind*) are involved in almost every movement experience. On a day when the children had been talking about animals, their likenesses and differences, their eating habits, and their homes, the cues were obvious—this was a day to "dance" animals into their body language.

This is the *integrated approach* to creative movement.

Music and movement are like happily married partners, each able to function alone but with added joy when they are together. Children enjoy dancing to the music from their favorite classroom records or exploring space and motion with music from classical symphonies and ballets or modern jazz and rock records or tapes. If an onlooker gazes out the window and reports, "It's snowing!" the teacher can spark the class by saying, "We'll have to plow the streets and push out all the stuck-in cars." "Plows" and "tractors," "shovelers" and "sliders" may be accompanied by music, and they are moving—creatively.

In the phrase *creative movement,* it is the *creative* which scares away many excellent teachers. To them the word suggests artistic talent and the "I can never draw a straight line" attitude sets in as they slip away to sit and watch from the sidelines. This is unfortunate, because movement is as simple as bread and butter, as accessible as crayons and paint. Art and motion become graceful partners as children translate body motions on paper with brushes and paint or explore colors and "the way they make you feel."

Movement is for *everyone* who can nod his head, clap hands, wink an eye, shrug a shoulder. The popularity of modern dance has confused many into thinking that creative movement and dance are one and the same thing. Though modern dance *is* creative movement, creative movement does not exclusively mean *dance*. The *creative* simply means awakening the consciousness to the wonders of body motion. How does it move? Why? How fast or slow? How does the body come to rest? Awaken? What shapes can the body become? How does it stand when you are happy, terrified, or sad? Can the body be a carrot? A machine? A cat? A flower in the wind?

Can motion ever be separated from sight, sound, smell, touch, or taste? No, never! Children learn through sensory experiences. Through movement we can seek ways to feel letter shapes and numbers with our bodies. For example, "Think of a number of ways to express the letter 's.' Can you make it with your fingers? With your whole body? How could two people make it? Use two different parts of your body to make it." Or, "Think of some action words that begin with 's.' Which could you do standing? Sitting?" Use ropes to make an 's' on the floor. How could we walk on them? Around them? Make an 's' pattern into a dance. "What kind of music shall we use?" Put large sheets of paper on the floor and paint 's' with musical accompaniment.

Creative movement begins when teacher and children are just "doing what comes naturally," as Annie Oakley sang in *Annie Get Your Gun.* It may be as simple as, "What could we do with our fingers? How many different ways can we move them?" while seated around the table at juice time or at the beginning of rest, when each part of the body is relaxed, one at a time, ending with a soothing y-a-a-a-w-n. Whenever bodies, attached to imaginations, are involved in exploring and discovering, creative movement is happening! (Look under *Bodies* and *Motions* in the *Index* to Vol. 2.)

Reading to children
All nursery teachers read story books to their students, but with varying degrees of skill and effectiveness. The following suggestions will improve those skills.

Reading well
• Begin by reading the story first to yourself. Even the simplest story, intended and illustrated for children, should have the benefit of preview by the teacher.

• Set the stage. The group should be reasonably settled, quiet, and comfortable. The wigglers will settle down if the story captures their attention. If you will use props for sound effects or visual aids, have them nearby and organized, so you can find them when you need them.

• Hold the book open, facing the children, so all have a view of the pages as they are turned. Even if there are no illustrations, the children are learning that "those black marks" are telling the story.

• Use your voice as a delicate, refined instrument in reading or telling stories. You can express the drama, the suspense, the compassion, the humor, or the excitement of the story with an infinite variety of tones.

• Ask the listeners to share the action as often as possible. Being involved gives children the feeling of *reading* and *telling* the story themselves. "Farmer Hezekiah Brown doesn't know what happened to his carrots, but *we* do, don't we? Shh, don't tell!" (*Smokey's Big Discovery*, by Walek .) These listeners know the glee of a shared secret. They reach the end of the story before Farmer Brown and can't wait until he finds out what they already know.

Telling a story
• Take the time to learn a story and *tell* it to the children. You will know great satisfaction as you watch the expressions of wonder, awe, amusement, and surprise on the faces of the audience. Their response will inspire greater skill in the telling. An additional benefit is that you have a valuable teaching tool available for immediate use. When there is a five-minute wait or a group is "high," a well-told story may save the day.

• Do not tell a story as a word-by-word recitation. Instead, memorize the first sentence, learn the sequence of events, and memorize the last sentence. If you memorize an entire story and relay it back by rote, you will be so busy trying to remember the next line that your performance becomes a recitation, and your story will be a bore for your audience and for you. But keep the story clear: "Oh, I forgot to mention that ..." will confuse and maybe even lose your audience.

• Bring your stories to life whenever possible by eliminating third-person grammar. Instead of saying "The king told the people he would solve their problems," address the audience in the king's own voice. Use other tones for each of the other characters. Tell the rest of the story in a comfortable, pleasing narrating voice. When two people in a story hold a conversation, turn your face in either direction, giving the impression of two people talking. Telling a story with these embellishments is just as easy and twice as much fun.

• Use sound effects. In "Paddy's Three Pets" by Mary G. Phillips, found in the anthology *Told Under the Blue Umbrella* (Macmillan), Paddy's father comes home every night and jingles his key in the lock and whistles to let Paddy know he's home. Paddy might come down the stairs by way of the piano keyboard, or by way of the xylophone. A cymbal struck slowly becomes the tolling church bell, helping to create a visual image of people dressed up and walking in a slow, dignified manner to church. Have these sound effects produced by preselected members of the audience to add interest and excitement.

• Please! *Don't* moralize! It really isn't necessary to "heavy up" the ending with "So, you *see*, children, if Cinderella's sisters had not been so selfish, ..." or "I'll bet Goldilocks listened the *next* time her mother told her not to go out into the woods." The children will get the moral message if there is one, perhaps not the first time, or even the second, but eventually the story will take on layers of meaning which fit their growing experiences, and they should be allowed the excitement of such discoveries. They do not need spoon feeding or adult interpretations. Books should be treasure chests, holding beautiful stories and exciting bits of knowledge. They should not represent some strange square vegetable out of which teachers squeeze *learning* which the child is expected to digest. Young children will learn to love books, and will approach reading with joy and excitement, if they have good experiences in these early years.

• Most important of all, choose a story *you* really like, one which tickles your funny bone and stimulates your imagination. Then let your own pleasure unlock the silver chains around the treasure chest of enjoyment.

The captive audience Too often in the nursery school story time means that every child is expected to sit down in front of the teacher and "enjoy." Children should be given a choice in this as well as in other areas of curriculum. Their options must necessarily be limited to activities which will not disturb or distract those who do want to listen, but they should be given alternatives: "Those who want to hear the story come over here. If you do not care to listen, you may look at books in the reading corner, you may play quietly with this game, or you may have crayons at this table. You may *not* play in the doll corner, build with blocks, or play with trucks, because that would disturb us."

Many children in a captive audience will be disruptive and take away from the pleasure of those who wish to listen. It is true that "When they get to first grade, they will *have* to sit still and listen," but these children are not yet in first grade, and they have a lot still to learn before they get there. When children seem incapable of listening, the challenge rests with the teacher to seek ways to encourage rather than to force attention.

Props and visual aids

Finger puppets are a delightful visual aid to supplement stories, finger plays, poems, and songs. They might be elaborate puppets made by adults or simple creations made by children. Some "special" puppets might be kept in pretty little containers to be used with specific stories or songs or to be used on holidays, birthdays, and other special occasions. Here are some easy-to-make finger puppets:

Finger puppets

- Five Little Mice: gray gloves with ears, tails, and faces sewn on.
- Five Ghosts: facial tissues over the fingers, held on with elastic bands, and with faces drawn on.
- Witches: black gloves with tiny brooms sewn on and separate black hats.
- Faces of story characters painted on paper circles and glued to paper rings.
- Button puppets: faces painted on buttons sewn to elastic bands that fit over the fingers.

Velcro boards

A piece of stiff cardboard covered with Velcro, with a cardboard brace on the back so it can stand alone, is the latest version of the flannel board or the felt board. Make silhouettes of the characters from a story, attach a small piece of Velcro to the back of each, and use them to illustrate a story as you tell it.

Mounted pictures

If you are telling a story with a setting that is not familiar to the children, just holding up a large picture of a giraffe or a palm tree, a rain forest or a snow-capped mountain, may help the children understand and visualize the tale you are telling.

Poetry and the program

Fortunate are those who were introduced to poetry by someone who loved it and shared that enjoyment. Too often even the suggestion of poetry stirs memories of rote recitations droning on in a monotonous cadence, such as "Oc-to-ber's bright blue wea-ther" or "I shot an ar-row in-to the air" or "This is the for-est prim-e-val." Total language development includes an appreciation of the beauty of spoken and written words, and so poetry becomes an integral part of any language.

Introducing poetry

Many teachers have said, "I like poetry, but I don't know how to use it." Others complain,"When I read poetry to the children, they just don't respond." One of the basic theories of how children learn states that *we start where the learner is.* Reading, singing, dramatizing, and drawing pictures of nursery rhymes can become the first step in an appreciation of poetry. The children are soon eager to join in with the rhyming word or the word that completes the sentence: "Jack and Jill went up the ..."

Finger plays are another excellent way to enter into the world of poetry. We play "This little piggy went to market" on the fingers and toes of the infant. Preschoolers will giggle all over again when they meet this old friend at school. It can be their introduction to a host of finger plays fitting the seasons and new concepts throughout the year.

Children need and enjoy repetition. "This is the house that Jack built" and "The old woman and her pig" should be a part of the poetic offerings. The teacher who is bored with such rhymes will devise visual aids to add interest.

Fours in particular are at a stage in their language development when they have a real need to experiment with sounds. This need often manifests itself in bathroom talk and even more offensive words. One teacher, frustrated by this situation, used the poems of Edward Lear: "A is for Apple Pie, Pidy, Didy, Widy ...."

Limericks are another style of poetry which children enjoy, but the sensitive teacher will lead children from such literary pabulum into enjoying more sophisticated poems: poems which express emotions ("Pierre" by Maurice Sendak); poems which take one into a world of fantasy ("Knitted Things" by Karla Kuskin or "Fish with a Deep Sea Smile" by Margaret Wise Brown); and Rose Fyleman's delightful poems about fairies. There are poems which express delicate imagery ("First Snow" by Mary Louise Allen) and poems to tickle the funny bone ("If We Walked on Our Hands" by Beatrice Schenk de Regniers). Robert Frost wrote the poem "Last Words of a Bluebird." When it was read in a nursery school, one four-year-old asked for it over and over. In a very few days he was heard reading it accurately to others. We must never underestimate the ability of a child to appreciate the best!

Presenting poetry But how does the teacher include poetry, and why do some children respond? Appreciation expressed in the face and voice of the person making the presentation will carry over to children and become contagious. There are some basic rules:

• Never try to read a poem aloud until you have read it many times yourself. If you do not like it, do not attempt to use it. Your feelings will come through to your listeners.
• Decide in advance whether this poem should have a rhythmic cadence, as when "Christopher Robin went hoppity, hoppity, hoppity, hoppity, hop," or whether the story aspect is most important. Your voice is the instrument playing the tune. If it stops at the end of each line, often in the middle of an idea, a sing-song version with little meaning emerges.
• Memorize short poems. You will be rewarded for this investment of your time. Write a poem on a small card and say it while you make beds or drive to school. Keep the card with you for reference in case you get stage-struck. Just knowing the card is there will give you confidence.
• Write your poem on the chalkboard or on a paper you can fasten on the wall and use as television actors use cue cards. You might hang a favorite poem at child's-eye level beside an appropriate picture.
• Present each poem alone, as you would a lovely object. Do not confuse the children by reading four, five, or six poems about snow on the same day. Present them one at a time, savoring the imagery, humor, or emotional content. We dilute the appreciation of so many

experiences for our children by offering too much too soon. Small bites, well digested, will leave a pleasant and permanent imprint on the developing mind.

Language games There are many games, activities, and tools to help children learn words and concepts, enlarge vocabulary, and master the art of conversation. Some games are as simple as finding the rhyming word to a jingle; others are as difficult as arranging pictures to form a sequential story. The transitions and experiences of each day run more smoothly for the teacher with a game or simple activity for every occasion—to make waiting less tiresome when program hits a slowdown or snag; to play at the luncheon table; to while away the last half hour in late afternoon; or to play outside on the playground.

The keen observations of the teacher will serve as guides to know each child so that he can be helped with his individual language needs through the skillful use of a variety of language games. Each child has some key which unlocks his ability to express, communicate, and create. Never cease searching for those keys.

Tiny treasure box Imagine the delight of a small child at peering into a tiny box filled with miniature treasures—dolls, cars, a shiny jewel, a china kitten. Such tiny treasures act as spurs to language development and as relaxing peacemakers to an unsettled child during homesick moments. Miniature treasures in a box help to tell a story or serve as storytelling puppets.

We all see pretty boxes or containers and tuck them away for future use. Most of us are attracted to miniatures: china people and animals, charms, dime store and joke shop items, cocktail favors, advertising gimmicks, and doll house furnishings. Put these treasures into a pretty box and create a tiny treasure box. It is not used as a toy or as part of a daily activity, but is taken out only for special occasions. Children take great delight and pride in naming the items and finding a remembered object.

Sometimes the treasures are changed; new surprises are added from time to time. On returning from a vacation trip, the teacher gathers children around and, after telling of travel adventures, takes down the treasure box and from her pocket a tiny package. Inside the children find a pink seashell, and it too is added to the box.

Specialized boxes enhance language and other skills: a collection of rhyming objects; several round items; a box filled with soft touchables; seriated items from small to teensy or from light blue to dark blue. Kindergarten children might make up spelling boxes for items with names they can spell, such as cat, hat, cup, and pin. A treasure box might even have a joke to trick an unsuspecting teacher or child: a box within a box within a box within a box ... .

Chapter 38   **SCIENCE AND MATH**

Science   Words of teacher: "Oh, I can't teach science!"
Words of wisdom: "Nonsense!"

- Can you brush your hair and create static electricity? That's physics.
- Can you dig around a tree and find its roots, bugs, and worms? That's biology.
- Can you bring snowballs inside to melt? That's physics, too.
- Can you measure the ingredients and bake a cake? That's chemistry.
- Can you mix blue and yellow paint to make—what? That's chemistry and physics, too.
- Can you blow up a balloon and let it jet-propel itself around the room? That's physics and engineering.
- Can you plant seeds and watch them sprout? That's biology.
- Can you go to a chicken farm and watch chicks hatch? That's sex education.
- Can you find three different kinds of rocks on the playground? Geology.
- Can you give a demonstration on how to scrub your hands? Hygiene.
- Can you pick up nails with a magnet? Physics.

If you can do any of these things, *you* can teach science. Furthermore, you can and will become an expert on *exploring* and *explaining* the world around you. There is only one rule of self-training in science to follow: *Always ask "Why?"*

If you are lucky, your "Why?" will come before the child's "Why?" and you will have a chance to go to a library in search of the answers. There are hundreds of basic books on science written for those who say "I can't teach science."

Science surrounds you as does the air. Speaking of air, if you sneeze, yawn, or burp, *you* are a scientific experiment. Did you ask, "Why did I sneeze?" If not, you missed a whole unit of curriculum.

Science   What can you teach in your science center? To observe, to experiment, to test. When children learn to *observe*, looking at things carefully, noticing likenesses and differences, how things are made, how animals move and birds fly, which rocks are the heaviest, what happens when the wind blows—that is science.

When children *experiment*, planting seeds in various kinds of soils, seeing what floats and what sinks, discovering what happens when you put various things in water—that is science.

When children *test*, guessing that two colors of paint will make green, then trying it to see what actually happens—that is science.

Cooking is science, and it has a pleasant sensory factor. Children not only measure, mix, and discover what happens when various ingredients are put together, they can also smell and taste the results.

Teachers should go to the children's room of the local public library and look at children's science books. These books will expand their vision of what science can be for young children. A teacher who arouses curiosity by bringing in rocks, shells, pine cones, seeds, birds' nests, feathers, or an old alarm clock, and helps children find answers to their natural questions, will have an active science program.

In Volume 2, *A Preschool Curriculum*, Science is one of the themes that runs through all twelve months. There are too many activities to list here, but if you look at the Theme Page for each sequence, you will see just which pages are devoted to science.

Mathematics With new knowledge of the capacity for early learning, teachers know that mathematical concepts are interesting and important to children. Math includes *recognition of numbers*, enabling the child to know her address and phone number. *Counting* is math, not for the sake of reciting numbers by rote, but when there is a reason for knowing "how many," as when counting out napkins or cookies. Math includes understanding the *concepts of quantity*. A child needs to assimilate "fourness," in addition to being able to recognize the numeral 4 and knowing how to make it.

Seriation is an important part of a math program. The child needs to know and comprehend *more than* and *less than*, *larger* and *smaller*, as she arranges objects and people in order of height or weight. We observe and sort colors from *dark* to *light*, listen to sounds from *loud* to *soft*, and gradually come to understand the total concept of differences in *gradation*.

Shapes in a math program help prepare the way for reading, starting with the simple shapes—the circle, square, and triangle. We lay the groundwork for recognizing the differences in letters (such as b and d) through this early recognition of shapes. Shapes help a child to order the environment, recognizing similarly defined areas. We refer to "that round box" rather than "that thing on the table."

Much of this curriculum is not new; many have taught such ideas in the early years. The difference is that we are consciously looking to specific goals and objectives, to give children a solid foundation which will later alter their attitudes toward education and learning. Not "You have to *know* this for first grade" but "You have *discovered* a new idea!"

The people theme   People! This is a major theme in our curriculum, which follows a natural sequence related to the life experiences of the child. In the beginning, when children are venturing into a whole new world, we try to
help them begin to see themselves in the context of a larger society. We
concentrate on that which they bring with them.

The teacher's task with every new child is to enhance and
strengthen the child's own self-image. His name is important to him.
It is uniquely his—the label which distinguishes him from others. We
capitalize on this symbol of person by exploring names in many ways.
(Look under *Names* in the Index to Vol. 2.)

Next we talk about the immediate family, remembering that the
Dick and Jane family of primer fame—mother, father, sister, brother,
and baby—are not always typical. Joe becomes the envy of his peers
when he announces that he has *four* grandfathers and *four* grand-
mothers. This fact is especially impressive to those keen enough to add
up presents! Many children are being brought up by single parents, and
some of the single parents are the fathers, not the mothers. Children
can cope with what is true in their lives if they are told the truth.
Preschool children have not lived long enough to know what is
different from the norm. The attitudes of parents and other trusted
adults will be the factors that disturb or effectively guide the child.

Extended family   As Thanksgiving draws near, we begin to hear about members of the
extended family. In family gatherings children meet aunts, uncles, and
cousins and explore new relationships. It is a real surprise to some
children to learn that Mummy was once Grandma's little girl. A child
listens eagerly to tales of "when Daddy was just as big as you are now."

In December we introduce the holiday customs of people in other
countries and cultures. Most of these customs will include some form
of caring and sharing, giving gifts, and meeting friends and relatives.
We stress what we have in common, yet respect the right of differences.

Likenesses and   These differences gradually flow into a discussion of *likeness and differ-*
differences   *ence.* We introduce the idea of differences in people, starting with such
things as hair and eyes, height and weight. We go on to differences in
skin color, culture, language, and physical makeup, including the
physically challenged. Talk of places, such as Alaska and Florida, may
lead to differences in what people wear and eat and how they live.

The work people do   We talk about what people do. Starting with fathers and mothers, we
invite adults to school to tell what their work is. Sometimes we go to
visit Wayne's dad at the gas station, or Dina's mother at the motel she
manages, or the big building where Juan's mother has an office.

We visit the people in our own school: the secretary, who lets us try the typewriter or adding machine, the custodian, the cook. If the school does not have a library, we visit a big library. A mail carrier shows us a mail bag and invites us to visit the post office. We extend our knowledge of people to community helpers—firefighters, hospital workers, police personnel.

With the coming of spring, we can find out how we get the food we eat. A trip to the vegetable section of the grocery store, followed by a trip to a market garden, helps children to a new understanding of the people involved in providing our food. If a dairy farm is within trip distance, it is a valuable learning experience to find out how milk gets into the little containers we use.

The child is thus gradually led from his own egocentric concept to a broader realization of where he fits into the total scheme of "people-ness." He acquires a social awareness which will help him to adjust to new situations and which will enrich the quality of his life.

Multicultural concepts
Since the first edition of this book was published in 1976, there have been enormous changes in our world. Television has brought us into instant visual contact with places and events. We have been exposed to people who look different, speak different languages, eat different foods, and wear clothing which would look out of place on Main Street, U.S.A. We cannot, within the limitations of this book, explore all the possibilities this expanded world offers, but we do suggest a plan.

The plan
Use the following questions as the basis for discussion. There are a lot of feelings to bring out in the open and attitudes to examine. Your role as director is to listen, respect everyone's ideas and opinions, and give ample opportunity for expression. The goal is to help everyone gain a better understanding of some of the children you may be teaching.

• Do you believe that people who come from other countries to live here *should* adopt the American way of speaking, dressing, thinking, and behaving?
• Do you see multicultural education as another imposed chore or as an opportunity to broaden your own horizons?
• How can we enlist the support of our parents in gathering information about the cultures they represent?
• If yours is a center on Main Street, U.S.A., with virtually no "foreigners," do you see any need to introduce other cultures to the children? Why or why not?

It is important to remember that we are not trying to teach children about the actual location of Africa or the distance from here to Japan. We explore and extend each child's contacts with other cultures and customs through other children in the center, through trips to restaurants, and through movies and videotapes. Recognizing and understanding that cultural differences are interesting and exciting is a vital part of expanding the child's world. (For specific activities, look under the heading *Multicultural* in the *Index* to Vol. 2.)

Chapter 40   **FIELD TRIPS**

Things to consider   In planning field trips, review goals and objectives based on the developmental square. Are all four sides of the square involved? What social experiences will be derived? Will the buddy system enhance new relationships and build friendships? Will parents participate? Children need time to express thoughts, ask questions, and digest details. They need plenty of time for conversation and observation. Small children should not be taken into crowds and rush-hour situations. Consider the anxiety and fear of a child lost, even for a brief time, in a strange and crowded place.

Climbing a hill, taking a hike, following a nature trail, or walking on a beach are good scientific expeditions as well as excellent physical activity. Children are doers, not watchers, so trips should take them where they can touch, taste, smell, and listen, or crawl into, get on, or climb over. A field trip is not just an excuse to go somewhere, and calling it one will not magically turn it into an educational experience. Simplicity of content, time to enjoy, and plenty of help are good rules to follow. A well-planned trip is an adventure.

For the littlest ones   Special thought should be given to the length and value of a trip for the littlest ones. Where the fours and fives may go to the post office, twos will find a trip to the nearest mailbox exciting enough. Imagination should be used to make trips exciting, even though they go no farther than the corner of the school yard, a neighbor's yard, or a short walking distance. Just leaving home to go to school is an adjustment, and taking them to other places may only arouse fears and anxieties.

Permission slips   At the beginning of the year, parents are asked to sign slips giving the school permission to take children away from school property. These forms will be sufficient for walking trips, and teachers should have lists of any children whose parents have refused permission. Use a more detailed form, such as the one at the end of this chapter, each time children go someplace in cars or buses.

When parents drive their own cars, list the names of the children in each car, the driver's name, and the license plate number, and leave the list in the office. Do *not* change children—or allow them to change—from one car to another for the return trip.

Supervision   There should be a minimum of one adult for each five children, and one to four is preferable. Since that many teachers cannot normally be spared, it is a good idea to invite parents to help.

Beforehand   •   Have a teacher and/or a parent make the trip in advance to decide on the best route, observe points of interest along the way, and discover possible hazards.

• Have this adult talk to the host or manager about the ages of the children, the purpose of the trip, and safety requirements, and find out what sensory experiences may be possible—things to touch, manipulate, taste, or listen for. Suggest that the host need not lecture to the children, just present a few bits of information and answer the children's questions.

• With the staff, talk about how you help children get the most from the trip. Ask the teachers to think of questions which let children discover, and warn them not to expect too much response at once.

• Ask for suggestions for ways to enhance the trip.

• Invite the parents to come beforehand for coffee and a discussion of plans.

• Make tags for adults and children. Code the tags by color, so the parent with the green jacket is responsible for the children with green name tags, and the colored jacket will help a child recognize his guide. Put the school's name and phone number on the tags, but not the children's names. That information should not be accessible to strangers. A child is all too likely to trust a stranger who calls him by name.

Teachers' prep
• Use books and pictures in advance to build interest.

• Talk to the children about the rules necessary for the entire trip, door to door. Keep the rules simple but explicit.

• Decide in advance which adult will take slide pictures, which will be invaluable in recalling the trip with the children.

• Make a list of things to look for on the way and share it with the children. "We will pass a big red brick building. Who will see it first? Who will tell us what it is? Then we will cross some railroad tracks with a warning sign. See if you can tell us what it says. Try to remember all the kinds of animals you see. We will go over a bridge. Who can tell us why we have to have a bridge there?" This kind of advance preparation will greatly reduce behavior problems on the trip.

After the trip
• Do not expect immediate reaction or response. Give the children time to let their impressions jell.

• Do not, as soon as you get back, insist that every child make a picture of something seen on the trip.

It happened:
> *On a walk, one boy muttered to another through gritted teeth, "Don't look! Don't look! You'll have to make a picture of it!"*

• Remember that children are tired just from the excitement of leaving school. Let them rest before expecting feedback.

• Later, divide the children into small groups to write stories. Read the stories from each small group to all the children. See how they are the same and different. Did one small group remember things another group did not? Some children may want to make pictures to illustrate their group's story. Put the stories and pictures into a book that can be read and reread.

• When the slides come back, have a show. Encourage the children to compare what they wrote with what they have just seen.

• Place some object in the block area that relates to the trip, such as a garden trowel, a pair of firefighter's boots, or a mailbag, each of which may stimulate block building.

• Introduce a science experience related to the trip.

• Encourage the children to recall sounds they heard or the moving machinery they saw. Sounds and motions can lead to dramatic play.

• With the children, write a thank-you letter to your host. This is a must. You may want to enclose pictures the children drew or stories they dictated that indicate the impressions they received.

Walking trips If there are more than two children, one holding each hand, there must be two adults, even if the trip is only across the street. For larger groups, there should be at least one adult for every four children.

Special walks It is just as easy to *plan* a special walk as it is just to *take* a walk. Here are some examples:

• *A color walk*—"Today we are going to look for things that are red or orange." An adult with paper and pencil writes them down as the children see them. If possible, the children collect samples.

• *A sound walk*—"Let's see how many sounds we can hear." List the sounds because, even if you take a tape recorder, you may not be able to recognize them when you listen later.

• *A smell walk*—Plan to pass a bakery or a restaurant. Smell weeds, trees, or the water in a puddle!

• *A taste walk*—Not as easy to arrange, but you can do it with some forethought.

• *A feeling walk*—"What can you find that feels smooth? Or rough?" The bark of trees, stones, milkweed, pine needles. Carry paper bags and let each child collect items to feel (keeping conservation rules in mind). Compare the items when you get back. Set up a table for the rest of the children to look at and touch. Make a "Feely Box" using items the children have found.

Destinations The following were all destinations for preschoolers' field trips:

Library	Gas station	Park	Pet shop
Post office	Museum	Farm	Apple orchard
Bakery	Airport	Building site	Horse farm
Supermarket	Zoo	Lumber yard	Photographer
Fire station	Aquarium	Produce stand	Turkey farm
Police station	Factory	Bottling plant	Greenhouse

Unusual destinations Some destinations can be made to seem exotic to the children:

• *The highway department garage*—The workers allowed the children to sit on the big trucks and showed them how a snowplow, a sander, a street cleaner, and a sewer dredger work.

- *A train ride*—The children were driven to the railroad station, rode on the train to the city and back again on the same train. At another school, the children were put on the train at one station and taken off at the next.
- *A motel*—The manager invited the group to have refreshments in the coffee shop after a tour of the facility.
- *A Chinese restaurant*—The owner opened early and talked to the children in Chinese, gave them tiny parasols (from cocktails) and fortune cookies, let them sample fried rice and other foods, and wrote the Chinese characters from 1 to 10. Each child was given his name written in Chinese. After they returned to school, the children made Chinese costumes. One child wore her costume when she was driven back to the restaurant to deliver a thank-you letter.
- *A hospital*—One mother, a doctor, demonstrated many kinds of medical instruments.
- *The dress rehearsal* of a high school drama—The children watched older boys and girls putting on makeup and costumes.
- *A weather station*—A mother, a meteorologist, showed how weather radar works and demonstrated other weather instruments.
- *An airport fire station*—The entire group of sixteen children could fit inside the cab of a huge foam truck. The children were allowed to try on the helmet of a fire-fighting suit.
- *An artists' studio*—The parents, both artists, showed their studio, then provided a picnic in their back yard.

Reverse field trips

Instead of going to the fire station, police department, or construction site, invite their workers and equipment to come to you. Interesting and exciting visits can have many beneficial side effects.

- *A fire truck*—The children were allowed to climb on the truck, sit on its seats, and try on a firefighter's helmet. The firefighters explained the use of their equipment and gave a talk on fire safety.
- *An ambulance*—Some children were afraid of this vehicle, which they associated with sirens, accidents, and trouble. When they were allowed to walk inside, holding tightly to a teacher's hand, they saw that it was not as fearsome as they had imagined. If these children ever have to travel in an ambulance, they will be better prepared.
- *A police attack dog*—The police handler who brought him allowed the children to pat him, but only while she held the dog tightly on his leash. She then gave a demonstration of the animal's training. It inspired a discussion of the need for such trained animals.
- *Construction machinery*—A parent who owned a construction company had workers stop by the center on the way to a job. The children were allowed to climb on the machines and learned about their uses.

FIELD TRIP CHECKLIST

Group: _____ Leader: _____ Date: _____

Site to visit	Phone	Contact person	Time expected
_____	_____	_____	_____
_____	_____	_____	_____
_____	_____	_____	_____

Transportation arranged and extra help secured:

Driver	Phone	Assistant	Phone	Bus	Car	License
_____	_____	_____	_____	☐	☐	_____
_____	_____	_____	_____	☐	☐	_____
_____	_____	_____	_____	☐	☐	_____
_____	_____	_____	_____	☐	☐	_____

Special needs: _____

_____

_____

_____

Parent notices issued _____

Site arrangements complete _____

Tags prepared _____

Planning forms for all adults _____

First aid kit ready _____

Bag of tricks ready _____

Snack for trip ready _____

Permission slips returned _____

Permission slips not in _____

Children not participating _____

Arrangements for them _____

Signed: _____ Approved: _____

FIELD TRIP PERMISSION FORM

I give permission for my child,　＿＿＿＿＿＿＿＿＿＿＿＿＿＿＿＿＿＿＿＿＿＿＿＿

to be taken on a field trip to　＿＿＿＿＿＿＿＿＿＿＿＿＿＿＿＿＿＿＿＿＿＿＿＿

on　＿＿＿＿＿＿＿＿, leaving the center at　＿＿＿＿＿＿　am/pm and returning by　＿＿＿＿＿
am/pm.

I give permission for my child to be transported in a　☐ bus ☐ car, license number　＿＿＿＿＿＿＿＿,

driven by　＿＿＿＿＿＿＿＿＿＿＿＿＿＿　and assisted by　＿＿＿＿＿＿＿＿＿＿＿＿＿＿＿.

I understand that each child in this vehicle will be secured by the required seat belt or other safety restraint at all times while the vehicle is in motion.

Enclosed is $　＿＿＿＿＿＿＿　for admission and $　＿＿＿＿＿＿＿　for transportation

I understand that you need permission for each child individually, even members of the same family.

Signed: ＿＿＿＿＿＿＿＿＿＿＿＿＿＿＿＿＿　　　Date: ＿＿＿＿＿＿＿＿＿＿＿＿＿＿＿＿＿

Chapter 41   **PROGRAM PLANNING**

A good curriculum must develop and change with each group of children, each individual child, each individual teacher. It must *react* to experiences, events, accidents, chance visitors, and other distractions. It must have eyes and ears on all sides and sensitive antennae which constantly say to the child and teacher, "Hey, look!" or "Shhh, listen!" It can never remain constant, since life is always in motion, changing, growing or shrinking, looking ahead or looking backward. Such a curriculum will change from day to day, month to month, year to year—and, often, minute by minute. Curriculum takes into account the needs of developing children, but cannot be administered as medicine forced upon a sick patient.

How to use   The curriculum ideas in this book are intended only as road maps.
a curriculum   They help tell where the children are at a given time; they suggest ideas and point out alternate routes; and they help show where the children have been and where they are going. It is not intended, it is not even desirable, that any teacher follow them exactly. Each person must bring to this curriculum fresh, original, current ideas, following leads within each group and taking cues from each individual.

Program planning Visit any three child care centers and you may find at least three different theories about good program. The truth of the matter is that there is no *right* way, or totally *wrong* way. The important thing is to have a *reason* for the plans.

In one center, during the first weeks of school we may see children playing with blocks, painting at easels, and making collages, and we may think, "This is a good school: the children are busy and seem to be learning." But, if we return to that school several months later and the children are building with blocks, painting at easels, and making collages in the same way as before, we are almost certain to witness boredom, aimless ambling about, and probably some negative behavior. The teacher has provided the right environment, but has neglected to *extend* it as the children have developed.

In a second center, we ask, "Do you have a curriculum?" "Oh, yes, it includes science, music, drama, art, and language development." This center is an improvement over the first one, where not much is stirring, but there is still something missing. The teacher has found enough ideas in the resource books to plan daily projects. The children are learning—their faces probably show evidence of interest—but the teacher does not know *why* she chose her projects. The *interrelationship* between one act and the next is lacking.

In a third center, the teacher *relates* planning to *what* the child should learn, *how* he learns, and *why* he learns. She presents experiences in a definite, *planned* sequence, and both student and teacher are learning. This teacher asks, "What can be added to the environment which will bring about the desired learning?"

Planning a learning experience

In planning a learning experience, these steps may be considered:
- Exploring with the senses
- Relating to the familiar
- Seeing relationships—likenesses and differences
- Classifying—separating into categories

For example, take the apple. The teacher shows a round, red, shiny apple. Her goal is to help each child assimilate "appleness." The children *touch* it, *feel* its roundness, and *smell* it. The teacher cuts it into pieces and they *taste* it and *hear* the crisp crunchiness.

The teacher says, "Tell me about an apple."

"It's round," says Tommy.

"It's red," says Sue.

"It's white inside," observes Mario.

"Those little things are brown," Jim adds, pointing to the seeds.

"It's sweet, but kind of sour," says Nina.

"It tastes something like a pear," José adds.

The teacher instantly asks, "How are an apple and a pear alike?"

"They both grow on trees. They are both fruit," some children say.

The teacher asks, "Can you think of anything else that is round and red?"

"A balloon," "A ball," and so on.

On subsequent days the teacher introduces stories, songs, and poems about or including apples; plans cooking experiences with apples; visits an orchard or market to buy apples; displays a granny doll made from a dried apple; deliberately leaves an apple outside during a frost; cuts one up and leaves it to dry; and so on. In so doing, she has made apples a part of every area of curriculum: language, science, math, music, and art. The children see apples in a variety of ways. They have begun a process of learning which can be carried into each new learning experience. Such planning rewards the teacher with the excitement of observing growth and development as the child absorbs new knowledge.

The best things just happen

A word of caution about planning: *Teachers should be careful not to become so involved with carrying out their plans that they are insensitive to the learning that comes about spontaneously.* In the words of one teacher, "The best things just happen."

In the well-planned approach described in the third center, the teacher is acting on the child, deciding what, when, and how he will learn. But does this approach allow for curiosity, discovery, and self-directed activity? What about the premise that we learn best and retain longest that which we have a need or a desire to know? When does the learner get a chance to act on the environment? Should the children simply be exposed to a rich environment while teachers wait for something to happen, or should they be fed carefully with a well-balanced, well-planned program? The answer is clear—both approaches working together will offer children the most successful kind of learning environment.

Listen for cues A chance remark or happening in a classroom of young children is often the spark to set off a whole series of creative explosions which can be called learning experiences. Teachers must be watching for such cues, ready to motivate and nurture them. Materials and guiding words or hands should be available at a moment's call. The teacher knows just where the right item has been stored which will stimulate and extend a child's thinking.

It happened:

Some fours had been making trains with their seat blocks for several days. The teacher, seeing their lasting interest, added a suitcase to the block corner and an old fur jacket and bathing suit to the dress-up collection. She did not call attention to the new additions. She waited. She would not have been concerned if the children had not made any connections, but of course she was delighted when they did. The added items stimulated conversations about "Where shall we go?" and "What shall I wear?" Children were busy acting: "What shall we take along?" "It's warm enough to swim there."

One conversation fused a whole new series of discoveries: "I'm going to Denmark, where my daddy went." "How will you get there?" asked the teacher. "Oh, on the train," was the response. The teacher brought in the globe and helped the children find the water parts and the land, the United States and Denmark. Soon one of the children discovered that a train could not travel from the United States to Denmark. Their train might take them from New York to Chicago (road maps verified this fact), but to get to Denmark, they would have to take a ship or a plane. Ticket sales, train conductors, air travel—the program for that group flowed, branching off in many directions, but coming back to the generalized theme of transportation.

Using teachers'
special talents Each teacher has a specialty, a forte, and developing it will bring creative zest to the classroom. Some teachers always have a good story or poem ready to illustrate or motivate; some use pictures to extend an idea; others are collectors of "elegant junk" and seem to know how to turn such items to magic uses. Children everywhere love and respond to music, rhythm, and rhyme, and the teacher who has memorized a repertoire of songs and rhyming patterns offers an extra sparkle of joy to the classroom.

In an interest-centered classroom such as the one we describe in Chapter 31, team teaching brings the best results. Teachers share their ideas *and* the work involved in developing program around those ideas. Their individual talents may be the keys to what each teacher contributes.

In a center of about a hundred children, team teaching achieved excellent, relaxed, creative results. The *director* met with *lead teachers* once a week to discuss and plan the following week's objectives. The *lead teachers* then met with their *teams* to plan. In a center where several teachers interact with the same children at different times of day, such planning is essential if teachers are to pick up where others have left off and to extend each activity.

Each teacher assumed responsibility for a particular aspect of the program, some of them focusing on a special area, such as music, science, or cooking. They discussed plans and objectives so that each knew the other's plans and could help to extend them.

For example, the fours were working with winter animals. One teacher planned a field trip to an aquarium where they could see seals and penguins. She made all the arrangements, including reservations, transportation, parent volunteers, snacks at the aquarium, and the like. A second teacher gathered materials for a related art activity, such as cotton balls, black and white construction paper, bits of furry cloth for making animals, and so on.

A third teacher assumed the responsibility for picking up related film strips and slides at the library and reserved a projector and projection room for a certain day. She made certain that the person who would operate the projector checked out the extension cord, an extra bulb, and the screen before the appointed show time. A fourth teacher went to the library for books, pictures, and videotapes and searched for special events, such as television programs.

The teachers planned related outdoor activities, such as building with snow blocks. "Where are the small shovels stored?" "Does everyone have boots and mittens?" As each task was completed, it was indicated on a checklist held by the director or lead teacher.

Director and staff could enjoy their weekends off, knowing that seldom would anyone be besieged with last-minute requests, such as "I forgot the toothpicks! Can I dash out now?" or "Where's the black construction paper? I can't find more than six sheets!" Nor were there minor irritations, such as "I was planning to read *that* book and surprise my group with the film strip, but Janya is using the projector!" and, of course, the inevitable "The bulb in the projector is burned out and my children are all waiting. It was fine when I used it last week!"

Planning ahead—which a team can do—is a wonderful cliché which should be part of every day. It smooths out the wrinkles in the program and on the face.

Holidays   For many teachers, holidays are the crutch with which they can limp through a year's program devoid of spontaneity, with little or no learning taking place. In the fall, they go from pumpkins, witches, black cats, and ghosts in October to horns of plenty spilling out fruits and vegetables in November. The great competition is to devise a new method for converting materials and objects into simulated turkeys. In December, hurrying to get ahead of the advertisers and department stores, they overwhelm their charges with trees, sprigs of holly decorated with carefully placed red berries, bells, candles, wreaths, and toys spilling out of Santa's pack.

January is easy if you live in the north—walls and windows are covered with snowmen. Then we have the hearts and flowers of valentines, which are soon replaced with Easter eggs and bunnies. A short fling with spring and at last, with a sigh of relief, the harried teacher ushers her children out of doors, where she puts them out to grass, throws aside her holiday crutches, and settles down to relax.

We are not suggesting that holidays should be eliminated from the program entirely. They are a part of our cultural and ethnic heritage and help to promote mutual respect and understanding among people of varying backgrounds. But they should not be the foundation on which we plan; rather, they should be one of the themes which add interest and sparkle.

The sequences in Volume 2 suggest ways of relating holidays to emotional growth. For example, Halloween lets a child dabble in the experience of fear while resting in the safety and security of family. Thanksgiving invokes a whole new concept of gratitude. This idea is extended with the giving and sharing of Hanukkah and Christmas, and so on through the year.

The teacher will be constantly on the alert for opportunities to integrate the principles of health into daily program.

Chapter 42   **HEALTH**

Parents display enormous trust when they leave their child in a child care center. No precaution can be overlooked, no procedure neglected, which justifies that trust. Here we have outlined the basics. In your center you may face special circumstances that indicate the need to extend these policies. We have not tried to outline procedures for the care of infants in this book. The subject is far too important to treat lightly, but far too vast to do justice to here. We strongly recommend that you seek this information from reliable sources.

Before enrollment   Before you admit a child to your center, you must have written assurance from a licensed physician that she is able to participate in the normal activities that are part of your program. (See Chapter 20, *Children with Special Needs*, for exceptions.) Regulations and supervision of compliance with them vary from state to state and even within some states, but *you* will be motivated by concern for the child more than externally imposed rules. You will need the following information before the child can be accepted:
- Report of physical examination.
- Evidence of required inoculations.
- Parent information sheet.
- Written permission for emergency medical attention.
- Names and phone numbers to be used in an emergency.

Health inspection   Each day, as the child arrives, she should be carefully checked by the nurse, a teacher, or you. It is important to have the same person make this check every day, for two reasons. First, it establishes a relationship of trust: the child feels that someone really cares for her and is watching over her. Second, a person who really knows the child can recognize chronic conditions and notice any changes.

The inspector, using a flashlight or standing under a direct light, looks inside the child's throat for redness, irritation, or white patches, at the same time feeling both sides for swollen glands, then looks at the child's face for rashes, sores, bruises, flushed cheeks or unusual pallor; at her hands for rashes, sores, or poor skin tone; and at her eyes for redness or runniness. The inspector also listens for a cough or wheeze and makes sure the child's nose is not running.

During the day, a teacher will report to you immediately if he observes any unusual behavior or symptoms. He is concerned if a child becomes listless, sleepy, restless, or irritable, if she makes frequent trips to the bathroom, if she stumbles or falls easily, or if she complains of aches in her stomach, head, or ears.

Health concerns and procedures apply to every member of your staff, even the ones who consider themselves non-teaching: the receptionist, the custodian, and, of course, the cook.

Letter to send to parents This is a letter we have sent home to parents. Please read it carefully. Whether or not you agree with our thoughts about clothing, it is most important that your plan for illness and accidents be at least as stringent as ours. You, rather than the nurse, should sign the letter.

Dear Parents,

Our concern for your child will not be limited to learning, but will encompass the physical and emotional sides of his or her development, as well as the social and intellectual. We ask for your complete cooperation in accepting the rules we have made for the health and safety of each child, and in turn we pledge to you our diligence in maintaining good practices. If at times you are inconvenienced, we ask you to remember that in protecting someone else's child, you will also help maintain a safe environment for your own.

Sickness: Please keep your child home under the following conditions: he or she seems listless or unusually irritable, complains of a headache, stomach ache, or ear ache, or seems to be unusually pale or flushed. It is better to be overcautious than to risk the health of your child or the chance of exposing other children to contagion.

Keep your child at home for forty-eight hours after a temperature goes down and for twenty-four hours after a minor upset.

If your child is exposed to a contagious disease here, we will send you a written notice, with instructions for keeping him or her at home. If you are aware that your child has been exposed elsewhere, please consult with me about procedures to follow.

Accidents: In the event of an accident, or if your child becomes ill at school, we will follow these procedures:

We will administer first aid for minor cuts or bruises, and I or your child's teacher will report this fact to you before the child returns home. If we cannot reach you, we will send a written report home with the child. We are required to have at least one person on the staff who has a current first aid certificate and is available at all times.

If stitches or further treatment seem necessary, we will keep the child quiet while we call you at home, call you at work, call the emergency number you have given us, or call your child's doctor.

If time seems to be important, we will call an ambulance, or I and one other adult will take your child to the hospital, while someone else begins making the calls mentioned above.

It may reassure you to know that, because we are so conscious of health and safety, these procedures rarely have to be used. All staff have been trained in the procedures to follow, and written instructions are posted in my office.

Clothing: *It is better to have too much rather than too little. Trust the teachers to use their judgment as temperatures change.*

Please send an extra set of indoor clothing (underwear, top, pants, and socks) and a pair of slippers or sneakers. It is possible for a child to get wet from without as well as from toilet accidents, and we do not want the children to sit in wet clothing. If we must send soiled clothing home, please wash and return it as soon as possible.

Our children play outside all year round, and in all kinds of weather. Please send your child dressed for active participation, with raincoats and rubber boots on rainy days and ski pants, boots, and mittens in the winter. On very cold winter days, we will stay in at first and go out later, when the sun is higher.

We teach the children how to dress and undress themselves. Please encourage your child to do so at home as well. Try to allow him or her enough time, and express your pride in your child's accomplishments. "I can do it myself" is the natural tendency of the child. When you cheat him or her out of this satisfaction, you also cheat yourself.

Changes from the norm: Incorporated into our curriculum are basic principles of cleanliness, knowledge of the parts of the body and their care and functions, and the body's need for food and rest. Our teachers see your child functioning in many ways and under various conditions and in comparison with other children of the same age. If they observe what appears to be a deviation from the norm, however slight, they will report it to me. If I observe the child and consider it a matter worthy of concern, I will report it to you.

On the other hand, we appreciate it when you share with us any information relating to your child's physical or emotional health. It is particularly important for us to know if you are going away on a trip, if there is serious illness or a death in the family, or if you are contemplating a move or change in family patterns. We respect all such information as confidential, but we know that children are often uncomfortably aware and will express their insecurity in their behavior.

Sincerely yours,

Medications Do not mention that you are willing to administer medications in the letter to parents. We strongly recommend that medicine *not* be administered by child care staff unless you have a nurse. The child's doctor should be encouraged to prescribe medication in dosages that would avoid the need for you to do so during the hours that the child is in the center—that is, to use long-acting drugs where possible.

If you choose to administer medicines, review each case separately and write procedures specifically for it. Ask yourself these questions, put the answers in writing, and discuss them with your staff:

• Do you have a medication permission form, signed by the child's doctor and the child's parent, specific to the medication being given?

• Is the medication in the original container, with the name and strength of the medicine and the name of the child to receive it?

• Who will administer the medication? Should more than one person at the center be allowed to do this?

- Has the medicine been given at home, so parents could watch for any side effects?
- Do you have a log book for medications given? Who signs it?
- Where can you store medicines when they are not in use so they are out of reach of children at all times?
- Who will check prescriptions for expiration dates?

The possibility of litigation is always a consideration. You should ask for legal advice if you are concerned about administering medications .

Personal care The teacher will be constantly on the alert for opportunities to integrate the principles of health into daily program. It is not necessary to preach. Learning basic facts can be as interesting and as much fun as acquisition of any other aspect of learning *if* the teacher sees program as everything the child has a need and a desire to know.

Children do not automatically know how to use a tissue, wash and dry their hands carefully, or care for toilet needs. The teacher should accept the responsibility of *teaching* these skills, using every available method. The teacher tells, shows, demonstrates, role plays, uses pictures, provides dolls, and makes health and weight charts.

First aid In most states, licensing requires that at least one person trained and certified in first aid be available at all times. It is your responsibility to provide training when necessary. First aid should be just that—only minimal treatment until professional help is available.

A daily log *must* be kept of every incident and treatment, however trivial. We suggest that you use a hard-cover bound book, rather than a loose-leaf notebook, and that you keep records almost indefinitely. A parent cannot sign away the child's right to sue after reaching twenty-one, and it is possible that a claim will be brought for an injury at a much later date. The report should not be limited to "Johnny fell and got a bump on his head. Applied ice." It should state how, where, and what part of the body was injured (tip of right index finger), and the information should be recorded immediately, not at the end of the day.

Procedures for emergency treatment *must* be *written, discussed,* and *posted* in a conspicuous place. Part of the training of each new employee should include going over this plan.

Cleansing It is not unreasonable to ask members of the staff to take turns cleaning the major problem areas in the center. You will need a basic washing solution (a tablespoon of bleach in a gallon of water), which should be stored in a tightly covered container in a locked cabinet. The designated member of the staff should use the following routine:
- *Once a day*—using the washing solution in a spray bottle, along with disposable wipes, wash counter tops, table tops, chair seats, cabinet doors, door knobs, and the wall surfaces around the changing area and the food preparation area.
- *Twice a day*—wash sinks and faucets, drinking fountains, and toilet seats.

• *After each use*—clean any toys children put in their mouths, as well as sponges and mops used for cleaning up.

• *At least weekly*—disinfect cribs, cots, blankets, mats, and play-pens. Wash sheets, blankets, other sleep coverings, and any machine-washable soft toys.

It happened:

"What is that child doing?" a supervisor asked as she watched fourteen-month-old Josh pick up a wooden toy, toddle over, and drop it in a bucket. "He's putting the toy in the bucket because it was on the floor," was the response. "The toys in the bucket will be disinfected." Joshua was learning health procedures at an early age.

Staff health It is your responsibility as the director to make certain that each staff member has some periods of relief during the day. However, a teacher cannot just drop everything at a specific break time. The needs of children do not fall into neat time slots. The timing of a brief respite should be determined by the members of a teaching team, and abuse of the privilege or disagreements about it should be handled at weekly team meetings. It is family business, to be managed within the family.

When a staff member has an hour off at noon, urge him to get away from the building, at least for a short walk. Have a cot or couch in the staff room or your office for staff use. You should give out medication to members of the staff, instead of leaving it in the medicine chest. A teacher who calls for aspirin every day bears watching.

Provision should be made for the teacher who is too sick to be with children, but not sick enough to stay home, especially when sick days with pay are limited. This person might help with clerical duties.

Keep careful records of staff absences, stating the reasons. You may need them in future evaluation conferences.

Hand-washing for teachers Teachers who are meticulous about teaching children how to wash their hands are, unfortunately, often careless about practicing what they preach. It is mandatory that teachers wash their hands:
• Before and after assisting children in the bathroom.
• After using the toilet themselves.
• After sneezing or coughing.
• After caring for a sick child.
• After caring for animals or their equipment.
• After any cleansing procedure.
• Before handling food.

Attendance A director who keeps a finger on the daily attendance has it also on the pulse of the school. Recording the reason for absence will give evidence of spreading infection. An analysis of why a cold spread through an entire class often helps in developing adequate precautions. A graph will show absentee patterns which have implications for staffing and for planning vacation periods.

Safety in the child care center is the responsibility of every member of the staff, teaching and non-teaching.

Safety at all times It is absolutely essential that someone be responsible for every single child at all times. Each child, in the beginning, needs to identify with *one* adult, and should be able to break this tie at *his own* speed, leaving for a time, but always free to come back for reassurance. This kind of supervision can be subtle and unobtrusive—certainly we do not want children clinging to adults, or feeling shadowed or over-protected by them; nor do we want to interfere with the flexibility and fluidity of our program, but there can never be any relaxation of responsibility.

A visitor to a child care center watched an outdoor program with many interesting activities going on. Staff were placed reasonably well throughout the play area, and yet *no one* saw a little girl go outside the gate. If the visitor had not seen her, and if the child had continued on her way toward a busy street, *no one* person would have felt responsible. Each one could have said, "But I thought you were watching her."

Supervision in the director's absence The immediate health and safety of the children is usually the responsibility of the teaching staff, but the overall supervision of a school rests on your shoulders as director. Therefore, it is essential that you make provision for supervision at every moment of the day, from the time the doors open in the morning until the last child leaves at night. No director can be there all the time, but some *one* person must accept the responsibility in your absence, even if it is only for fifteen minutes while you are out on an errand.

It is not enough to say, "When I'm out in the morning, Kirk will be responsible, and when I'm out in the afternoon, Beth will take over." You must hand over the reins every time.

What are the things this person needs to know? Put the answers to these questions in writing.

- What do you do if a child is hurt?
- Which member of the staff is trained in first aid?
- When do you call the parents?
- What do you say to avoid alarming them unnecessarily?
- Where is the fire alarm? (Someone from the fire department may arrive at any moment and ask for a fire drill.)
- How do you turn off the alarm? (In one case, it went off because of a short circuit and no one knew where it was.)
- How do you shut off the water if a pipe bursts?
- Where is the toilet plunger and how do you use it?
- Who understands the total transportation setup, in case problems arise?
- What do you do if a teacher reports a child missing?
- Where is the director and how can you reach her?

Your plan for supervision should be written down and posted in a conspicuous place. Practicing emergency procedures through role playing at staff meetings will firm up the need for such precautions.

Supervision of the playground

Sometimes it is best to assign certain areas of the playground: "For the next hour, Chris, you watch the sandbox area. Tony, you cover the gate and the children playing in the gate area. Lynn, you take charge of the swings and climbers. Yvonne, you stay indoors. We will let children enter only through this door, and it is up to you to know what is going on in there."

One person—*at all times*—*must* be in charge.

Supervision includes stopping disruptive actions before they go too far. Children do not need to scream at the tops of their lungs to be happy. When they do, they are actually infringing on the rights (as well as the nerves) of others. The nearest adult *goes to the child* and says very quietly and directly *to* him, "You are going to give us all headaches if you make so much noise. Find another way to have fun."

Finally, teachers who *teach* have little time for conversation with other adults, indoors or out, while they are on the job. When they are not involved in program activities, they are observing, making mental notes about behavior and new skills, storing up information, and thinking of the developmental needs of the children.

Supervision is everyone's business, but the responsibility of one individual.

Safety checklists

Safety in the child care center is the responsibility of every member of the staff. There are dangers inherent in every aspect of program, in every moment of the day, and adequate protection calls for constant vigilance. The following suggested plan requires cooperation, concern, and conscientious observation.

At initial staff training, give each member copies of the checklists and discuss each item fully, with examples. Many members of the staff may not know—unless you tell them—that spongy food items such as hot dogs and marshmallows are dangerous because they cannot be forced out of the air passage with the Heimlich maneuver. Toddlers may choke on pieces of balloon or pieces of nuts, and children under three are likely to get glitter on their hands, then rub it in their eyes.

Each week, assign a different staff member to do a thorough inspection of all facilities. Have that person check each item and give details of incidents observed or faulty equipment. These inspection tours should take place at various times of the day. Assemble the safety reports and discuss pertinent items at monthly staff meetings and report on action taken.

Facility Checklist

I. ACCESS TO THE BUILDING
1. Are doors that permit access from the outside kept locked?
2. If playground gates are locked, is there a plan for escape in an emergency?

II. SURFACES
1. Are floors slippery from wax, sand, or spills? Are floors dirty or splintery?
2. Are outdoor surfaces icy or cluttered?
3. Are there hard surfaces under climbing equipment or swings?
4. Are passageways clogged? Obstructions in front of doors?
5. Is equipment broken or dangerously worn?
6. Is equipment unsuited to the ages of the children using it?
7. Are handrails on stairs at the wrong height for children?
8. Do doors open in instead of out? Do heavy doors not have crash bars? Are there inside locks in closets or toilets?
9. Are windows at child level made of breakable glass? Do sliding glass doors lack decals or designs to prevent children or adults from walking into them?

III. HEAT
1. Are heaters, fireplaces, and radiators covered?
2. What is the temperature of the hot water coming from faucets the children use?

IV. PLAYGROUND
1. Are pools fenced and locked when unsupervised?
2. Are there depressions in the surface which hold rain?
3. Are any poisonous plants growing on the playground?
4. Is the equipment sturdy?
5. Have any parts begun to work loose?
6. Are there exposed nails, screws, sharp edges, or points?

V. KITCHEN
1 Are stove knobs and burners out of reach of children?
2. Are pots and pans on the stove out of reach of children?
3. Is there any evidence of insects or rodents?
4. Are cleansing agents, insect poison, and other dangerous materials in locked storage?

VI. LIGHTING
1. Are play areas and passageways clearly lighted?
2. Are electrical outlets either four feet from the floor, covered, or equipped with safety covers?

VII. FURNITURE
Are all free-standing bookshelves and racks of cubbies securely fastened to the floor so they cannot tip over?

Program checklist   I. SUPERVISION
1. Did you see children unattended? Children in forbidden areas? Children in dangerous play?
2. Did you see an inadequate adult/child ratio?
3. Did you see children hurting other children?
4. Did you see children inadequately or inappropriately clothed?

II. PROGRAM
1. Are children using dangerous items, such as glitter?
2. Are children eating hot dogs, nuts, or marshmallows?
3. If children are cooking, are they separate from the kitchen, but close to the hand-washing area?
4. Are they using clean, safe utensils?
5. Have all small pieces of games, toys, and puzzles been checked with a no-choke tube?
6. If children are using an electrical appliance, is its cord arranged so no one can trip over it?
7. Are materials on the walls or bulletin boards secured safely, without tacks or pins?
8. Have substitutes or new members of the staff been trained to follow emergency and accident procedures?
9. Are emergency phone numbers posted next to all phones?

III. RECORDS
1. Are sign-in and sign-out sheets visible and current?
2. Are emergency treatment permission slips readily available?
3. Is each emergency treatment permission slip signed?
4. Are all inspection reports filed?
5. Are emergency accident procedures posted properly?
6. Is the accident/incident log complete and up-to-date?
7. Is the evacuation drill log current?

Fire precautions Procedures for fire drills should be explained and practiced at pre-opening training. Thereafter, you should hold a fire drill at least once a month. You should use only one signal—and use that signal for that purpose only. Children should be alerted to the sound of that signal prior to the first drill (Vol. 2, p. 21). They should be taught that they *must not* stop to gather their belongings or to put on outside garments. Those few seconds could be crucial.

Timing is of the utmost importance. If you stand with a stopwatch and commend those who get out of the building promptly, children will take pride in competing with their own record.

Hold fire drills at various times of day and in all kinds of weather. Assign each class, group, or team a meeting place. Plan the procedures for counting, checking attendance, and reporting to you, and have the teachers practice them. The last adult to leave the building should check all areas—this check is crucial in centers where children come for different hours in the day or days of the week.

Test smoke detectors regularly. Replace the batteries once a year on some memorable date, such as the anniversary of your opening.

Post emergency evacuation procedures in every area and go over them with the teachers. Hold some fire drills in which, without warning, you block some exits with large signs saying "The fire is here: go another way." Record how much longer than usual the staff and children took to clear the building.

The secretary should keep a log recording the date, time of day, and time taken to clear the building in each fire drill. She should also maintain a list of the locations of the fire alarm system and all shut-offs (for electricity, gas, water, and heat) in the building. It would be wise to invite the fire chief to send someone to review the procedures and suggest improvements, if needed. If inspection is not automatic, the fire chief or his representative should look over the property.

Safety for infants Ideally, infants should be on the ground floor, with direct access to the outside. You will need *evacuation cribs* to hold as many infants as your center cares for. These cribs, with reinforced wheels, can be rolled out quickly, each one carrying four to six babies. Identify these cribs by painting their ends red.

If your infant room is above or below ground level and you cannot roll cribs out, you must plan carefully for evacuation. Consider with the staff the possible "what ifs"—What if the person assigned to carry out two babies has gone home sick? Will her replacement know?

If the fire is real You have to be ready for a real fire, which means that you have to plan where the children will go in bad weather and how you will get them there. You must arrange for this shelter *in advance* with the person in charge there—the principal of the local school or the manager of a nearby office building or mall—and you must be certain that the building will be open at any hour your center is open. Put this information in the parent handbook and on parent bulletin boards and repeat it in parent bulletins.

Other disasters may threaten—a smog alert, a hurricane or tornado warning, a dangerous person on the loose, or a lost child. Review procedures for dealing with them with the staff.

Local resources At your new center, do not wait for disaster to strike to make contact with all of the services you might need. One of your first tasks would be to call upon the local police. Tell a little bit about the center and its purpose, its hours, the ages of its children, and other pertinent topics. At the same time, ask that a police officer come to school to talk to the children about safety, and ask that a police cruiser check during off hours for vandalism, especially at night or on weekends.

You should also make contact with the local hospital or medical center. If you plan to use a local hospital as one of your resources, visit it to determine the exact location of the emergency entrance and to find out about any special requirements.

You will need a local doctor as your first resource in a medical emergency. You should have a written agreement with the doctor and should have information about office hours on file.

You and the secretary should have on hand the telephone numbers for the nearest poison center and other emergency services.

School traffic You have to plan and practice procedures for parents to deliver the children when they arrive and to pick them up when they go home.

Traffic flow If your center is located on a busy highway, the location and angle of the entrance road are of prime importance. They should be carefully planned and measured. (With a new building, local authorities may have standards for access. When an existing building is to be used, you may have to sacrifice some playground space for new driveways or exits to other streets.).

It is usually best to have one-way traffic in the driveway. The convenience of the parent who is hurrying on the way to work must be balanced with provisions for the parent who wants to stop to speak to you or a teacher. If the line of cars cannot move smoothly at the busy hours, drivers may become angry or confused.

Drop-off time The following procedures are suggested. A staff member, properly attired for the weather, should be assigned as a greeter. She will:
• Open the car doors and assist children in getting out, making sure that they have all their belongings. A pleasant greeting for driver and child are both important.
• Have the parent or driver sign the child in.
• See that the children go straight into the building or playground and are received by another adult.
• Collect written messages from parents or drivers and convey them to you or a teacher, as appropriate.
• Take oral messages from parents or drivers, put them in writing at the time they are given, and convey them to you or a teacher.
• Make sure that one parent does not hold up traffic while talking or while stopping to enter the building.

Signing in and out Sometimes parents who are concerned about being late for work are inclined to take lightly the need for personally seeing that their children are delivered to responsible adults at the center. It is essential that every parent or driver be required to sign a log book when dropping off a child and when picking up a child. It is equally important for members of the staff to make a note in the log book if the child leaves the center at any time other than the regularly scheduled one.

Grace Mitchell writes:

On a visit to an inner city child care center, I was appalled when I saw a father leave his four-year-old daughter on the sidewalk in front of the school, which was located on a busy city street. She went to a side entrance and through a gate. I followed her as she made her way into the center, through a classroom, and up to the second floor. Although she passed several adults, *no one* greeted her—and *no one* questioned why she was walking about the building alone. And this was in a licensed, community-funded center!

Pick-up time Shortly before a child is due to leave, the teacher should make sure he is ready—clean hands and face, papers and messages in one place and clipped together, and outer clothes ready. Time-consuming items such as snowpants and boots can be put on if the parent does not usually come in. A staff member should watch for the car, help the child with last-minute items, and deliver him to the car, handing the driver the sign-out board. *Never* allow children to wait outside by themselves.

Transportation Between the security of the home and the safety of the child care center lies the public way, over which the child is conveyed twice each day. Many parents do not find it convenient to drive their children to the center every day. Some schools provide transportation as a service. In others, the concerned director tries to help find satisfactory solutions to this frustrating problem.

Car pools Many parents may be willing and able to share the responsibility for getting their children to the center. They will need help in making such arrangements. You can set up lists and provide addresses and phone numbers. You may also offer guidelines for car-pool parents. However, one member of the car pool should act as coordinator to call a meeting to establish rules and policies and to deal with problems.

Hired drivers In some cases the parents may prefer to hire drivers. Some areas may have taxi or bus companies interested in providing this service. However the drivers are hired, the following questions must be considered:
•   How can you be assured that the vehicles are properly maintained and checked regularly for safety?
•   Will drivers attend driver training and monthly meetings?
•   Are drivers for hire required to obtain special licenses? Have their past driving records been checked?

Center-owned vehicles When the center owns the vehicles, you have control over the factors that relate to safety. Parents also feel more secure when they know that the center can set the rules for selecting and training drivers, maintaining vehicles, planning routes, and setting costs. It is an advantage to have a vehicle on hand to provide before- and after-school care. It is not unusual for a child care center to own or lease one or an entire fleet of station wagons or mini-buses. Automobile manufacturers are at last recognizing that this is a needed service and are making mini-buses with built-in safety features, such as reinforced sides and tops, padded seat backs, and seat belts for all children.

If your center owns a vehicle, you must arrange for maintenance and regular safety checks. Worn windshield-wiper blades, brakes that squeak, unusual noises—all should be reported and taken care of.

Requirements for drivers Some states require, and we strongly urge, that all drivers be at least twenty-one years of age and have at least five years of successful driving experience. They should be in good physical condition, with no restrictions or limitations on their licenses. As representatives of the center, they should be neat and clean in appearance. (An unkempt, unshaven man in a dirty sweater or a woman wearing inappropriate clothing would not inspire the confidence of parents!) Drivers should be emotionally stable. They should be able to stay calm under stress and to exercise good judgment when quick decisions are necessary.

These are nebulous qualities, not easy to ascertain, and you must use all of the tools available to seek the right person.

Substitute drivers Whenever possible, a substitute driver should be introduced to parents and children in advance. In a large center which maintains a fleet of vehicles, it may be worthwhile to employ one full-time substitute driver who learns all the routes. Substitute drivers must meet all the requirements that apply to regular drivers.

Meetings with drivers At the beginning of the school year, it is as essential to meet with drivers as it is with teaching staff. The children are, in effect, in your teaching and caring environment from the time they leave the security of their homes, and it takes only one thoughtless statement or act to counteract the efforts of the teacher at the center.

During the year, you should meet with the drivers at least once a month. A good time for this meeting is 9 a.m. This is a time for listening, for sharing problems. Drivers who are treated with this kind of respect and who are, after a trial period, salaried and given the same fringe benefits as the teaching staff, will stay on year after year. Veteran drivers often help to find and train new drivers and may offer valuable insights into children's behavior. They are usually deeply respected and loved by children and parents.

Chapter 44   **KEEPING YOUR CENTER GREAT**

Your center is well established. You have a long waiting list of eager parents and a stable staff, and all is going well. When you approach your building, you feel a justifiable glow of pride. Can you now draw a sigh of relief and rest on your oars? Never!

Before you are even aware of it, you may drift off course into the swift and dangerous currents of a changing economy. An unexpected reef may loom before you in the form of an accusation of child abuse. When you don't watch your course, you may venture into shallow waters and glide onto the sandbar of complacency, and you may not be able to back off without serious damage.

How can you protect yourself?

Take another look   You may think that you constantly appraise your center, but the old adage, "Familiarity breeds contempt," applies here. When we see something every day, our eyes have a tendency to glaze over, and details lose their sharpness. Like the horse with blinders, we see what is directly before us, but fail to take in the entire picture.

Approximately every six months, you should stand off and take a good look at your total organization—the people, environment, and program. This inspection will be most effective after you have had a brief vacation, after you have visited some other centers, or after you have attended a convention where you were exposed to the latest in equipment and a wealth of new ideas.

Be objective   You may find it easier to be objective if you take off your director's hat and don that of a parent seeking child care, or a licensing agent on an unannounced visit. Imagine that you are a competitor, seeking comparisons, or a representative of a corporation that gives vouchers to employees and is creating a list of quality centers.

Seek another   Some of the time you may want to assign this task to a lead teacher or
opinion   one of the staff, someone who can look at the total situation from a different perspective. If you have an established network, you may exchange evaluation visits with the directors of one or two other centers.

Look at the people   You should, on an ongoing basis, observe the members of your staff just the way you ask them to observe children (described in Chapter 15). If you have been doing this, your evaluation process will be quite easy. You are looking at their relationship with the children and their fellow teachers, their general attitude, and signs of professional growth. This process will coincide with the teachers' six-month appraisal conferences, so you will be accomplishing two things at once.

Children What about the children? Do they come happily in the morning? Do they participate with interest and sometimes excitement? Are they learning how to get along together? Are emotional problems working out? Is general behavior improving?

Look at environment Before you start to evaluate environment, fine-tune your sensory equipment. Look! Listen! Smell! Touch! Taste!

Start on the street. As you approach the building, do you find that it looks inviting or forbidding? Well kept or neglected? *(That shrub needs replacing.)* If the playground is visible from the street, does it look enticing? *(I can see rusty toys in the sandbox and a naked doll lying on the grass.)* Are there children on the playground? What are they doing? What about supervision? Are the teachers just standing around, or are they involved with the children? *(Two are talking with their backs to the children. One is huddled up, obviously cold and uncomfortable.)*

When you enter the building, what are your very first impressions? Light, bright, and orderly? Look around the foyer. Do you see a bulletin board? Is it current? Attractive? Informative?

As you walk around, look for signs of neglect or wear. Did that stain-proof carpeting live up to its promise? Are the walls in need of a fresh coat of paint? *(In spite of the rules, I see that teachers have been taping things to the walls, and the paint has come off when they took the things down. Those little chairs which were so bright and attractive are really dirty. No more of that pebbly surface—it's too hard to keep clean.)*

Your mistakes will show if you failed to invest in top-quality equipment. Replace anything that is broken—you can't afford to let a shabby environment counterbalance your good program.

Listen Do you hear fighting, shouting, or crying? Or do you hear cheerful voices, laughter, and singing? Are teachers' voices dominating the room?

Smell Are there good, home-like smells coming from the kitchen? Do you occasionally catch a whiff of soap? Or is an unpleasant odor reaching your nose? Has the cleaning of the bathroom been neglected?

Taste Given the opportunity, sit down at snack time or lunch time and engage in conversation with the children.

Grace Mitchell writes:

"It was a small center where a hot lunch was prepared on the premises. As I sat at a low table with the children, enjoying a plate of delicious spaghetti and meat sauce, a five-year-old boy sitting across from me looked up, beamed, and exclaimed, 'Is this food great, or *what!*'"

Touch   Do you see a variety of surfaces—and are the teachers providing opportunities for kinesthetic experiences? What about people touching—a comforting arm, a loving pat on the shoulder?

Order   One final factor encompasses every aspect of your center—order. It is much more than "a place for everything and everything in its place." The parent feels it when the morning teacher is calm, confident, and smiling, and when picking up a clean, contented child, waiting with all his belongings—no hunting for a mitten, a boot, or the toy he brought that morning. The staff member feels it when she knows exactly what is expected of her and is provided with all the tools to do her job. The child feels it when the adults around him offer stability, security, and loving care.

Environment is more than a facility—it is the ambience created within a facility by the people and the program. It is that indefinable quality that makes you feel that this is a wonderful place for children —or makes you uneasy.

Look at program   Take a good look at the interest centers. If you were a visitor who knew nothing about early childhood education, would you be able to determine the learning taking place in each one? Can *you* tell what is happening? Does each interest center provide for a range of abilities? Do the planned activities leave room for the children's own ideas to develop? Are displays of the children's projects attractively arranged? Are they current? Most important of all, do they reflect the *children's* work, rather than the teacher's?

The goal of evaluation   The object of your evaluation is not to score a hundred points and win a star. Your goal is to see where things can improve and how you can help the teachers grow. A good way to use what you have learned is in a series of workshops. Keep these workshops general, addressing a problem you have noticed and suggesting—or drawing from the group— ways to deal with it, but never overpraising one teacher or criticizing another.

Keep up with the world   Making a thorough evaluation of your own center is your most important key to maintaining quality, but it is not the only one. You should not ignore the second key, which might be called keeping up with the world. The director of an agency-operated center has the benefit of a community to call upon for support and encouragement. If you are the owner-director of a proprietary center, you may feel isolated, sheltering the uneasy feeling that something may be changing "out there" of which you are unaware. What can you do about it?

• Join a professional association—and get involved! The two major organizations are the National Association for the Education of Young Children (NAEYC) and the National Child Care Association (NCCA). They both have legislative committees that keep on top of legislation and notify their members of pending action. If you do not know how to locate the nearest local chapter, write the national headquarters. You will find addresses for these two organizations in the Bibliography under Resources.

• Read periodicals that will keep you informed about developments in the world of child care. Several are listed in the Bibliography.

• Organize a network with other directors and meet on a regular basis to discuss common problems and share good ideas. Occasionally the owner of a small center will choose to avoid this contact with the competition, unwilling to share trade secrets with anyone. Acting on this narrow point of view will backfire—there are *no* trade secrets among those who are truly dedicated to the cause of young children! Far better is the attitude of the director who said, "When I hear that a new center is open, I call on the director, in the same spirit in which I would call on a new neighbor, taking a book or record as a gift, and wish her well."

All this reaching out is intended to keep you off that sandbar, to make certain that you are constantly seeking ways to improve your center. In addition, you need to develop a plan for continual ongoing self-evaluation. To measure your own operation, you will need a yardstick —something to measure against.

A yardstick for quality
You should seek accreditation for your center from the National Academy of Early Childhood Programs, a division of NAEYC, which administers the only professional, voluntary accreditation system. Its standards represent the current consensus of the early childhood education profession on defining a high-quality program for young children. Accreditation is a three-step process: self-study, on-site evaluation, and commission decision on final acceptance.

We urge you to send for accreditation materials and begin the first step, an in-depth self-study in which you, your staff, and the parents of your children work together to measure your practice against the Academy's criteria. It is up to you to determine when you are ready for the on-site evaluation. This program is time-consuming and hard work, but the rewards in terms of team building, increased communication, and benefits for children are immeasurable.

When you and your staff feel that you are ready, you apply to the Academy for an on-site evaluation. Accreditation decisions are made by a three-member commission. Members of the commission may grant accreditation or defer it until you make certain improvements. One hundred percent compliance is not required. Accreditation is valid for three years.

The news that you have received accreditation is a cause for celebration and a mark of distinction. You can use it for valuable free publicity. More and more parents seeking child care will look for the symbol of an accredited center.

Another yardstick
If you are not quite ready to engage in this program, what else might you use as a measure of quality? The authors of this book have developed *The Early Childhood Staff Training Center*, a ten-hour videotaped

program that covers the basic elements of quality child care. It is listed in the Bibliography. Books and an instructor's manual are included with the tapes, which cover the following topics:

- A Philosophy—The Foundation
- Staff: Finding Them and Keeping Them
- Parents as Partners
- Creating the Environment
- Schedules, Routines, and Zoning
- A Fresh Approach to Discipline
- Developing a Curriculum
- Ages and Stages of Child Development
- Regulations: Guidelines for Health and Safety
- Progress Reports: A Measure of Quality

This program gives you a tool for ongoing staff training. You can have your coach use it in training a new staff member, and it is always available as a source of reinforcement and new understandings. A center in which all members of the staff have completed this program can approach the accreditation process with great confidence.

Conclusion It was not our intent to frighten you with warnings or to overwhelm you with the magnitude of your task, but to remind you that you are involved in a very important profession in a period of time which promises exciting new changes. The children who are with you right now will be making crucial decisions in the not-too-distant future. That future will be profoundly affected by the *care* you provide now, and we hope this book will help you to make sure that *care* is *great*.

BIBLIOGRAPHY

There are so many books! How do you choose? Selecting the books that will help you and your staff to grow in your profession is a personal matter. In this very limited list, we have included a few favorites—books that we consider a must.

Joining one or more of the organizations recommended here will give you a starting point. The articles you read will guide you in selecting the books you need.

When you attend a conference, set aside time to look carefully at the books and exhibits. Talk to the people you meet and ask them about their favorites. A good book is a friend—seek introductions to them with the same interest with which you enlarge your circle of social and professional friends.

Books

People: Infants

Badger, Earladeen. *Infant/Toddler*. St. Paul, Minn., Redleaf Press. (Redleaf Press, 450 North Syndicate # 5, St Paul, MN 55104-4125)

Bailey, R., and E. Burton. *The Dynamic Infant*. St. Paul, Minn., Redleaf Press.
Focuses on development, physical activity, and creating an environment that stimulates learning.

Castle, Kathryn. *The Infant and Toddler Handbook*. St. Paul, Minn., Redleaf Press.

Harms, Thelma, Debby Cryer, and Richard M. Clifford. *Infant-Toddler Environment Rating Scale*. St. Paul, Minn, Redleaf Press.

Wilson, La Visa Cam. *Infants and Toddlers: Curriculum and Teaching*. St. Paul, Minn., Redleaf Press.

Growth and development

Ames, Louise Bates, and Frances Ilg. *Your One-Year-Old. Your Two-Year-Old. Your Three-Year-Old*. New York, N.Y., Dell Publishing Co., 1976.
This series of small books, one for each age up to eight, were written primarily for parents, but offer easy readings with useful descriptions of children at various stages.

Bender, Judith, Charles H. Flatter, and Barbara Elder Schulyer-Hass. *Half a Childhood*. Mt. Rainier, Md., Gryphon House. (Gryphon House, PO Box 275, Mt. Rainier, MD 20712)
A valuable book for child care centers that include school-age children. Covers developmental characteristics and activities.

Boden, Ruth K., et al. *School Age Child Care*. St. Paul, Minn, Redleaf Press.

Bredekamp, Sue. *Developmentally Appropriate Practice*. Washington, D.C., NAEYC, 1986. (NAEYC, 1834 Connecticut Avenue, Washington, D.C. 20009-5786)
The guidelines in this book will help teachers, parents, program ad-

ministrators, policy-makers, and others make informed decisions about the education of young children.

Miller, Karen. *Ages and Stages.* Chelsea, Mass., TelShare Publishing Co., 1985. (TelShare Publishing Co., 24 Breakwater Drive, Chelsea, MA 02150)
Developmental descriptions of children from birth through eight years. Offers a guide to reasonable expectations of children at various ages and developmental stages

Rubin, Richard R., John J. Fisher, and Susan G. Doering. *Your Toddler.* New York, N.Y., Collier Books (Johnson & Johnson, 1980.
Three books in one. Part One covers growth and development; Part Two, personality and behavior, including common toddler problems such as negativism and temper tantrums; Part Three, play.

White, Burton. *The First Three Years of Life.* New York, N.Y., Avon Publishers, 1978.

Environment
Greenman, Jim. *Caring Spaces, Learning Places: Environments that Work.* St Paul, Minn., Redleaf Press, 1988.

Harms, Thelma, and Richard M. Clifford. *Early Childhood Environment Rating Scale.* St. Paul, Minn., Redleaf Press, 1980.
Answers many questions about the adequacy of early childhood settings.

Miller, Karen. *The Outside Play and Learning Book: Activities for Young Children.* Mt. Rainier, Md., Gryphon House, 1989.

Vergeront, Jeanne. *Places and Spaces for Preschool and Primary: Outdoors.* Washington, D.C., NAEYC, 1987. Publication 311.

Program
Bos, Bev. *Before the Basics: Creating Conversations with Children.* Mt. Rainier, Md., Gryphon House, 1983.
A practical guide for using language and music to encourage creativity and self-esteem in young children.

.... *Don't Move the Muffin Tins: A Hands-Off Guide to Art for the Young Child.* Mt. Rainier, Md., Gryphon House, 1978.

Brown, Sam. *Bubbles, Rainbows, and Worms: Science Experiments for Preschool Children.* Mt. Rainier, Md., Gryphon House, 1981.
Sixty-two hands-on, active experiments with air, animals, plants, water, and the senses.

Clemens, Sydney G. *The Sun's Not Broken, A Cloud's Just in the Way: On Child-Centered Teaching.* Mt. Rainier, Md., Gryphon House, 1983.

Honig, Alice. *Playtime Learning Games for Young Children.* Syracuse, N.Y., Syracuse University Press, 1982.
Uses games to convey ideas, language, and behavior.

Lasky, L., and R. Mukerji. *Art: Basic for Young Children.* Washington, D.C., NAEYC.

McDonald, Dorothy. *Music in Our Lives: The Early Years.* Washington, D.C., NAEYC, 1979.

Miller, Karen. *Things to Do with Toddlers and Twos.* Chelsea, Mass., TelShare, 1984.

.... *More Things to Do with Toddlers and Twos.* Chelsea,

Mass., TelShare, 1989.

These two books give hundreds of developmentally appropriate activities for toddlers and twos, along with information and insights about this age level.

Paley, V. G. *The Boy who Would Be a Helicopter*. Cambridge, Mass., Harvard University Press, 1990.

By describing a year in a preschool classroom, Vivian Paley demonstrates the power that personal stories have for children and the vital role that the teacher can play in story development.

Pitcher, Evelyn, S. Feinburg, and D. Alexander. *Helping Young Children Learn, 5th ed.* Columbus, Ohio, Charles E. Merrill, 1989.

Schiller, Pam, and Joan Rossano. *The Instant Curriculum: 500 Developmentally Appropriate Activities for Busy Teachers of Young Children*. Mt. Rainier, Md., Gryphon House.

Williams, R., R. Rockwell, and E. Sherwood. *Hug a Tree*. Mt. Rainier, Md., Gryphon House, 1983.

Helps children learn to love and appreciate the natural environment. Each learning experience has a suggested age level.

.... *Mudpies and Magnets*. Mt. Rainier, Md., Gryphon House, 1987.

One hundred and twelve ready-to-use science experiments providing hands-on learning activities.

For parents and teachers

Dodge, Diane Trister, and Joanna Phinney. *A Parent's Guide to Early Childhood Education*. Teaching Strategies.

Greenberg, Polly. *Character Development: Encouraging Self-Esteem and Self-Discipline in Infants, Toddlers, and Two-Year-Olds*. Washington, D.C., NAEYC.

Hymes, James. *Teaching the Child Under Six*. 3rd ed. Consortium Publishing.

First published in 1968, this book has passed the test of time. It should be required reading for all early childhood professionals. Covers the state of the profession, based on concern for the individual child.

Le Shan, Eda. *Conspiracy Against Childhood*. New York, Atheneum, 1974.

Helps teachers explain to parents that pushing their children to develop skills before they are ready is cheating them of their right to childhood and may backfire in later years, defeating their original purpose.

Mitchell, Grace L. *A Very Practical Guide to Discipline with Young Children*. Chelsea, Mass., TelShare, 1982.

Describes many typical behavior problems of children of all ages and gives adults possible solutions that preserve the dignity of both parties.

Periodicals

Child Care Information Exchange, PO Box 2890, Redmond, WA 98073.
Bi-monthly. A must for directors. It offers accurate information based on reliable research and on-site observations.

Interracial Books for Children Bulletin. Council on Interracial Books for Children, PO Box 1841, New York, NY 10023. Valuable newsletter for selecting books and activities that fairly represent sex, age, culture, handicaps, and other human qualities.

Pre-K Today, PO Box 54814, Boulder, CO 80322-4814. Eight times a year. Directed to the teacher-caregiver of preschool children. Filled with good ideas and information covering every aspect of the job. Subscribers eagerly watch for it and usually want their own copies.

School Age Notes, PO Box 120674, Nashville, TN 37212. Deals specifically with care for children between the ages of five and twelve. Includes activities, developmental characteristics, and behavior management.

Young Children. NAEYC. Six times a year. The official journal of the organization. A valuable resource for anyone involved in programs in early childhood education.

Professional organizations

National Association for the Education of Young Children (NAEYC), 1834 Connecticut Avenue NW, Washington, D.C. 20009-25786

A respected and growing network of more than 75,000 members in 380 affiliate groups. Membership services include the journal, *Young Children;* books, brochures, videos, and posters; an annual conference; membership action grants; insurance plans; public policy information; and materials to celebrate the Week of the Young Child.

We strongly recommend that all staff members take individual memberships—it is their lifeline to the profession.

National Child Care Association (NCCA), 1020 Railroad Street, Conyers, GA 30207.

Specifically for the private, licensed child care community, with 23 state affiliates. It offers programs in accreditation, credentialing, education and training, and government relations. It holds an annual conference.

Videotapes

Mitchell, Grace, and Dewsnap, Lois. *Early Childhood Staff Training Center.* Chelsea, Mass., TelShare, 1985.

A ten-session staff training program, with five related books, an instructor's guide, pre-tests and post-tests, and certificates of completion.

INDEX

Must Reading for Early Childhood Educators

I Am! I Can! (New and Revised)
    Volume One *Keys to Quality Child Care: A Guide for Directors*
                by Grace L. Mitchell, Nancy C. Bailey, Lois F. Dewsnap
    Volume Two *A Preschool Curriculum: Activities for the Classroom*
                by Harriet Chmela, Grace L. Mitchell, Lois F. Dewsnap

A Very Practical Guide to Discipline with Young Children
                                by Grace L. Mitchell

The Day Care Book   by Grace L. Mitchell

Curriculum Planner for Early Childhood Teachers
                by Nancy C. Bailey and Marcia Bennett-Hebert

Ages and Stages   by Karen Miller

Things to Do with Toddlers and Twos   by Karen Miller

MORE Things to Do with Toddlers and Twos   by Karen Miller

Also available:

Early Childhood Staff Training Center
                by Grace L. Mitchell and Lois Dewsnap
  A ten-session videotaped staff training program with an Instructor's Guide, a Test Packet, and five related books.

For information about the training program, write to:

      TelShare Publishing Company, Inc.
      24 Breakwater Drive
      Chelsea, MA 02150

Or **phone:**   **1 (800) 343-9707** (outside Massachusetts)
             (617) 884-4404 (inside Massachusetts)